The Boy General

Francis Channing Barlow as a major general, c. 1865. Library of Congress.

The Boy General

The Life and Careers
of Francis Channing Barlow

Richard F. Welch

The Kent State University Press
Kent & London

©2003 by Rosemont Publishing and Printing Corp.
All rights reserved

Library of Congress Catalog Card Number 2004056911
ISBN 0-87338-835-6
Manufactured in the United States of America

09 08 07 06 05   5 4 3 2 1

Library of Congress Cataloging-in-Publication Data

Welch, Richard F.
The boy general : the life and careers of
Francis Channing Barlow / Richard F. Welch
p.   cm.
Originally published: Madison, N.J. : Fairleigh
Dickinson University Press, 2003.
Includes bibliographical references and index.
ISBN 0-87338-835-6

1. Barlow, Francis C. (Francis Channing), 1834–1896.
2. Generals—United States—Biography. 3. United States. Army—Biography.
4. United States—History—Civil War, 1861–1865—Campaigns. I. Title.

E467.1.B25W45 2005
973.7'3'092—dc22
[B]   2004056911

British Library Cataloging-in-Publication Data are available.

For Kate and Jack

Contents

List of Illustrations

ILLUSTRATIONS

MAPS

Acknowledgments

No one writes a book—especially a work of history—by himself. This book could not have been possible without the aid, support, and enthusiasm of many individuals and institutions. These individuals and institutions shared their expertise and provided me with the means necessary to navigate the sometimes poorly charted currents of Francis Channing Barlow's life. Thanks are due to several libraries, historical societies, and other repositories of historical documents, that have generously allowed me to use letters and documents from their collections. The Massachusetts Historical Society kindly made available the Francis Channing Barlow Letters, the prime resource of Barlow material for the Civil War years. The staff at the Houghton Library, Harvard University was most helpful in guiding me through their Barlow family collection, and in allowing me to quote from it. I also wish to express my gratitude to the Manuscripts and Archives Division of the New York Public Library, the New York Historical Society, the Yale University Library, and the Perkins Library, Duke University for making their Barlow-related letters available. I am indebted to the United States Military History Institute, Carlisle Barracks, Carlisle, Pennsylvania for supplying both photographic material and permission to quote from manuscripts in their possession.

Donald Pfanz, historian at the National Battlefield Park at Fredericksburg and Spotsylvania, provided documents from the Park's own collections as well as making useful suggestions for further research. Williams C. Sparks, Jr. was most considerate in allowing me to quote from the letter of his ancestor, Robert Robertson. I also wish to thank Anna Barlow Nielsen of Center Moriches, Long Island and Robert Sullivan of the Brookline Public Library, Brookline, Massachusetts, for their help in illuminating Barlow family connections. The reference staff at the South Huntington Library, Huntington Station, New York, was most accommodating in securing uncommon titles through interlibrary loan. I am also indebted to Miesko and Kamila Lis, who rendered valuable assistance in negotiating bottlenecks in Cambridge,

Massachusetts. Likewise, thanks to Wally Broege, Director of the Suffolk County Historical Society, who graciously allowed me to read the *Official Records* of the Civil War in the comfort of his office in Riverhead, New York. A special note of appreciation is due Don Richard Lauter of Disputanta, Virginia, who unhesitatingly made available material from his Barlow collection and who freely shared his knowledge of Barlow and his circle. Don's enthusiastic interest and generosity were of immense help.

It is always helpful for an author to get feedback on his work, and I wish to express my appreciation to those who read and critiqued the book in its various stages. I am beholden to Wilbur Miller, History Department, University at Stony Brook, Stony Brook, New York, and Chris Calkins, Historian at the National Battlefield Park at Petersburg, Virginia for their helpful comments and suggestions. In this regard, let me extend my deepest gratitude to George Collins, Professor Emeritus of History, Wichita State University, Wichita, Kansas, who took on the entire volume in its early form, and, as always, made pertinent and valuable recommendations for its improvement. Thanks are also due Beverly Welch, who proofed the entire book and helped me clean up many grammatical and technical errors.

Lastly, let me express my fond appreciation of my family, who tolerated my long hours at the word processor and pretended that they believed the project would really be completed. Needless to say, any flaws remaining in the book are the sole responsibility of the author.

Introduction

THE AMERICAN CIVIL WAR PROVIDED THE OPPORTUNITY FOR many individuals to demonstrate talents in organization, leadership, and combat, which might otherwise have lain dormant. Throughout the four years of war, both sides encouraged and rewarded such men with promotion, official recognition, and public acclaim. A few of these, primarily army and corps commanders, although occasionally exceptional or infamous leaders of smaller or irregular units, achieved a place in the national consciousness which survived the demise of the Civil War generation. Others, whose exploits had made them household names and sectional, if not national, heroes, slowly faded from the public awareness and fell into obscurity, largely unknown except by specialists and enthusiasts. One such man was Francis Channing Barlow, known to his men as "The Boy General."

The nickname derived from his youthful looks and clean-shaven face, unusual among Civil War officers. Slight of frame, unprepossessing in appearance, only his gaze betrayed the implacable energy and formidable spirit which burned within him. His men, superiors, and opponents soon learned that the young countenance masked a hard and agile mind, unshakable self-confidence, indomitable will, and an acid tongue. These characteristics, combined with an innate aggressiveness and fearlessness, made Barlow one of the most successful field and general officers in the Army of the Potomac.

Experiencing army life on several levels, from private to general, Barlow served in almost all the major operations in Virginia between 1862–65. He quickly proved his capabilities as a fighting man. He was repeatedly promoted to higher rank and entrusted with greater responsibility. The young general was increasingly handed assignments of crucial importance to the success of Federal arms, and he commonly thrust his way into much of the hottest and deadliest combat in the Virginia theater. By the time he mustered out of the United States Army in 1865, Barlow had compiled a record of achievement and distinction on the regimental,

13

brigade, and divisional level, which few could match and none could exceed.

Barlow was a man of his class, region, time and, perhaps, ethnicity. His outlook was shaped, if not determined, by his New England roots, which, in turn, were nurtured and strengthened by a Boston Brahmin upbringing and education. Under the circumstances, it is unsurprising that Barlow never seemed to question the validity and superiority of his own assumptions and values. It seldom, if ever, occurred to him that those who took positions other than his own might be acting from convictions held as deeply and honestly as his.

The young commander's relations with the two largest non-British ethnic groups of the mid-nineteenth century ranged from uncertain to contemptuous. Barlow's Yankee Protestant background probably led to the ambiguous attitude he seems to have taken with the Irish. During the Peninsula and Sharpsburg campaigns, he fought with the redoubtable Irish Brigade and commanded it during the 1864 Overland Campaign and through the first months at Petersburg. In conversations with one of his political mentors, the Irish-American Judge Charles Daly, Barlow recounted tales of the Irish Brigade's bravery and resolve, but accounts from members of the brigade suggest a more distant and troubled relationship.

Barlow spoke and probably acted with open scorn toward the German troops he commanded at Chancellorsville and Gettysburg. Whatever negative attitudes the young general might have held towards the German troops before 1863 were reinforced by the rout of many of the XIth Corps' German units during Stonewall Jackson's surprise attack at Chancellorsville, and their disintegration on the first day of Gettysburg, when he went down with a serious wound. Although Barlow's natural honesty led him to exempt some German-born officers from his general contempt, by his thinking these were the exceptions that proved the rule. Generally, Barlow consistently rated native American troops the highest, although he was hardly the only officer in the army to do so. While his evaluations were generally derived from his own demanding appraisals, it seems, at least at times, that they were skewed by his personal ethno-religious biases.

Yet Barlow held himself to the same high standards he demanded from others. His effectiveness as a field and general officer, demonstrated consistently over four years of war, was anchored in his unshakable confidence in himself and his cause— if not necessarily those who led it. Respected, although seldom loved, he was not an easy commander to soldier under. Yet his arrogant and caustic personality were complemented by a resolute bravery and ferocity, which transformed him from a young lawyer into one of the most formidable combat leaders produced by either side during the war.

1

The Apprentice Warrior

THE FUTURE "BOY GENERAL" SPRANG FROM AN IMPECCABLE YAN-kee lineage. The American branch of the Barlow line probably began with George Barlow, who arrived in Sandwich, Massachusetts in the seventeenth century.[1] His father, the Reverend David Hatch Barlow, the son of David and Sarah Hatch Barlow, was born on 31 January 1805 in Windsor, Vermont. David Hatch Barlow's began his career auspiciously. He graduated as first scholar in his Harvard class of 1824, and completed divinity school as an ordained Unitarian minister in 1829.[2] In addition to his preaching duties, Hatch Barlow wrote verse—he had been his class poet at Harvard—and composed hymns as well.[3] One of his musical creations was sung at the ordination of Ralph Waldo Emerson as junior pastor of the Second Church of Boston.[4] At about the same time he was completing his theological education, he met and wooed Almira Cornelia Penniman of Brookline. Almira, born in 1810, was widely regarded as "a famous beauty" whose good looks were matched by an engaging personality and taste for expensive fashions.[5]

The couple wed on 10 May 1830. At first the marriage went smoothly and David and Almira were "regarded as the handsomest couple that had been seen in town."[6] Their first son, Edward Emerson (named for Edward Bliss Emerson, a close college friend of David's) was born 5 August 1831 in Lynn, Massachusetts where David had a parish.[7] Possibly exhibiting early signs of a troubled personality, Barlow left his position at Lynn and moved to Brooklyn, New York, where, on 17 September 1834, he began his tenure as pastor of the First Unitarian Church.[8] It was there that Francis Channing Barlow was born on 19 October 1834. Francis Channing Barlow's New York birth proved a portent of his future as his professional, military, and governmental careers were all in the service of his natal state. Nevertheless, Francis would spend his formative years in the Bay State. When he was two years old, his parents returned to his mother's hometown, where he was raised. Here, another boy, Richard D., was born in 1838.

The Barlow family was solidly entrenched in the Unitarian-Transcendentalist circle, which dominated social and intellectual circles in the Boston area during the antebellum years. Unitarianism, a rationalist variation of Christianity, originated in Boston around 1800 and quickly spread through the Congregational churches in eastern Massachusetts, supplanting what was left of the traditional seventeenth-century Calvinism that had so long dominated New England. David Hatch Barlow's own clerical career personified this theological transformation. Transcendentalism arose among the heavily Unitarian intellectual elite around 1836. Taking its name from Immanuel Kant's "transcendental" ideas, it was heavily influenced by German and English Romantic thought. Critical of industrialization, the Transcendentalists believed the divine was present in both man and nature. Moving away from Unitarian rationalism, they maintained that human intuition was the highest form of knowledge. Its optimistic attitude towards human development led the transcendentalists to emphasize individualism, self-reliance and human progress. The transcendentalists were also committed to social reform and embraced the abolitionist movement. The influence of transcendentalism proved strongest in literature. Followers of the movement included essayists such as Ralph Waldo Emerson and Henry David Thoreau, and novelists Herman Melville and Nathaniel Hawthorne.

Perhaps the most ambitious attempt by the New England transcendentalists to put their beliefs into action was the founding of Brook Farm in West Roxbury. Operating between 1841 and 1847, Brook Farm was an attempt to establish a self-supporting commune based on a union of labor and culture.[9] The Farm was founded by George Ripley, a former Unitarian minister who had been forced to give up his church due to his passionate advocacy of Emerson's transcendentalism.[10] Despite the conscious intent to combine work and thought, the community's intellectual activities life proved far more significant and enduring than the experiments in communal living or cooperative agriculture. Hawthorne, Charles A. Dana, and Isaac Hecker were among Brook Farm's members, while Emerson, Margaret Fuller, Horace Greeley, and Orestes Brownson visited frequently. The Brook Farm commune also ran a school, officially titled the Brook Farm Institute of Agriculture and Knowledge, which operated along the principles later advanced, for good or ill, by John Dewey. Students who attended school in the morning were expected to carry out their farm chores in the afternoon while students who studied in the afternoon worked in the morning.

The Barlows' deep New England roots and membership in the Unitarian-Transcendentalist network proved no defense against personal and family disintegration. By the time of the Barlows' return to Brookline, David was exhibiting signs of emotional instability. His behavior, which may have been belligerent at times, quickly affected his family and career.[11] He was forced to give up his pulpit in Brooklyn due to "mental stress"[12] and, as one chronicler delicately phrased it, "his habits became irregular [and] he remained but a short time in any place."[13] In 1840, two years after the birth of their youngest child, Almira and David separated. David remained in the Boston area for a few years and then drifted south to Pennsylvania, abandoning any of his paternal responsibilities. While it is not clear whether Almira legally divorced David, the two had little contact after their separation, and none once he left Massachusetts sometime after 1844.

When David Hatch Barlow left Massachusetts he also turned his back on his children, who apparently never saw him again. Towards the end of the Civil War, Francis, by then a well-known Union general, discovered his father's whereabouts near Philadelphia and attempted to make contact with him. Before the two could meet, however, David Hatch Barlow was killed, and whatever chance existed for a father-son rapprochement died with him.

Almira Barlow rose to the challenge of keeping herself and her three sons in the social milieu to which they were accustomed. Moreover, she was determined to see that her sons' prospects remained open. Shortly after her husband's desertion, Almira and her children became boarders at the Brook Farm commune. Almira's immediate reason for making the trek to West Roxbury was her desire to have her children continue their education under Ripley's tutelage. Edward, Francis, and Richard had been enrolled in Ripley's Boston school, and when he moved it to Brook Farm Almira followed him to West Roxbury.[14] She and her sons lodged in two rooms on one side of "The Hive," the large farmhouse which was at the heart of the community.[15] As enrollees in the school, Francis and his brothers were introduced to some of the foremost thinkers and writers in antebellum America. The Brook Farm experience seems to have made a great impression on young Frank—as he was known to his friends and family—and he felt a sense of affection for the commune and its members

Almira Penniman Barlow, possibly by Francis Alexander. *Courtesy Don Richard Lauter,* **"Winslow Homer and Friends in Prince George County, Virginia, 1864."**

for the rest of his life. His sentiments were reciprocated, and many of Brook Farm's luminaries, such as Emerson, retained a fondness for the fatherless boy and an interest in his future.

In addition to securing a first-rate education for her sons, Almira was probably drawn to Brook Farm by the frequent presence, and possible encouragement, of her old friend, Margaret

Fuller. Fuller was the preeminent woman writer-intellectual of her day. An ardent feminist, Fuller had begun her career by giving lecture seminars to—mostly—female audiences in Cambridge and Boston, and went on to establish herself as a writer, editor, book reviewer and, ultimately, foreign correspondent for the *New York Tribune*. Almira, whose beauty masked a keen intellect, had become acquainted with Fuller before her marriage and according to one source, the two vied for the leadership of a coterie of young intellectuals, "Margaret claiming it by right of intelligence [Almira] by right of beauty."[16] The two remained in contact with each other after Almira's marriage, visiting and corresponding. On 9 March 1834 Fuller, feeling somewhat isolated at her family's farm in Groton, Massachusetts, wrote to Almira who was then living in Brooklyn. The letter, composed as a mock-classic lament, not only sheds light on the women's friendship—and, Fuller's presumption of preeminence—but also reveals Almira's own forays into public discourse:

To Mrs. Almira B.
Are you not ashamed o most friendshipless clergywoman not to have enlivened my long seclusion by one line? You can write to Mistress Mary Hedge, forsooth! to her you confide the history of your intellectual efforts, of your child's mental progress and various maladies, and of your successes in Brooklyn society. . . . Can the Brooklyn Society have exercised so depraving an influence on your heart and tastes? Or does the Author of the 'Lecture delivered with much applause before the Brooklyn Lyceum' despise and wish to cast off the author of 'Essays contumeliously rejected by that respected publication the *Christian Examiner?*' That a little success should have the power to steel the female heart to base ingratitude! O Ally! Ally! Wilt thou forget that it was I (in happier hours thou has full oft owned it) who first fanned the spark of thy Ambition into a flame? Think'st thou that thou owest nought to those long sweeps over the insignificant, inexpressive realities of literature, when thou wert obliged to trust to my support, thy own opinions, as yet scarce budding from thy heels or shoulders. . . . Still remains enveloped in mystery the reason why neither you nor my reverend friend came to bid me good-bye before I left your city according to promise. . . . I had treasured up sundry little anecdotes touching my journey homeward, which, if related with dramatic skill, might excite a smile on your face, O laughter-loving blue stocking. . . . My love to your reverend husband, and four kisses to Edward, two on your account, one for his beauty, and one abstract kiss, symbol of my love for all little children in general. Write of him, or Mr B's sermons, of your likes and dislikes, of any new characters, sublime or droll you may have unearthed, and of all other things I should like.[17]

Despite, or because, it was so heavily patronized by intellectuals, Brook Farm had its share of incongruities. Among these was a whistled greeting/recognition signal. The "Brook Farm Whistle," begun among the children and adopted by the adults, functioned like a fraternity sign and young Frank's was noted as "shrill and trill like a fife."[18] Towards the end of the Civil War, John van der Zee Sears, who knew Barlow from the farm (and who claimed to have introduced the whistle to the commune) caught sight of then General Barlow striding down Pennsylvania Avenue in Washington "at his usual breakneck pace."[19] Rather than call out a greeting, Sears gave out with the "Brook Farm Whistle." "[Barlow] came to an abrupt halt," Sears recalled, "answered my greeting [with the counter whistle] and dashed across the Avenue with both hands extended. Neither of us had more than a short allowance of time, but we could do no less than adjourn to a convenient resort for a good hearty talk about the old days in West Roxbury."[20]

Almira and her brood were gone from Brook Farm by 1844 when Ripley tried to convert it into a socialistic "phalanx," a type of organization devised by the French theorist Charles Fourier.[21] The problem was not disagreement about the Farm's possible new direction, but Almira's beguiling effect on the male members and visitors. The recently separated Mrs. Barlow was well-known as "a famous beauty in Brookline and of a lively and attractive disposition."[22] Almira enjoyed the attentions of men drawn to her "vivacious" personality and soon acquired a circle of admirers.[23] Among these was Nathaniel Hawthorne, who may have based the character of Zenobia in his *Blithedale Romance* on Almira.[24] Shortly after meeting Almira at Brook Farm in the wintry early months of 1841, Hawthorne wrote Sophia Peabody that she looked "as if her ample person were stuffed with tenderness, as if she were all one kind heart."[25] Almira certainly invited masculine attentiveness and often praised the work of Hawthorne in a style which can only be characterized as flirtatious.[26] While male members and visitors to the Farm were first attracted to her physical beauty and charm, they soon found she was well capable of holding her own in conversation with Ripley, Fuller, Orestes Brownson, Hawthorne, and the other members of the literati.

Almira had an especially devastating affect on Isaac Hecker, who worked as a baker in the "Hive's" kitchen where Almira also labored. Hecker, who later converted to Catholicism and founded the Paulist fathers, placed notes on Almira's plate to which she responded on perfumed stationery of her own. Nevertheless, as seems to have been her usual style, Almira's notes were less ardent than Hecker's.[27] Hecker confided his love for Almira in his diary, but apparently she deflected any overt protestations of affection on his part. In the end, Hecker proved more attracted to spirituality than erotic attachments and he drifted off into a friendship with Thoreau before following a religious vocation.

The most besotted of all Almira's admirers was John Sullivan Dwight, who was on his way to becoming a noted promoter of music, especially that of Beethoven. After leaving the Farm he founded *Dwight's Journal of Music,* which became the nation's most influential periodical of music. Six years Almira's junior, Dwight's lovesick attentions became embarrassing, and Almira finally told him that he had become too attached to her. She tried to let him down gently by telling him she valued him as a friend. Dwight asked if she was sure she did not love him, to which she replied, "Oh very sure, Mr. Dwight."[28] Dwight persisted in pledging his love and suggested that in time she would love him, but Almira told him bluntly, "that is out of the question."[29] Apparently the interchange cooled Dwight off, but he still corresponded with Almira after she left the farm, and she, feeling he had come to accept the boundaries of their relationship, allowed him to visit her at Concord.[30]

Almira's beauty and "fondness for the society of men" made her the subject of a great deal of gossip.[31] The other Brook Farm women, perhaps out of jealously or feeling she was pushing the envelope of acceptable behavior, took a dim view of her flirtations. The atmosphere of feminine disapproval made Almira's position increasingly untenable and she was asked to leave Brook Farm by 1 June 1843.[32] How far Almira went with her romantically inclined admirers is unknown. In the absence of evidence to the contrary it seems she was expert at infatuating men while simultaneously holding them at arm's length. A single mother with three small children to raise had to think several steps ahead in an age when full legal rights and power belonged only to men. Whether any of her Brook Farm admirers would have married a divorced woman is impossible to say, but not likely. Having been burned once, Almira never remarried, although undoubtedly she had her opportunities. She correctly saw the role of a mistress as a dead end and a potential humiliation for her children, whose interests seem to have been foremost in her mind. There is no reason to doubt that she genuinely enjoyed the company of the opposite sex. But, if her coquettries were also designed to build a network of influential and potentially useful men for herself and her children, it was a game she played well. The lesson was not lost on her middle son.

The new regime at Brook Farm did not suit the tastes of many of the Transcendentalists, who began to leave the commune for the more agreeable environment of rustic Concord. By the time Almira settled in the village in 1843, its intellectual and cultural life was dominated by Brook Farm alumni and sympathizers. The Concord community included such luminaries as Hawthorne, Emerson, Thoreau, as well the two Curtises, Burrill and George William. Apparently none of her West Roxbury critics were present at Concord—significantly, almost all the Concord group were men—and she quickly resumed an active social and cultural life.[33] George William Curtis, who later became an influential essayist, was especially attentive. He had also been smitten by Almira at the Farm and remained a warm admirer and fast friend at Concord.[34] She was still in the village in 1850, when she was listed with Edward and Richard in the 1850 census. By that time, Frank was headed to college.

How Almira made ends meet is unclear, but it seems her family and personal connections served her in good stead and she managed to raise her brood on her own. Certainly, young Francis benefited from his Brook Farm education and made what seemed a natural progression to Harvard.[35] Money, however, might always have been tight, and there is no evidence that David Barlow ever contributed to the support of his family. On 29 March 1843, Almira wrote to her cousin E. P. Clark and asked to borrow $100 dollars to establish a livelihood.[36]

How young Francis and his brothers reacted to the fracturing of their family is uncertain. He seems to have appreciated his mother's difficulties and her efforts to raise him successfully. During the war, whether in camp or in the field, he corresponded regularly with Almira and was always solicitous as to her comforts and needs. Perhaps Barlow's unstinting sense of duty and resolute commitment to principle derived, at least partly, from his reaction to his father's desertion.

Although the Barlow family situation lacked key elements of stability and cohesion, they held on to the security of place and position which the family name and influence could bestow on the children. This assumption of place and prerogative would have reinforced whatever sense of self-confidence, intellectual and social, Francis received at birth. Perhaps too, the Unitarian-Transcendentalist emphasis on self-reliance and the primacy of one's own beliefs helped shape young Frank's natural self-assurance.

Francis Channing Barlow developed into an alert, quick-witted, bright young man who entered Harvard College at 17. Little is known of his Harvard career other than what might be surmised from his graduating as valedictorian in 1855. Despite his later fastidious commitment to military discipline and ritual, Barlow took part in undergraduate pranks and fired a piece of artillery in the state arsenal yard during his freshman year. Indeed, a Harvard classmate later recalled that there was nothing "in his personal bearing nor his tastes which foreshadowed in any degree a military career."[37]

But it was neither his intellect nor occasional mischievousness that struck most acquaintances about him. By the time he graduated Harvard, he was already noted for his highly polished ego and strongly opinionated personality, characteristics which led him to freely express his disdain for people, behavior and ideas he considered ignorant or inferior. According to Edward H. Abbot who knew Barlow at Harvard,

> He always perceived existing facts and relations with a singular precision and quickness. He prided himself in college upon having no illusions, and was resolved to see things as they really were. He then, and afterward, spoke his thoughts without restraint, and with a singular and almost contemptuous disregard of consequence. He indulged throughout his life in a very unusual freedom, not to say, license, of speech. He acted and spoke, without seeing any regard to what man could do, or say, or think about him.[38]

Barlow's unfiltered frankness was complemented by another signal component of his character—an innate and unhesitant physical courage. As was true of his readiness to express his opinions, Barlow's natural and unreflective pugnacity was noted early in life. The other students at Brook Farm often called him "Crazy Barlow," due to his tendency to make a "headlong rush at whatever object he had in view."[39] Others who knew him as a youth were likewise struck by his aggressiveness. When Barlow enlisted in the army at the onset of hostilities, Edward Barry Dalton, whose family was well acquainted with him, wrote to his brother, "I am, with you, very much afraid for Barlow, for as we know, he is not only brave, but reckless. I think I never knew anyone so perfectly without fear of physical injury."[40]

Shortly after graduating Harvard, Barlow joined the large number of New Englanders seeking the wider opportunities available in the burgeoning metropolis of New York. His decision to leave Boston was viewed with regret by some of his friends and mentors who had hoped to add a promising young man to the roster of distinguished Yankees. On 27 August 1855, Ralph Waldo Emerson wrote his former pupil expressing such sentiments. "My dear Frank," the noted essayist began, "I am resigned to your going to New York where so many opportunities glitter for your ambition but I am sorry you do not decide for Massachusetts humble but finer. Perhaps you will after looking at Broadway."[41] Emerson would be disappointed in that hope.

Like many of his class and generation, at least those unattracted to a religious career, Barlow trained as a lawyer. After a year in which he earned his living as a tutor preparing young men for college and business, he joined the firm of William Curtis Noyes, but soon moved on to Wheaton and Livingston. Working for someone else's law practice held little allure for an ambitious young attorney, and once he passed the Bar examination in 1858, he entered into a legal partnership with George Bliss. In addition to his work with Bliss, Barlow moonlighted as a law reporter and editor for the *New York Tribune*. His mother and brothers joined him in New York, and all were listed as living in the City according to the 1860 census.

Before launching his legal career he dabbled in teaching, and in the summer of 1855 he tutored college-bound students. Among these was Robert Gould Shaw, who later fell while leading the 54th Massachusetts in their doomed assault on Fort Wagner, South Carolina.[42] The Shaws were another prominent Boston family who had been connected with the Brook Farm experiment. Indeed, Robert's father, Francis G. Shaw, had been one of the commune's first supporters. In the late 1850s the Shaws had relocated to Staten Island in order for Robert's mother, whose sight was failing, to have more immediate access to leading eye specialists. When young Robert decided he wanted to get into Harvard, his parents sought a tutor to prepare him for the entrance examinations. The "crammer," as Robert called him, turned out to be the old family acquaintance, Frank Barlow. Barlow's tutoring bore fruit and Shaw was admitted into Harvard, though he was not able to skip a grade as he had hoped. Barlow's friendships with the Shaws and his other Boston friends and acquaintances lasted throughout his life. After the war, Barlow's connection with the Shaws became more intimate when Robert's sister became his second wife.

From the beginning of his adult life, Barlow seemed well aware that the friendship of influential families could prove advantageous politically and professionally. Barlow's Harvard background and Boston connections may have opened doors in New York—Emerson provided him with an introduction—and his promising law career introduced him to many of the more prominent politicians in his new city and state. During the War, for example, Barlow proved himself totally at ease in corresponding with New York's governors, offering advice on promotions and other military matters, and, not incidentally, keeping his name and exploits fresh in their minds.

Perhaps the most important acquaintance made by Barlow before the war was of Judge Charles Patrick Daly. Daly, son of Irish immigrants, began life in poverty and rose to prominence by virtue of his intellect, diligence, and personality. When Barlow first met him, Daly was a justice on the Court of Common Pleas, then the highest and most important court in New York City. Daly was later appointed Chief Justice of the New York State Supreme Court. Throughout his lengthy career on the bench, Daly held the enviable reputation of being the "incorruptible judge." The jurist was also active in the intellectual and cultural life of the City and was a founding member and long-term president of the National Geographic Society. Not surprisingly, he was active in Irish causes, but he was also on good terms with the City's Jewish community as well. Daly married Maria Lydig, a member of an old-money German-Dutch family, when they were both in their 30s. Maria was an influential figure in New York Society in her own right, and Barlow cultivated them both. While Barlow's feeling of friendship towards the Dalys seems heartfelt, there is little doubt that he appreciated the advantages which the judge's influence and patronage could bestow on him, and he took pains to keep his relationship with the judge and his wife warm and constant throughout the war.

Although he was well on his way to a flourishing legal career, Barlow dropped everything and quickly enlisted in the army after Lincoln called for volunteers in the wake of the Confederate bombardment of Fort Sumter. Bliss kept the law firm going during the War. Barlow not only remained in contact with him, but occasionally did some legal work while on leave or convalescing.

Barlow's motivation for rushing to the colors seems straightforward. He was a man who tended to see the world in terms of right and wrong. To him, the Union was inviolate, secession evil, and his course clear. As he put it in a letter written many years later, "In all ages of the world it has been supposed that it is the duty of citizens to come to the defense of their country."[43] Evidence indicates that he was a moderate abolitionist, but not necessarily a believer in racial equality, common enough at the time (see chapter 4). "No one rejoices more than myself in the overcoming a rebellion the design of which was to destroy this Government for the purpose of maintaining the monstrous institution of slavery," he later wrote, identifying the dual causes of union and abolition which impelled him to enlist.[44] Certainly an anti-slavery outlook would have come naturally to a man raised in the Unitarian-Transcendalist tradition and an alumnus of the Brook Farm School to boot.[45] During the War he expressed his belief that only those on the Federal side who fought the war "on antislavery grounds" possessed the earnestness and nobility of the Confederates. His personal commitment to "antislavery grounds" was demonstrated by his interest in commanding a black regiment or taking a position with the Freedmen's Bureau during the war.

The secession crisis and Lincoln's call for volunteers coincided with Francis' marriage to Arabella Wharton Griffith. Arabella, known as Belle to her friends, was a native of Somerville, New Jersey. Her father, William R. Griffith, had been trained as a physician, but was reported as a merchant at the time of his marriage.[46] Money seemed to be a chronic problem and he borrowed frequently. He was in debt when he married Arabella's mother, 21-year-old Ann Marie Wallace Howell, on 21 September 1819. Whatever personal affection he may have felt, Ann Marie's attractiveness to William was probably magnified by his financial embarrassment in contrast to her family's wealth.[47] William's money problems, perhaps intensified by intemperance in alcohol, did not cease with marriage. Creditors, including his own father-in-law, hauled him into court.[48] Three children were born during the couple's turbulent marriage. Two sons, John and Edward, were born in December 1820 and February 1826, respectively. Arabella, the middle child, was born 29 February 1824.

Like Francis, Belle was fated to come from a broken home. The same month her younger brother was born, the Griffiths separated. The couple divorced in November, and William was lost at sea the following year.[49] With the immediate family fragmented, Arabella was sent to live with an elderly relative, Eliza Wallace, her maternal grandmother's cousin. She became so close to Eliza that Francis later referred to Arabella as Eliza's adopted daughter. When Miss Wallace died in December 1861, Arabella received a small inheritance.[50] Arabella remained under Eliza's foster parenting for about twenty years during which time which she was educated at St. Mary's Hall. She soon went off on her own to New York, where she was living by December 1846.[51]

During the pre-war years in New York, Arabella was living in Manhattan at the residence of prominent merchant and ship-broker, Peter Nevius, at 19 Waverly Place, where she was likely employed as a governess.[52] Arabella soon became a member of a circle of middle-class socialites and artists, which included inveterate diarist George Templeton Strong, and his wife, Ellen. Strong met Arabella during an evening at the Lydigs. "Tea at the Lydig's tonight," he recorded in his diary account of 29 March 1855, "where the Rev. Mr. Weston and Miss Arabella Griffith, of whom I've heard so much from the Lydigs; certainly the most brilliant, cultivated, easy graceful, effective talker of womankind, and has read, thought and observed much and well."[53] Arabella quickly became a part of this socially distinguished set of doers and thinkers. She was a frequent guest at the Strongs' home and sometimes attended Trinity Church with them. Her deep intelligence and keen perceptions impressed those who came into contact with her, although some men clearly did not know what to make of her. On 6 May 1855, Strong noted that Arabella accompanied him and his wife during two sermons at Trinity. Afterwards she returned to the Strongs and passed the evening with them. "Mr. Ruggles here, much fascinated by the lady [Arabella] (men generally don't affect her a great deal, say she talks conversation and isn't natural)."[54]

Winslow Homer (a distant cousin of Barlow's) who was already making his name as a popular artist, maintained studios across the street from Waverly Place at the University Building. Homer's friend and fellow artist, Eastman Johnson, was a friend of the Strongs, who were well known in the City's art circles, and he probably introduced the Strongs, and Arabella, to Homer. Exactly how Barlow entered the picture is not entirely clear, but the young, ambitious lawyer had a knack for befriending prominent and influential people, and he may have met the Strongs through his legal work. He might also have tied into the Lydig-Strong circle through his friendship with Judge Daly who was married to Maria Lydig. On the other hand, Barlow had gone to Harvard with Homer's brother, and he was acquainted with Homer from his Boston days.[55] Possibly he met the Strongs and Arabella through Homer.

On 20 April 1861, Barlow enlisted in the 12th New York Volunteers, a three-month unit, and married Arabella that evening

at St. Paul's Chapel in New York City. The couple had little time
to savor the pleasures of married life as, in Strong's words, Barlow "married Miss Arabella Griffith at St. Paul's Chapel Satur-
day Evening, left her at the church door and went to Washington
yesterday."[56] Arabella was 10 years older than Frank, an unusual spread in ages which apparently concerned them not at all.
Having been raised by the vivacious and capable Almira, marriage to a strong, dynamic older woman might have been a natural step for Frank. But if Belle and Frank seemed oblivious to
their age difference, fresh acquaintances were sometimes struck
by the disparity, which was probably exaggerated by Barlow's
slim build and youthful face. Maria Daly once recorded that when
her maid admitted the couple to the Daly house during the first
year of the War, she reported to her mistress that "a young soldier and his mother [were] in the parlor."[57]

Arabella and Francis were destined to enjoy only intermittent
periods of time together during their married life. Nevertheless,
Arabella was absolutely devoted to her husband and his career.
She once told Maria Daly that "women rule everything," a statement which reflected her belief that wives could effectively act as
advocates and lobbyists for their husbands' careers, effectively
managing their careers—and maybe them as well.[58] She whole-
heartedly joined in the work of maintaining Barlow's political
connections and friendships, especially during times when he
was unable to do so. In November 1861, shortly before Barlow returned to the Army after a brief return to civilian life, Arabella
complained to Maria Daly that sharing a soldier's life was a burden, but Daly thought her complaints mere pretense. "I know
that in her heart it is just the thing she would choose and has, no
doubt, had much to do in urging Frank to return."[59]

Arabella strove to keep in as close proximity to Francis as the
turmoil of war would allow. Perhaps influenced by her friend,
George Templeton Strong, who became prominent in the United
States Sanitary Commission, a forerunner of the Red Cross,
Arabella enlisted in the organization as a nurse. Her medical duties not only allowed her to serve her country and cause, but also
permitted her to join her husband for varying lengths of time,
depending on the military situation. She was usually with him
or nearby when he was in one camp or position for any time, but
the exigencies and uncertainties of the war made anything resembling a stable married life impossible. The only significant
exceptions to the often-separated state of their union came in
the months after Frank's two woundings, which required lengthy

convalescences. During these periods, she took leave from her nursing duties at military hospitals to devote herself whole-heartedly to her husband's recovery. Unfortunately, neither her letters to Frank nor his to her have survived. Consequently, only glimpses of this remarkable woman can be gleaned from the letters Barlow sent his own family, plus a handful of letters she sent friends and scattered remarks in diaries and memoirs. The lack of material unfortunately obscures and diminishes the importance she must have had in Barlow's life during the war.

Having barely had enough time to exchange vows with his bride, Barlow left with his regiment for Washington.[60] The 12th New York saw no action, but was stationed in the defensive perimeter surrounding Washington. The soldiers' time was spent mastering the rudiments of drill and organization, while the tedium of camp life soon blunted the fresh recruits' initial flush of enthusiasm. Probably due to his education and background, not to mention his profession, Barlow was offered a lieutenancy when he enlisted. He declined the offer on the logical grounds that he had never handled a gun in his life.[61] Service as private, however, quickly grew old and Barlow soon accepted his first commission. His relatively quick decision to leave a private's life may have been partly motivated by his conclusion that life as an enlisted man was unsuitable for a man of his class, education, and abilities. Such an attitude was hardly unusual among members of his social strata. While many of the social and economic élites joined the colors, many others never served in any capacity. Some, such as Theodore Roosevelt, Sr., father of the president, and J. P. Morgan, took advantage of provisions permitting substitutes or cash payments as a way of avoiding the draft when conscription was implemented in 1863. Additionally, Barlow quickly turned his critical eye on the leadership abilities of many of the officers above him and found them wanting. His own self-confidence, temporarily checked by his lack of experience, resumed full vigor after a brief taste of army life and the realization that few of the ranking officers he encountered possessed any more experience than he had. Barlow likely concluded, correctly as events bore out, that he could do the job as well as most and better than many.

Receiving a lieutenancy did not reduce Barlow's dissatisfaction with army life. In May, he pronounced the weather at Camp Winfield Scott as "enervating." He missed his friends, family, and Arabella, and complained about the lack of intelligent companionship. He was also unhappy with his colonel, Daniel Butterfield, whom he later denounced as a "snob," who did not know how to treat his men or officers.[62] The only bright spot was a visit, the first of several throughout the war, of his brother, Edward. "This sort of life is not pleasant," he wrote his mother, "but I did not come for pleasure and can endure anything for three months."[63]

Always quick to vent his opinions both in writing and conversation, Barlow rarely held back from expressing exactly what was on his mind at any given time. On several occasions, exasperation, frustration, and disgust at army life and the conduct of the War led him to threaten retirement from his command as soon as his term of enlistment was up. Such explosions were usually short-lived, and sober reflection and logical thought usually followed his outbursts. This pattern appeared early in Barlow's military career. In summer 1861, for example, he confided to his brother Edward that he would return to "New York the moment our time is up & I shall not enlist again at least at present—I am sick of this damned Regt."[64]

Barlow's unhappiness at the time contained an element of simple homesickness and camp boredom. He complained that he saw "no one," by which he evidently meant friends or acquaintances. He was also irritated that he had not been able to go anywhere. While he grew increasingly concerned with his ability to command, he showed no inclination to develop any rapport with his men, a shortcoming which remained the greatest single flaw in his performance as an officer throughout the war. "I have commanded the company with credit," he boasted in his June 18 letter "& feel competent to be capt—with the exception of one thing—that is I have not the desire to make the damned scoundrels like me & I do not think they do especially."[65]

By early July, Arabella had traveled to Washington and the couple might have found some time together. Their meeting was short, however, as Barlow's unit was finally put into motion. The 5th and 12th New York broke camp and were transported by a circuitous route to the head of the Shenandoah Valley where they reinforced Federal forces already deployed in the area. The Union troops converging at the end of the Valley were part of an overall strategy aimed at driving the Confederate forces from northern Virginia and opening the way to Richmond. While General Irwin McDowell prepared to strike the Confederates under General Pierre G. T. Beauregard at Manassas, the Shenandoah force under General Patterson was to advance against General Joseph J. Johnston who was encamped near Winchester and prevent his going to Beauregard's aid. Since the Confederates had blown up the bridges at Harpers Ferry, the 5th and 12th New York were

transported to Baltimore where they changed trains and proceeded to Hagerstown, Maryland. From Hagerstown, they
marched to Williamsport where they crossed the Potomac and
linked up with Patterson's command near Martinsburg, (West)
Virginia. The chance for action had revived Barlow's spirits and
he optimistically predicted that the entire Federal Army would
"march on Richmond from all sides."[66]

The 35,000 or so troops under Patterson moved to Bunker Hill
and Barlow expected that a battle would soon be fought at Winchester. The Federal push was halted, however, and the troops
pulled back to Charlestown where John Brown had been hanged
two years previously. While denied a taste of combat, Barlow
took advantage of the pause to evaluate the different regiments
in the army. He boasted that the 12th New York was—with a
single exception he found later—superior to the others, laying
out their tents "with regular streets ... [while] ... the others were
all straggling and unmilitary."[67]

Despite the fact that they were in the field and within a short
march of Confederate troops, the 12th New York found time to
hold dress parades, which "shamed" the other regiments into
following suit. Barlow threw off some of the tedium and irritation of camp life and learned to appreciate the attributes of at
least some of his men. He reacted favorably to the soldiers' singing while marching and decided that there were "several amusing men in the ranks who make a good many amusing jokes ...
and really have a good sense of humor." On the other hand, apparently to his surprise if not necessarily disapproval, Barlow
discovered that "the style of profanity of the whole regiment is
frightful."[68]

During the "phony war" at Charlestown, Barlow took advantage of the lack of action to visit old friends in the Massachusetts
regiments in his camp. While clearly proud of his own unit, he
pronounced the 2nd Massachusetts "much the finest in the Volunteer service." Barlow was happy to discover himself among
friends and rode over to a Massachusetts camp to visit his former
student, "Bob" Shaw, who was, unfortunately, asleep when his
old tutor came calling.[69]

The time spent in the Martinsburg area was Barlow's first real
taste of the South and he took note of the nature of the Virginia
countryside and the character of its inhabitants. Although the
Shenandoah was, and remains, one of the granaries of the South,
Barlow was unimpressed. Although his previous knowledge of
Virginia was confined to the areas around the army camps and a

few villages across the Potomac from Washington, Barlow felt expert enough to dismiss Charlestown for being "like all Virginia towns . . . slovenly and wretched with occasionally some large old pleasant looking place and houses . . . . The country is generally poor with a worn out look and the people very ignorant."[70]

The novice officer found the secessionist spirit strong, especially among the women, whose rebel sentiments were laced with good, if acid, humor. Most of the military-age men were away in service with the Confederate Army, and Barlow was treated by one woman to the stereotypical boast that any of her three brothers could whip three Yankees. Another woman volunteered that she would like to become a cook for the northerners so she could lace their food with arsenic.[71]

While Barlow was learning how to get his men to lay out their tents in street-like patterns and march well in formation, he still had little knowledge of the primary purpose of his enlistment—combat. By the time he arrived in the Shenandoah, he had acquired some rudiments of military practice and wrote to his brother from Charlestown, apparently in response to a question, explaining that the officers ordinarily remained in the rear of companies and

> of course in the firings are there. In charging a battery or in charging bayonets I suppose the officers or at least the commandant leads his men up to the object on an enemy to be attacked but he must fall back, I should think, before bayonets are crossed as he would stand little chance with his sword against a bayonet.[72]

Barlow was candid about the state of his military expertise at the time. "I confess I understand but little of the practical duties of an officer in battle & no one else here does. We ought to be instructed in it. In battle I shall obey orders when they were given & use my discretion when they were not."[73]

Though Barlow was clearly concerned about the overall lack of training he and his fellow officers and men received, the time had not yet arrived for him to face the ultimate test. Through timidity, hyper-concern for the capital's safety, or the incompetence and age of its commander, a War of 1812 veteran, the Federal forces in the lower Valley never advanced against Johnston's force at Winchester. Instead, Johnston withdrew his forces from the Valley by rail through the Manasses Gap in the Blue Ridge Mountains and joined Beauregard in time to turn back the Federal attack at First Manasses. Barlow was spared the experience of being caught in the northern rout and was mustered out of the Army when the three months' enlistment of the regiment expired on 1 August.

Barlow kept his word and did not reenlist in "this damned regiment." Nor could he have done so as Federal forces were totally reorganized; three-month units were abolished and a new system of three-year regiments inaugurated. Barlow took his time, three months, before joining up again. Some of his lag in donning a uniform anew may have been due to the time necessary to arrange a new system. More probably, Barlow was enjoying his marriage and arranging a superior rank. He also seems to have spent some time doing legal work with Bliss at their 50 Wall Street office.[74] By October, if not earlier, Barlow was lobbying the governor for a position as major in a new regiment. The commission had not arrived by 25 October, when he affected not to care whether he received it or not.[75]

On 9 November 1861, Barlow reenlisted in the 61st New York as its lieutenant colonel. Once again, he found himself posted to Washington's defensive perimeter where his regiment was assigned to Howard's Brigade in Israel Richardson's division, which became part of Edward Sumner's II Corps the following March. Barlow met his new regiment at Camp Kendal Green in Washington, though they soon transferred to Fort Worth near Camp California on the Virginia side of the Potomac. One of the men in his regiment, Charles A. Fuller, who fought under Barlow until the latter's wounding at Antietam, was not overly impressed on his first look at his new lieutenant colonel. "He was not at first sight an impressive looking officer. He was of medium height, of slight build, with a pallid countenance, and a weakish drawling voice. In his movements there was an appearance of loose jointedness and an absence of prim stiffness."[76]

From the beginning of the war, Barlow understood that the North could not prevail without qualified officers and competently trained men. His efforts to identify and promote capable officers and remove those lacking the requisite military aptitudes were part of his personal campaign to improve the military prowess of the Federal forces, and he stayed at it throughout the conflict. Despite his innate self-confidence, Barlow was aware of his own inexperience and took steps to educate himself in military science. During the winter of 1861–62, he applied himself to the study of military affairs, and his friend Nelson Miles recalled that Barlow made good use of his spare time in the first winter of the war to acquire a "useful knowledge of military history ... [and] ... made himself absolute master of military tactics."[77] Barlow's regimen of study and instruction dovetailed with the reorganization, refitting and training program directed by the Army's new commander, Major General George McClellan. The II Corps commander, Edwin V. Sumner, may have been old but knew what was necessary to convert raw recruits into battle-ready soldiers. "We are drilling violently from morning to night," Barlow reported home, adding, "General Sumner says he shall not be so strict when we are better drilled."[78]

Sumner's training schedule fit Barlow's inclinations perfectly. The 25-year-old lieutenant colonel worked his men hard and took steps to impart what he had learned to his subordinate officers. His measures and methods did not make him loved, but increasingly, especially after the regiment saw combat, his men came to appreciate his insistence on training and preparation. Charles Fuller approvingly recollected the effects of Barlow's leadership on his regiment.

> At once schools and drills were established for commissioned and non-commissioned officers and rumor credited Barlow with their establishment. Discipline became stricter; the duties of a soldier were better explained and the men sensibly improved. There is no doubt to whom is due the credit for the change. In a short time there was a feeling in the air that the strength of the regiment lay in the person of the Lieutenant Colonel. He knew the details of his business; he had the military instinct; and he was fearless. At first from his exacting requirements and severity he was quite disliked, if not well hated; but as time went on, and it was seen that he knew more than any man or set of men, in the regiment—that he knew how to work his men to the best advantage and would see that they had what the regulation prescribed, and, that when danger was at hand, he was at the head *leading* them, this animosity turned into confidence and admiration.[79]

That Fuller's assessment of Barlow was common, if not universal, is supported by the recollections of Samuel S. Parmalee of the 1st Connecticut Calvary who first met Barlow on the Peninsula in early 1862:

> I remember when I first saw [Barlow], looked about nineteen, was lying on a bed as lazy as a Turk. 'What' says I' 'you a colonel?' The men found out he was a Colonel. He would put a man in the guard house for coming from a right shoulder shift to a present, without coming first to a shoulder etc. break a corporal of the guard for not instructing better the deficient sentinel. He once broke [a soldier], one of the

best Sergt. he had for handing a man a cup of water on the march . . . .
His old regt. hated him as they hated anything, but he was the man
after all they wanted to go into a fight with.[80]

Understanding and respect for Barlow's tough methods may
have come to many of his troops after battle, but while they
trained in camp large numbers clearly considered him an inflexible martinet. The young lieutenant colonel's stern discipline
quickly achieved notoriety both within and beyond the army.
After hearing reports of Barlow's severe training, Robert Gould
Shaw's sister, Effie, wrote her brother criticizing Barlow for treating his men harshly. Shaw replied that all his sister's complaints
had done was "to show that [Barlow] was a better Field Officer
than 9 out of 10 in these two divisions."[81] Word of Barlow's unbending ways even reached New York City circles where Maria
Lydig Daly reported, "Barlow, they say, is very cruel to his men.
He may, however, be only a stern disciplinarian."[82]

Most of Barlow's men ultimately developed a fierce pride from
belonging to one of the most stringently trained and possibly best-
prepared units in the army. More importantly, Barlow's methods
bore fruit when his regiment—and later brigade and division—
was sent into combat, and his troops won a place among the most
effective warriors in the Army of the Potomac. There were, however, others who felt that Barlow's drill and training regimen was
excessively harsh and unbending. In any case, Barlow's understanding of his duties as an officer, and the standards he set for
his troops, seem fully developed from the time he assumed his
first command. While experience on the battlefield led him to
alter his tactical deployments and maneuvers, the demands he
placed on himself and his men changed little over the course of
the war. His style of command seems to have sprung naturally
from his own personality and upbringing, coupled with whatever
military science he garnered from the texts which he studied
over the cold months of 1861–62. When he put his concepts of
leadership and organization the test, they worked, and he found
no cause to doubt himself, or reconsider his methods.

Barlow's dedication to the professionalization of his unit did
not lead him to ignore his creature comforts. During the winter
of 1861–62, he had a log house (of about 16 by 12) constructed,
which was sealed with dry plaster to keep out the winter winds.
Windows were installed in his camp abode and Barlow claimed
that ". . . with a good fire it will be as comfortable as a house."[83]
Nor did the young Brahmin want for personal assistance. He

retained an "excellent servant" and a "first rate cook for our mess."[84] As a field-grade officer, Barlow also owned and rode a horse. All in all, Barlow made himself about as comfortable as a man of his rank could under the circumstances.

Fort Worth, like most Civil War camps, was plagued by sickness and disease, especially in the winter months, when men were in close proximity to one another in confined and frequently badly ventilated quarters. Additionally, neither the sanitary standards nor the medical knowledge of the time could deal satisfactorily with a host of contagious pathogens. While Barlow managed to remain healthy throughout the winter, 140 out of his 675 men fell sick and three had died by the end of the year.[85] In order to re-plenish the regiment's strength, a recruiting detail was formed in early 1862, which set up headquarters on Broadway in New York City. The effort was not overly successful and only about a dozen new enlistees were secured, leaving the regiment well be-low prescribed strength.[86]

With his snug cabin completed and servant at hand the only thing Barlow needed to make his winter household complete was the company of his wife. On 12 December he wrote his mother that he had not seen Arabella since leaving New York and did not expect her yet for a few weeks. He also encouraged his mother and brother Edward to visit him in Virginia. He told his mother that she could stay with Arabella when she arrived, as "Arabella always manages to find some good place."[87] When Arabella fi-nally reached Alexandria in late December she found lodgings near Fort Worth with a family named Richards. After her arrival, Barlow wrote home that he "generally" went up to the Richards and "sat awhile with her."[88]

By January 1862, the weather had turned raw. The ground was covered with snow which turned the earth into mud when-ever there was a thaw. The overall weather conditions made the daily routine of drill, picket duty, and general camp life increas-ingly onerous. To break the tedium and gloom, Barlow occasion-ally went out to practice shooting with the revolver he carried at the time, even though he doubted its usefulness in battle.[89] But even riding was difficult and twice he was thrown from his horse as the animal tried unsuccessfully to negotiate ice and mud. On 23 January, Barlow endured a four-day stretch of picket duty, which was made more unpleasant by the fact that "we have not seen the sun for ten days."[90]

Even Arabella's presence nearby could not dispel Barlow's mid-winter gloom. "On the whole it is a damned stupid life," he complained. As was often the case, once he fell into a bitter mood, he became temporarily despondent, and vented his spleen at any target which came to mind—including his own cause. "I hardly think this disgusting country is worth fighting for," he snarled.[91]

Barlow was frustrated by the lack of action, a situation that frequently set off his hair-trigger temper. Having spent much time working to improve himself and his men, he wanted to put both to the test. He erupted in indignation at anything, which suggested weakness or incompetence in the United States government. The release of Mason and Slidell, Confederate emissaries to Britain who had been captured by the navy, infuriated him. He expressed his outrage in a letter to his brother, stating he would prefer a war with "the whole of them" by which he apparently meant the Confederacy, Britain and anyone else who got in the way of the Union cause. Then, and throughout the War, Barlow insisted that the North could only prevail through an unswerving commitment to total victory. "We are lost if we show any cowardice or want of spirit on any point. I also believe that a war with England would bring out a spirit which this war never has."[92] Fortunately, cooler and wiser heads than Barlow's were directing United States diplomacy at the time.

Concern over the competence of Federal officers again drew Barlow's attention. He expected much from himself and refused to accept anything else from others, including his brother officers in the 61st New York. Early in December, he had decided both the regiment's colonel and major were lacking in "any capacity whatever . . . for overseeing the command of a Regt." "I do it all," he declared, and he was right.[93] The following month the colonel's shortcomings led to a revolt among most of the regiment's officers. Barlow was a leader in the effort to have the colonel, Spencer W. Cone, removed. The discontented officers drew up a petition charging Cone with nine counts of incompetence. All the officers except Cone himself, the major, whom Barlow had also branded as a dud, the quartermaster, and one second lieutenant signed it.[94]

The disgruntled officers submitted the petition to Colonel Cone, and asked the thunderstruck man to forward it to higher authorities. After consulting with General O. O. Howard, then brigade commander, the hapless colonel seemed to accede to his own removal and claimed he had intended to resign anyway. Barlow remained skeptical, saying he would believe it when it happened. He maintained that he personally found Cone a pleasant and "genial man," but contended that he was "utterly unfit for his place and under him the regiment is going to ruin & private feelings must be sacrificed to public good."[95] Nevertheless, the colonel was still in command in February, though Barlow believed that Howard and Sumner were about to remove him. Cone was finally dismissed from the service on April 14, 1862 and the name of the 61st New York's new colonel was announced—25-year-old Francis Barlow.[96]

As the weather slowly warmed in March, Barlow continued to pursue the life of a garrison soldier. He had the enjoyment of Arabella's presence, and often drove her out into the countryside, socializing at times with higher-ranking officers and their wives. These included the spouse of General Francis Meagher. Meagher had organized the Irish Brigade, a unit Barlow would have the opportunity to know well in the future. His corps commander, General Sumner, also entertained the Barlows. After Joseph Johnston had pulled the Confederate forces out of Centerville and prepared a new defensive perimeter south of the Rappahannock, Francis and Arabella drove out to inspect the Confederate fortifications which had been considered formidable by the Union command. "They have deceived us and kept us at bay with the terror of a name," Barlow concluded grimly after examining the empty Southern works and the "Quaker guns"— painted logs designed to resemble cannon and intimidate Yankee attackers.[97]

The coming of spring must have made Barlow, seemingly stuck in interminable camp duty, increasingly edgy. Like many soldiers, he had joined the army to subdue the southern rebellion and "see the elephant"—experience combat. As the ice- and mud-filled winter slowly released its grip, General George McClellan, commander of the Army of the Potomac, made ready to launch his massive, superbly equipped army against the Confederate capitol. Barlow was to get his wish at last.

2

Initiation in Blood

FOLLOWING THE UNION DEBACLE AT FIRST MANASSES, ABRAHAM Lincoln looked about for a commander who could retrieve the situation, restore the confidence of the demoralized Federal troops, refit and retrain the Army, and take the Confederate capital at Richmond. George McClellan seemed the logical choice. He had bested Robert E. Lee in the pro-Union counties of western Virginia, brought that area under United States government control, and set the stage for the creation of the new state of West Virginia. McClellan had superb credentials as an engineer, had served as an observer during the Crimean War, and achieved the Federal government's only notable success to that date. Moreover, McClellan exuded confidence, striking Napoleonic poses and assuming an air of intellectual superiority and military sagacity—especially around Lincoln. Initially, Lincoln gave him control of all Federal armies. "I can do it all," the "Young Napoleon" replied when Lincoln asked if the task might be too much for one man.[1]

In the end, McClellan could do only one thing, although he did it well. Through the winter of 1861–62, McClellan amassed a huge military force of approximately 100,000 men.[2] He saw to it that they were clothed, equipped and, to the best the Federal government could procure weapons, armed. The drills and parades, in which Barlow participated, were designed to erase the sting of Manasses, restore morale, instill pride, and create a military force capable of defeating the rebels in Virginia and seizing the Confederate capital. Barlow's own regimen of regimental training and preparation fit well with McClellan's overall policy, though his disciplined pursuit of military knowledge seems beyond that found among most of his peers. By early 1862, the Army of the Potomac, as the United States government's major eastern army was now called, had been fashioned into a powerful military instrument. It was then that McClellan's major, and fatal, weakness as a commanding general began to appear. The army's commander understood how to organize an army, inspire it, and create a sense

43

of personal loyalty to himself that in some cases endured long
after his incapacities were proven, but he froze when the time
came to do the job he was selected to execute—lead his army into
battle and defeat the enemy.

While McClellan was at work restoring and rebuilding the
army, Lincoln tolerated his general's contemptuous and insulting
conduct towards him. But by early 1862, with McClellan unwilling to explain his plans for taking the war to the Confederacy,
Lincoln's forebearance reached its limits. First, he removed Mc-
Clellan from overall command of all Federal forces and then ordered the Army of the Potomac to move forward on 22 February,
Washington's birthday. Faced with the necessity of committing
his troops to action, McClellan countered Lincoln's desire for a
direct movement against the rebel lines in Virginia with a proposal to move most of the army from its camps around Washington and land them near Urbana, forcing Johnston to pull south
from his Centerville lines thus providing McClellan with the opportunity to strike at Richmond from a shorter distance. The plan
was sound, though Lincoln, nervous about Washington's security,
insisted that McClellan leave about 40,000 troops in the forts and
works ringing the northern capitol. McClellan reluctantly agreed
to the stipulation, but immediately began convincing himself that
Lincoln was forcing him to take the offensive with a numerically
inferior force.

However, on 8 March, anticipating exactly such a move as
McClellan was preparing, Johnston withdrew from his lines at
Centerville and took up a position further south behind the Rappahannock River. This new defensive line, which became the default position for Confederate forces for most of the war, allowed
Johnston to move south to cover Richmond or remain in place to
blunt a northern offensive from Washington. With the military
situation now totally changed, McClellan decided on a more ambitious movement. The Federals had retained Fortress Monroe
on the eastern extremity of the York Peninsula between the York
and James Rivers. McClellan determined to take advantage of
this northern toehold and transport the Army of the Potomac to
the York Peninsula by ship and disembark his men within the
Federal defensive perimeter. Once the Army of the Potomac was
ashore he intended "by rapid movements to drive before me, or
capture the enemy on the Peninsula, open the James River, and
push on to Richmond before he could be materially reinforced from
other positions in his territory."[3]

Either through leaks or deduction, the outline of McClellan's plan became known to the soldiers. As the lead elements of the Army of the Potomac left Alexandria for Fortress Monroe on 17 March, Barlow wrote his mother "the whole army is to descend the river in transports and land somewhere and march thence to Richmond."[4] He confessed he did not know exactly where the army would disembark. The 61st New York, part of the largest military organization the United States had yet created, arrived on the peninsula no later than 11 April. Despite the necessity of leaving behind enough troops to allay the politicians' fears for Washington's security, McClellan's army contained 121,000 men, 44 batteries of artillery, and 14,592 animals to haul the various types of wagons and artillery limbers.[5] In contrast, the Confederate forces facing him under General John B. Magruder numbered only 13,000 men.[6] What Magruder lacked in means he made up in heart. Determined to brazen it out in front of York-town, the Confederate commander ordered his men to march and countermarch behind their position, allowing the Union troops to glimpse what seemed like fresh troops entering their lines, when in fact they were the same men were simply moving in and out of their works. The maneuver deceived McClellan. Now thoroughly convinced that he faced a large, well-entrenched enemy force, the "Young Napoleon" dug in, and he called for his siege artillery. The "rapid movements" that he projected earlier were abandoned, and the Army of the Potomac commenced a laborious, almost glacial, advance towards Richmond whose character and outcome was determined by the timidity of its commander.

The officers and men of the 61st New York, part of General O. O. Howard's Brigade of Sumner's II Corps, were quickly introduced to the hot, humid, and wet conditions typical of the warm season in the Tidewater. While some small unit actions occurred in April, Barlow's regiment remained behind the lines in reserve. Although he felt vindicated by his promotion to full colonel, Barlow's arrogance and disdain for those he considered inferior socially and intellectually tended to isolate him. Not surprisingly, he sometimes seems to have experienced a sense of loneliness, especially since he had left Arabella behind in Alexandria. His loneliness was relieved by visits from his brother, Richard, and his old friend, brother of a former classmate, and distant cousin, Winslow Homer. Richard had come, hoping to see a battle, while Homer, already making his name as one of the nation's foremost

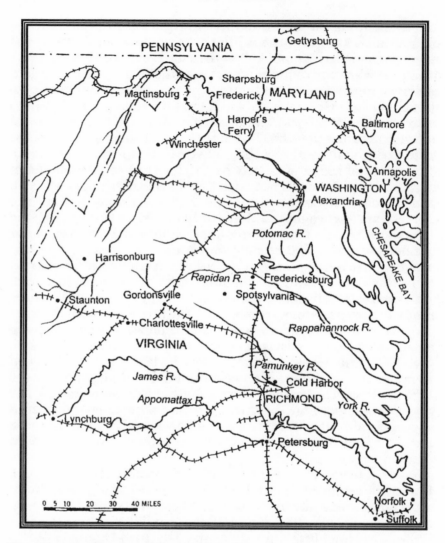

The Virginia Theater of War, 1861–1865.

illustrators, sought the firsthand observation of the war that would give him new material for his art.[7]

While the rear echelon work of building roads and staking out encampments went on, Barlow continued to live the life of an officer-gentleman, and complained of the lack of servants available in the area. He allowed his two guests to do the cooking while they observed the army ponderously prepare to close with

the Confederates. Richard left for home on 18 April without seeing any fighting, but Homer stayed on awhile longer, his presence
cheering the young colonel. "I have not laughed so much since I
left home," Barlow confessed, discussing his visitors. "It is very
tedious living here so many months with men who are so little
companions as our officers are. There is not one who I am at all
intimate with or who is any companion to me."[8] When Homer and
Barlow were not reminiscing, the young artist took his sketch-
book to the front lines and drew scenes of Army life, some of which
appeared in *Harper's Magazine,* while others formed the basis for
Homer's more famous Civil War paintings, such as *Camp of the
61st New York.* If he did any studies of Barlow at the time they
did not survive, although his soldier friend would later appear in
one of Homer's best-known wartime paintings. Homer's sketch-
ing had led some to suspect his intentions and fears arose that
his drawings, if published, might somehow find themselves
across enemy lines and provide useful information to the rebels.
On 23 April, Barlow reported that Homer's "occupation is gone,"
that is, he was unable to continue drawing scenes of Army life.
Despite that, the rising artist hoped he could stay until a battle
was fought. Homer had shaved his head and in Barlow's words
he "look[ed] like hell."[9]

Barlow did not reveal why Homer had shaved his head but it
might have had something to do with the conditions of camp life.
Soldiers, even officers, often found themselves beset by lice, and
Barlow reported being assaulted by wood ticks and "bites from
mysterious animals, which we never see, but know only from their
bites . . ."[10] In addition to the oppressive heat and humidity the
weather became increasingly rainy as April turned to May.
Streams and rivers rose, further slowing the movements of the
Army of the Potomac, and affecting subsequent operations.

Concluding that McDowell's troops around Washington were
not on their way south, Johnston pulled most of his men from
the Rappahannock line and finally reinforced Magruder, whose
performances continued to bedazzle McClellan. Nevertheless, the
Army of the Potomac vastly outnumbered the combined Confederate force, although McClellan doggedly insisted otherwise. His
perception of Confederate strength spread to his junior officers
and Barlow reported hearing that Johnston had 80,000 men under his command. Despite his personal apprehensions, McClellan
began advancing up the peninsula, gradually pushing the Confederates back on their capital. The first action of consequence
occurred at Williamsburg on 5 May. The Confederates fought a

successful rearguard action at Virginia's old, colonial capital, although they were forced to evacuate the old colonial town. The
possibility of breaking the entire southern line was lost when
Sumner halted Winfield Scott Hancock's brigade, which had taken
a position on the north of the Confederate defenses. Johnston,
who seemed always ready to surrender space for time and later
opportunities, retreated ever closer to Richmond, leading Jefferson Davis and his military advisor, Robert E. Lee, to grow increasingly emphatic that Johnston stop McClellan and drive him
back.

The 61st New York had still seen no action, although it was
moved closer to the front and Barlow looked expectantly for the
opportunity to put himself to the test. The heat, humidity, mud,
and rain made marching and drilling arduous enough even
without fighting. At times many men were seized with dizziness,
and fell while carrying out their duties.[11] Indeed, Barlow was
concerned that his command remained badly understrength. On
13 May, he wrote New York Governor Edwin D. Morgan request-
ing reinforcements for his regiment. He explained that while he
was carrying 700 men on the rolls, he had only about 500 present
for duty and he believed 50 of those should be discharged due to
physical problems.[12] Unless the 61st could be recruited up or
receive more troops, Barlow suggested that the regiment be consolidated with another unit.[13] Barlow's manpower problems were
shared by many regiments in McClellan's army and Morgan, who
probably felt there was little he could do in the middle of a military campaign, did not act on the young colonel's suggestion.

Although it seemed clear that the Confederates would not give
up Richmond without a fight, the lack of immediate action left
Barlow with time to deal with more mundane matters. He became involved in arranging support for the son of one of his men
after the boy was taken to one of the poorhouses established on
the East River islands in New York City.[14] He also consoled his
mother, whom he believed was languishing due to a lack of an ex-
citing summer itinerary. He was pleased to learn that she had
volunteered her services as a nurse, helping to care for soldiers
who had been sent home. Almira's tenure as a nurse apparently
did not last long as it was never mentioned again. The fact that she
attempted it at all might have been due to Arabella's example.

Barlow correctly foresaw a "good battle" in the immediate future, and suggested his mother might join him in Richmond. He
quickly reversed himself and concluded such a visit might not be
"practicable," since he thought it unlikely the Army of the Potomac

would tarry in the city after its capture, but would "move on" after any retreating rebel forces. On the other hand, Barlow believed that "if we are beaten . . . the North will give up."[15] As for his own immediate future, Barlow spoke of leaving the army as soon as a battle was fought—a course of action he predicted several times during the war, but one which he never acted upon.

By the end of May 1862, McClellan had reached the villages outlying Richmond with the grand prize seemingly within his grasp. The Army of the Potomac was divided by the Chicka- hominy River. The river was ordinarily not a major barrier to communication, but it had been greatly swollen by the frequent rains. The II, V, and VI Corps were situated north of the river with the III and IV Corps on the south bank near the Fair Oaks Station of the York and Richmond Rail Road.[16] The hamlet of Seven Pines lay nearby and the battle which shortly ensued is named after either location. Johnston's first major counterstroke was designed to take advantage of McClellan's separated forces. The Confederates planned to attack and destroy the IV Corps be- fore any significant reinforcement could be sent to its aid, thus unhinging the entire Federal alignment.[17] The attack began on 31 May, but unfortunately for the rebels, Johnston's plans were not carefully explained to his officers, and even worse, his major subordinate, James Longstreet, went down the wrong road to strike the Yankees. While the IV Corps was forced back from some of the ground they had held, the disjointed rebel assault was un- able to achieve any significant gains. More significantly, John- ston was wounded on the evening of the attack and his place was temporarily taken by Gustavus Adolphus Smith, who prepared to renew the attack on the following day, 1 June.

McClellan's reaction to Johnston's assault was characteristic of his performance as a field commander. He seemed paralyzed by the onset of combat, remained distant from the fighting, leaving the actual conduct of the battle to his subordinates, and issued only general, imprecise, and ineffective orders. Sumner, com- mander of the II Corps, might not have been the fastest-thinking general in the Army of the Potomac, but he had battle experience and was not afraid to send his troops to aid the IV Corps south of the Chickahominy. Using his own initiative he began shifting his units south of the river on the night of the 31st. Meanwhile, G. W. Smith found his efforts to organize another assault ham- pered by Longstreet, who was sulking because he was not given command of the Southern army after Johnston's wounding. Longstreet essentially refused to cooperate with his commanding general and it fell to General Daniel Harvey Hill to organize a Confederate strike force from the men of three Confederate divisions.

Barlow missed the first day's fighting at Fair Oaks. A few stray shells fell near the 61st New York's position as the men formed ranks and crossed the Chickahominy. They arrived on the battlefield at nightfall. About 4 A. M. the next morning, Barlow was ordered to prepare his men for battle. Howard's brigade was deployed on the left of the Federal line, where it guarded against any attempt to turn the left flank of General French's brigade. The 64th New York held the ground immediately to the left of Barlow's unit, and the 81st Pennsylvania held the ground beyond that. The 61st, part of the second line of Federal troops, was told to prepare to move forward in case the first line gave way or if Barlow saw an opportunity to hit the Confederates at a vulnerable point.[18]

If Barlow felt any doubts or misgivings about his ability to lead men coolly and effectively under fire, he hid it well. Under fire for the first time, Barlow exhibited the qualities which marked his leadership throughout the war—instinctive courage and resourcefulness, combined with a cool head and an aggressiveness which bordered on ruthless. Barlow began the action at Fair Oaks on horseback, but once the regiment entered the second-growth woods in their front he dismounted due to lack of maneuvering space. He had already taken to wearing the cavalry saber which became his preferred sidearm. He may have chosen the cavalry saber over a lighter officer's sword because it symbolized his own aggressive spirit. On a more practical level, he favored it because its weight had a greater impact on stragglers and shirkers who received the flat of its blade.[19]

Seeing his lead regiments running short on ammunition, Richardson sent Howard's brigade forward to ease the pressure on French. The 61st New York, which numbered only 417 in all ranks going into action,[20] formed up north of the York and Richmond Rail Road tracks. The railroad ran through swampy ground, and the heavily wooded country made visibility poor. Unable to determine exactly what lay before him, Barlow ordered his men to halt while he went ahead into the woods to reconnoiter. While he was gone, the men lay down to avoid stray bullets coming from the direction of the advancing Confederates. When he returned from his scouting, Barlow was furious to find his men hugging the ground. He quickly barked orders for them to get to their feet and led them across the tracks into the woods to the south.

The muddy ground and forested terrain slowed the advance,

and file closers and officers were kept busy keeping laggards moving forward. Personally fearless, Barlow held shirkers and cowards in deep contempt. Seeing some men from another regiment crouching in bushes, Barlow demanded an explanation for their failure to move forward. When they lamely replied that they had lost their muskets, Barlow tore into them, loudly condemning them as cowards.[21] He then took his men to the front of the Federal line, passing through the 53d Pennsylvania, which had been firing at Confederates. The Union troops pushed the Confederates back until they crested a small hill. From this vantage point, the northerners finally got a clear view of the rebel troops in front of them and quickly fired. The Confederates, probably the 3d Alabama, supported by the 12th and 41st Virginia, delivered a volley in return, which Howard later described as "rapid, well-directed and fatal."[22] Most of the losses the 61st New York suffered that day occurred in the ensuing firefight. Howard, who had accompanied the 64th New York during the attack, was hit by rebel fire and made his way back to the rear on foot with his arm in a sling from two wounds, which later necessitated the limb's amputation. Howard handed over temporary control of the brigade to Barlow, who was, in Howard's words, "immediately in the front . . ." The wounded brigade commander told Barlow to hold the position at all costs and call for reinforcements as necessary.[23]

The fighting raged fast and furious for some time, and Charles Fuller, now a sergeant, used the bodies of two of his fallen comrades as cover while blazing away at the Confederates. The sight of wounded, killed, and mutilated men shocked many of the green troops. Possibly the worst sight that confronted members of Barlow's regiment was that of a soldier named Sandford Brooks. Brooks was shot through the side of the head, and the force of the bullet threw his eyes out of their sockets without killing or even dropping him. Instead, the wounded man staggered around in the woods, his sight and reason lost, not dying until after the battle.[24]

The Confederates retreated before Barlow's oncoming troops, and the Yankees lost contact with them in the woods. As the southern fire slowly fell away, Barlow ordered his men to cease firing. Looking around, he was unable to detect any supporting regiments on his flanks. Barlow sent word for Colonel Brooke of the 53d Pennsylvania, which had replenished their ammunition, to come up for his support. There was growing concern that the two regiments Barlow now commanded had advanced so far from the main Federal line along the railroad tracks that Confederates might be able to slip in behind them and cut them off. At one point a "tremendous fire" opened on Barlow and Brooke's men from the rear, though no one was hit as Barlow quickly ordered his men to get down. Orders soon arrived by messenger from General Israel Richardson for him to withdraw his men back to the railroad tracks. Barlow proudly remembered, "We came out in beautiful order and were the last out of the woods."[25]

The Battle of Fair Oaks/Seven Pines was a tactical draw. The second day's fighting, in which Barlow and his men first "saw the elephant," was confused and inconclusive. Yet the 61st New York and its colonel had every reason to be satisfied with their performance. They had stood under fire and drove the enemy back, even if they were eventually pulled back. Barlow's drilling and training had borne fruit and in his official report he proudly stated that in accordance with orthodox small arms tactics of the time, "the greater part of the men stood firm and erect during the firing, and only stooped or went down when ordered to do so. I did not see one officer shirk or fail his duty, and all deserve praise alike."[26] Privately Barlow admitted, "Several times the line wavered and fell back a few paces but we always brought them right up." Experience would eventually lead Barlow—and most seasoned combat officers—to stop using massed lines of standing men in assaults. The increasing use of the rifled musket made such tactics both costly and ineffectual. In the meantime, feeling satisfied, if not smug, the young colonel favorably contrasted the conduct of his men with those of other regiments, especially the 64th New York that "had behaved so badly." "We were the only Regt of the Brigade which did not break or run at sometime or another,"[27] he boasted.

Barlow's unquestioning confidence in his own leadership and bravery was vindicated, and he did not shirk from seeking recognition, praise, or promotion. He was highly pleased with Howard's references to him, which the wounded brigadier included in his report of the battle. "I desire especially to notice the coolness and good conduct of Col. Barlow 61st NY," Howard wrote. Barlow underlined the word "especially" when he forwarded Howard's praise in a letter home, making it clear that Howard had done so in his account of the action.[28] Barlow's success in leading men in combat owed something to his study of military affairs, knowledge which would be greatly enhanced and expanded by the experience of war itself. But it also sprang from his unflinching bravery, coolness under fire and delight in combat. These attributes, which never deserted him during the war, seem innate. They were reinforced by yet one other element, which contributed to his drive and pugnacity in battle—a belief in his own invincibility. Barlow led from the front—by example—not only because he thought it was right, but because he could not imagine his own death. Shortly after the Battle of Fair Oaks he wrote his mother, "I am a lucky person you know and was not born to be killed in battle I do not think."[29] Nor were these just the words of a son trying to allay the fears of a parent. After the war, Charles Fuller met his old commander at a meeting of the 61st New York Association, a veterans' organization. During the course of their conversation, Fuller told Barlow that he "never went into a battle without an effort of will, and always expected to be wounded or killed. He [Barlow] said in his quiet way 'I never felt so. I never had an impression that I was to be hurt.'"[30] Arabella put it more dramatically when she told Judge Daly and his wife Maria that Frank "loves fighting for the sake of fighting and is really exceedingly bloodthirsty."[31]

Whatever their source, Barlow's combat abilities were recognized, and not just by his superiors. "My men are much pleased with me since the action," Barlow recorded, apparently happily.[32] Nor was this a false or conceited conclusion. According to Charles Fuller, "Before this battle, Col. Barlow was rated highly for his *military scholarship,* after the battle he was recognized by his superior officers as *one of the bravest of the brave.*"[33]*Not that the regiment's respect softened Barlow's style of leadership. He never allowed any familiarities. Nor did he ever forget his rank or relax his diligent imposition of military discipline. Indeed, in the same letter in which he related that his men were "pleased" with him he recorded having several punished for various infractions of the military code. Even Charles Fuller, who thoroughly admired Barlow, found himself under house arrest for failing to police camp at the appointed time.[34] It is doubtful that many men actually liked Frank Barlow. But when the shooting began they learned to appreciate how well he had prepared them for combat. Confidence in Barlow's leadership led to respect for Barlow and confidence among the men themselves. These attitudes engendered a high sense of morale in Barlow's units and made them formidable in battle.

*—unless otherwise stated, all emphasised words or phrases appear as such in the original quotation.

Barlow's men paid a stiff price for their initiation into warfare at Fair Oaks. About one-quarter of the already seriously under-manned regiment was lost. Official returns showed 27 enlisted men and four officers killed, 69 enlisted men and four commis-sioned officers wounded, with four enlisted men captured or missing.[35] Fair Oaks gave Barlow and his men their first look at the aftermath of battle. Like many soldiers, Barlow was able to recount the horrors of war while simultaneously becoming in-ured to them. "We have got entirely accustomed to dead, wounded and decayed men," he wrote, and "the Hospitals are shocking sights with men lying about out of doors with all manner of shock-ing wounds." The weather made the situation even worse. The heat, Barlow related, was "perfectly awful here. . . . the dead de-composed yesterday, it was dreadful work to bury them."[36] He would see a lot more of such work in the next two and one-half years.

3

Valor and Frustration:
The Seven Days

COMPARED TO THE CARNAGE THAT CAME LATER IN THE WAR, FAIR
Oaks was a small affair, with 5,000 Federals and 6,100 Confederates killed and wounded.[1] Nevertheless, the battle provided
the first combat experience for the mostly green troops and officers involved. Some, like Barlow, thrived in the environment of
smoke and blood; most simply survived, and some never saw
daylight again. Yet, the Battle of Fair Oaks decisively altered the
course of the War. Joseph Johnston's wound was severe enough
that it became clear that he could not continue as commander of
the Confederate Army blocking the Army of the Potomac's advance on Richmond. Jefferson Davis turned to his military advisor, Robert E. Lee, and placed him at the head of the force that
was soon to be named the Army of Northern Virginia. McClellan,
who remained haunted by reports and rumors of phantom Confederate forces building on his front, had been among those who
had not risen to the challenge of battle. He remained fixed at Fair
Oaks while he slowly recovered his nerve. For almost a month,
other than sending out skirmish lines, reconnoitering, and gingerly testing the Confederate positions, the Army of the Potomac
did nothing.

McClellan's profligate expenditure of time may have been based
partly on erroneous assumptions about his opponent. During
the West Virginia campaign of the previous year, McClellan had
bested Lee and ended Confederate attempts to control the mountain counties of western Virginia. If McClellan could have looked
at the situation objectively, he would have seen the situation in
West Virginia was very different from the one on the York Peninsula. In western Virginia, the population was generally pro-Union,
logistical factors favored Federal forces, and the Confederate
command structure was fragmented. Lee's failure in western—
soon to be West—Virginia might have convinced McClellan that

he was dealing with a general as cautious as himself. Lee would quickly prove him wrong. The new southern commander immediately began strengthening his lines, familiarizing himself with his new command, and setting plans to take the offensive at the first opportunity. While McClellan may have blundered in his assessment of Lee, the Virginian had taken McClellan's measure in full.[2] Lee only awaited the arrival of Thomas J. "Stonewall" Jackson's force from the Shenandoah Valley to launch his counterstrike.

The Federal troops and officers who saw action at Fair Oaks knew that they had given the Confederates at least as good as they received, and many were puzzled—and irritated—at the lack of aggressive action in the battle's aftermath. Barlow was among those who had begun to realize that however effective "Little Mac" had been at organizing and outfitting an army, he was miscast as a field commander. Two days after his firefight in the woods at Fair Oaks Barlow observed, "our generals are always more frightened than hurt."[3] Later in the month, still in the lines around Fair Oaks and trying to ignore the heat, Barlow groused that the Federal army seemed "acting on the defensive rather than the offensive."[4]

Always quick to anger, Barlow was also incensed that someone, he suspected his law partner, Bliss, had given his letters concerning the Battle of Fair Oaks to the New York newspapers. As a result, his remarks on the deficiencies of some of the other regiments were published, resulting in Barlow's concern and embarrassment. "It will do me harm here to have commented on the other Regts especially as I find my statements as to their running were much exaggerated. It is damned outrageous to have published the letter."[5] On the other hand, Barlow was pleased by the "very flattering notice of us [61st New York]" which, he bragged, was "generally considered here as being the crack Regt. in this fight."[6]

Barlow never showed much tolerance for camp life, especially when he was beyond the succor of his wife or family. Arabella had arrived at Harrison's Landing on 2 June and took up her duties as a Sanitary Commission nurse at the Harrison House, which had been put to use as a hospital. Barlow's duties at the front and the possibility of renewed action prevented the couple from meeting for a week.[7] Despite Arabella's presence, Barlow seemed depressed by the lack of activity after the exhilaration of battle. Not for the first or last time Barlow threatened to leave the army. "I shall certainly resign as soon as we get to Richmond," he wrote in a curious combination of annoyance and optimism. "I am sick of this life and have no idea of beginning to drill and discipline a Regt. over again which will have to be done if this [61st New York] is recruited up."[8] Ironically, Barlow kept his word in this regard. He did resign shortly after Richmond was taken, although it would take another three years to do so.

While Barlow chaffed at the lack of action, Robert E. Lee prepared to break the impasse. The Federal Army lying before Richmond remained divided by the Chickahominy River, which remained swollen from the heavy June rains. Lee's immediate target was the Federal V Corps, under General Fitz-John Porter, which was positioned north of the River. Once Porter was broken, the southern commander intended to attack the bulk of McClellan's army and drive it away from Richmond. Lee's ultimate objective, however, went beyond saving the Confederate capital. He aimed at nothing less than a decisive victory, a massive blow which would effectively destroy the Army of the Potomac as a fighting force.[9] Never one to place much hope in foreign intervention to save the Confederacy, Lee hoped such a victory would demoralize the North, sapping its will to continue the struggle. If the people of the North lost their resolve, the Union war effort would collapse. Lee's offensive, termed the Seven Days' due to its duration, was plagued by inferior staff work, lack of familiarity among officers and men, and the unexpected lethargy of Stonewall Jackson, a condition which had not been seen previously and would not recur after the Seven Days. Probably Jackson was temporarily burnt out by the rigors of his Valley Campaign, which had cleared northern troops from the Shenandoah Valley and which allowed him to join Lee before Richmond.

On 26 June 1862 the Confederates hit Porter north of the Chickahominy. Lee's plan fell apart and the southerners were repulsed, suffering 1500 casualties to Porter's 400.[10] Nevertheless McClellan, typifying his performance throughout the entire campaign, was not on the battlefield directing the army. Instead, he totally lost his nerve and ordered Porter south of the Chickahominy. Tactically, Federal forces had won a victory; strategically, the initiative had been conceded to Lee. From the moment Lee opened his attack, McClellan's only thought was to move his army southeast to the James River, abandoning his supply base on the Paumunkey River, as well as the Richmond and York Rail Road, which he used to move supplies to his units.[11]

McClellan ordered Porter to hold the north bank, while he began to shift his supply lines from White House on the Pamunkey to Harrison's Landing on the James. Lee struck Porter again the next day, 27 June, at Gaines Mill. The battle was another closely run affair, but finally, around nightfall, the massed Confederates, led by John Bell Hood's Texas Brigade, broke the Federal position in several places. Despite these penetrations, Porter's men withdrew in good order, although the position north of the Chickahominy was lost. As the Army of the Potomac pulled back towards the James, Lee kept up the pressure, anxiously seeking the opportunity to cut off and crush all or most of the retreating Federals before they could reach the safety of newly prepared positions braced by the heavy ordnance on the Federal gunboats patrolling the river.

Barlow and the rest of Richardson's division took no part in the actions at Mechanicsville and Gaines Mill, though they no doubt grew increasingly anxious as the sound of battle drew near. June 28 saw only small-scale action as the Federals continued marching away from Richmond and Lee sought to determine their route of retreat. The retreating Yankees soon reached Savage Station on the Richmond and York Rail Road. The station was the site of a northern supply depot and approximately 3,000 wounded troops were being treated in the hospital there. Orders were given to destroy the stocks of ammunition and supplies to prevent them from being captured by the Confederates. The flames and smoke from the torched depot revealed McClellan's line of retreat to Lee. The rebel commander responded quickly and ordered Magruder and Huger to attack the Federal force from the west while Jackson was directed to cross White Oak Swamp and assail on the Union force from the north. Fortunately for the Union troops, Jackson contented himself with bombarding the Federals while Sumner fended off Magruder's assaults.

Most of Richardson's division was in reserve during the battle. The 61st had been pulled from its previous position at 3 A. M. and witnessed the destruction of the stores at Savage Station. As Barlow's men were drawn up into a line of battle to provide support for northern artillery, rebel shells began dropping among the New Yorkers. While the Yankee batteries traded iron with the rebel gunners, Barlow sat calmly on his bay horse "Billy" and, in the words of one veteran, "observed the situation as coolly as if it had been a sham battle."[12]

But it was no sham. Heinzelman's and Franklin's corps had already crossed White Oak Swamp and the 61st New York, originally deployed to the west of the railroad station, hurried off with the division's other regiments towards the smoldering depot. Barlow characterized the march as *almost* a panic. My Regt.

marched in good order but some quite stampeded and we were all huddled in together."[13] With McClellan again absent from the field, responsibility for the fighting withdrawal rested with the corps, divisional, brigade, and regimental officers—not to mention the troops themselves. Though plagued by faulty staff work and poor coordination, the Confederate attackers had the advantage of Lee's superior leadership—not to mention his relentless determination to smash McClellan's army. The Confederate commander never surrendered the initiative and if one blow failed to achieve its intended effect he immediately prepared another. "We must lose no more time," Lee remarked grimly when he realized the action at Savage's Station had failed to cripple the Army of the Potomac, "or he will escape us entirely."[14]

The next day Lee again attempted to rip off a piece of the Union Army. The bulk of the Army of the Potomac was moving through an intersection called Glendale. McClellan realized the crossroads had to be held if his army was to retreat successfully. He ordered seven divisions to hold the position and then he rode off towards the promontory of Malvern Hill, leaving no one in overall command at the critical juncture. As the sun rose at Glendale, the 61st New York found itself placed next to the Irish Brigade. The day's fighting began with artillery bombardments and Barlow lost a considerable number of men to rebel shelling. Caldwell's brigade, to which Barlow's regiment belonged, was then pulled out of line and hurried off to support Kearney's division, which was being hard-pressed from determined southern assaults. In the swirl of battle with regiments and brigades shuffled from one position to the other as the action dictated, some Federal units mistakenly fired on each other. In the confusion following a friendly fire incident, the 61st New York became separated from the rest of the brigade. Deciding that it was less important whom he fought with as long as he and his men were in the fight, Barlow wasted no time attempting to locate the rest of his brigade, and instead reported to the first brigadier general he could find. This turned out to be General Robinson of Kearney's division, and Barlow placed himself under his command. Due to sickness, casualties and men on detatched duty, the 61st numbered about 150 men when it entered the fray.[15]

It was about 6 P. M. when Barlow and his men were sent into action through a wood of arching trees whose overhanging boughs created a tunnel-like effect. Emerging from the woods, they came to a fence which northern troops had been using as a parapet to fire on Confederate soldiers from Longstreet's division who were advancing against them. Robinson ordered Barlow to take his men over the fence, charge across the field that spread out before it, and seize a road which lay in the distance. Barlow explained to Robinson that he had only a few men, the numbers of the 61st having been sorely reduced. "Yes, but they are good ones," Robinson replied encouragingly.[16]

The New Yorkers clambered over the fence and stormed across the field with bayonets fixed and no shots fired. Light was poor and the Federals could not see the southerners clearly, but their rapid assault, probably unexpected, unnerved the Confederates who abandoned their position, leaving a stand of colors on the ground. The flag, which was retrieved, bore the battle honors "Williamsburg" and "Seven Pines." Barlow ordered it sent back to General Sumner. On reaching the opposite end of the field the regiment entered another woods and Barlow ordered the men to lie down. One of the rebels concealed in the trees in front of them called out, "what Regt is that?" An Irishman in the unit shouted back "61st New York." "Lay down your arms or I'll blow every one of you to hell" the southerner spat back. "Up and at them men," Barlow roared and the New Yorkers poured a volley into the Confederate positions and received one in return.[17] In the poor light of the murky woods the troops seldom had a clear shot at their opponents and both sides blazed away at muzzle flashes.

As the firefight grew hotter, Barlow called for reinforcements and the 81st Pennsylvania was sent to him for support. The sharp, if confused, fighting continued for some time with Barlow's men taking several casualties. Kearney finally pulled the 61st New York and 81st Pennsylvania back to the fence and told them to hold the line with bayonets, as their ammunition was almost gone. As senior officer on the field, Barlow was placed in command of both regiments. About midnight, having succeeded in preventing the rebels from punching through their lines, Barlow's regiments were ordered out of their position and fell in with the rest of the troops moving towards the James.

The Battle of Glendale proved yet another frustrating experience for Lee. The Federal forces engaged had been mauled, but their lines held, and they withdrew in reasonably good order. Again the Confederates had suffered heavy losses. Not that the northerners had gotten off easily, and Barlow's men had also suffered heavily. Approximately one-third of the 61st New York, including six of the regiment's nine officers, were casualties.[18] The necessity of leaving the wounded on the field for the Confederates to capture was especially galling to Barlow. Witnesses were struck at Barlow's tenderness in speaking to the wounded men he was forced to leave behind.[19] Barlow's confidence in his own invincibility was again vindicated. Although bullets had ripped his uniform, he had emerged unscathed from the fighting. Unfortunately, his horse "Billy" was not as lucky as his master and the steed was mortally wounded in the battle.

As at Fair Oaks, Barlow's courage and leadership favorably impressed his superiors. In his report of the battle, Brigadier General J. C. Caldwell wrote, "In mentioning officers worthy of particular commendation I can not fail to award the highest praise to Colonel Barlow. . . . In every engagement since [Fair Oaks] he has only added to the laurels there acquired. He possesses in an eminent degree all the qualities of a good commander—intelligence, coolness and readiness."[20] General Phillip Kearney, under whose direction Barlow fought at Glendale, also volunteered his admiration for Barlow's performance.[21]

Whatever gratification Barlow derived from such encomiums lay in the future when the after-battle reports were written and there was time to reflect on what had happened. In the meantime, along with the rest of the weary and beleaguered Army of the Potomac, Barlow and his men trudged off to their next position—Malvern Hill. Lee, desperate to break McClellan's army before it escaped to the defenses of Harrison's Landing and the Federal gunboats on the James, ordered an assault on the well-prepared artillery-studded Federal position. McClellan himself rode around the perimeter of the line inspecting its strength, but departed by boat for Harrison's Landing before the fighting commenced. Again he left no one in command although, as senior officer on the field, Fitz-John Porter found himself in charge through default.[22]

The men of the 61st had managed only about two hours sleep in their new lines on the hill before cannonading announced the opening of the day's contest. About this time one of Barlow's men, who had been on detached duty as a hosteller for field officers, approached his colonel with a woebegone face and explained that he was sick and asked to be sent to the rear. Sleep-deprived himself, preparing his men for another enemy onslaught, and in an especially foul mood due to the loss of his horse, Barlow quickly questioned the supplicant and concluded the man was a coward, a species of humanity he detested. Charles Fuller recorded Barlow's violent reaction:

> His wrath broke out vehemently. He cursed and swore at [the man] and called him a variety of unpleasant and detestable things and then he began to punch him with his fist wherever he could hit. Finally,

he partly turned him around, and gave him a hearty kick in the stern and said "Damn you, get away from here. You're not fit to be among my brave men."[23]

Not surprisingly, no one else dared ask to be excused from the coming fight. Or as Fuller put it, "I believe every man of us preferred to meet the rebels rather than the vocal scorn and denunciation of Barlow."[24]

The II Corps was deployed on the right flank of the Hill. The 61st New York and 81st Pennsylvania, now consolidated under Barlow's leadership, were placed between Palmer's and Abercrombie's brigades in support of Couch. Barlow's position lay in a field at the edge of the Hill close to Confederates who were massing for the attack in a wood to their front. It was hot and clear and several men fell sun struck during the day. As the Confederates surged forward from the concealment of the woods, Union artillery poured shot and shell into their lines, gouging great gaps in their ranks breaking the charge. Unfortunately, shells fired from the northern guns sometimes burst over Barlow's men or exploded behind them, which, Barlow commented dryly, "did not add to the pleasure of the occasion."[25] Even in the din and turmoil of the musketry and cannonading, Barlow detected the sound of bayonets being affixed to rifles and quickly prepared his men to face a new southern assault. As the rebels burst into the open again and raced for the northern lines, Francis ordered his men to hold their fire until the southerners were so close that virtually every shot would find its mark. When he was satisfied the charging Confederates had advanced close enough, he gave the long expected order to fire.[26] Barlow's lines erupted with rifle fire and a devastating sheet of lead ripped into the oncoming rebels. At first, the colonel ordered volley firing by ranks, then firing by files, and lastly firing at will. The troops shot so rapidly that their rifle barrels became hot and the men were forced to hold their weapons by their slings. Some men found the barrels of their weapons so fouled from the powder that the minié balls could not be rammed home. With ammunition all but gone and with the rebel intentions unclear, Barlow called out, "If the enemy make another attack, we will meet them with cold steel."[27] But repulsed at great loss by artillery and infantry, the attacking Confederates were about played out. A last rebel assault was turned back by a volley from the Excelsior Brigade, which had some ammunition, while Barlow and his men waited with bayonets ready.

The Battle of Malvern Hill, the most one-sided of the Seven Days' contests, was over. At about 11 P. M. Barlow and his men were withdrawn from the front line and lay down without supper. Before many had a chance to sleep they were ordered off the Hill with the rest of the army as the Yankees began the last leg of their retreat to the new base at Harrison's Landing. "I was awfully worn out," Barlow confessed, speaking for all his men and probably for the soldiers of both armies.[28]

The final march to Harrison's Landing took place in another of the frequent rains, which had added to the misery of the Peninsula campaign. Many regiments had lost cohesion and large numbers of troops found themselves mixed up with men from various other units. Nor surprisingly, considerable straggling occurred. Barlow deemed the march more of a rout than a "strategical movement," as McClellan claimed.[29] The young, but now veteran, colonel witnessed the Army's commander, accompanied by only one attendant, ride alongside the crowd of men who took no notice of him. Barlow was among the increasing number of officers and men who considered McClellan a disaster. "The whole army feel that it was left to take care of itself and was saved only by its own brave fighting," he commented bitterly.[30] Barlow's two tiny regiments reached Harrison's Landing about seven in the morning. For the first time since Fair Oaks the 61st was placed in reserve, and Barlow doubted that the Confederates would attack such a strong position.

Finally in a place he would not have to abandon in a few hours, Barlow took stock of his losses and found he commanded about 175 men, of whom about 60 were sick. Having been forced to leave the wounded on the field upset him intensely. Tolling up the numbers of killed and wounded, he was again struck by his own escape from injury. Others were also amazed he had avoided death or wounding, and he heard a soldier outside his tent proclaim that the colonel would be shot in the next fight.[31] The prediction proved true, though the battle lay two months in the future.

Though the Army of the Potomac had been driven back from Richmond and forced into a defensive perimeter, Barlow took consolation from his own and his men's performance. "This small Regt. has fought five fierce infantry fights and driven and held back the enemy and has every reason to feel proud," he maintained.[32] He was also satisfied with his own performance and was further pleased when he saw the positive reports on his leadership which were written by Caldwell and Kearney. General Howard continued to add his voice to those praising Barlow's performance on the Peninsula. On 4 September, as the Maryland campaign was beginning, Howard recommended Barlow for promotion in the most glowing terms: "I have the honor to recommend Col. Francis Barlow as an officer of unusual coolness under fire, a most excellent disciplinarian and tactician. I believe him to be *particularly well fitted* to command a brigade. . . . I would particularly call the attention of the War Department to this worthy man."[33]

Never one to ignore the political angle, Barlow was counting on his law partner to lobby New York's governor to push his promotion to brigadier general in Washington. He was also able to call upon political support from prominent men from Massachusetts such as Charles Sumner, and in New York he enjoyed the aid of Judge Daly. Barlow would receive his promotion, but not before he had fought another battle.[34]

While Barlow's superiors and friends pushed him for a promotion, Francis himself was engaged in lobbying New York Governor Edwin D. Morgan to advance Nelson Miles. One of his lieutenants, D. E. Gregory, the regiment's adjutant, was unhappy that Barlow refused to recommend him for a lieutenant colonelcy —the position he wanted for Miles—and Morgan had been apprised of the situation. Gregory was a brave and capable officer, Barlow admitted in a note to Morgan, but the 61st New York boasted other field-grade officers "of higher rank and equal bravery with him."[35] Shortly after contacting Morgan, Barlow heard that "influential friends" had recommended Gregory for an elevation in rank. On 13 July, Barlow sent another letter to the governor pointing out that Gregory's promotion had not been recommended by the regiment's colonel, that is, himself.[36] He also made it clear that not only did he not suggest Gregory for advancement to Lieutenant Colonel, but that as a lieutenant, Gregory had no claim to be jumped over captains.

The captain Barlow suggested for promotion to lieutenant colonel was his friend, Nelson A. Miles, about whom Barlow had apparently written Morgan previously. Barlow extolled Miles as a man on whom he could rely to take on the responsibilities of the regiment in the event Barlow was "disabled or separated" in any way. He also mentioned that Miles' "activity & energy & courage" were well known and that further endorsements could be obtained from Howard, Richardson and Caldwell. Barlow closed his letter stating it was his "hearty & earnest wish that Capt. Miles be promoted as soon as may be."[37] He got his wish and Miles rose to take second in command in the regiment.

Promotions and praise could only do so much to alleviate the dejection that accompanied the obvious failure of the campaign—a mood not helped by the incessant tidewater heat. His spirits were lifted by the arrival of Arabella, whose work as an army nurse had brought her to Harrison's Landing. Barlow was able to visit her at nurses' quarters, though it is unclear how much time they had together in private.

As the Army slowly revived, many of the troops and officers itched to renew the campaign and chaffed at being holed up at their base along the river. In the first week of August, Hooker led a reconnoitering expedition back to Malvern Hill, which many expected would lead to a renewal of fighting. But McClellan was not ready for another round with Lee and soon withdrew the force. Lincoln himself came down from Washington to see if he could prod McClellan into action. The president polled the officers and found that most wanted to resume the offensive against Lee and Richmond.[38] In contrast, McClellan continued to insist that he needed reinforcements. Lincoln sent some, but McClellan demanded more.

There were some soldiers in the Army of the Potomac who never lost their affection for "Little Mac," but Barlow was not one of them. Instead, he stood with McClellan's critics and his contempt for the Army of the Potomac's commander grew during the weeks of inactivity at Harrison's Landing. He was especially outraged by the contrast between McClellan's bombastic pronouncements and his actual leadership on the field. "McClellan issues flaming addresses though everyone in the Army knows he was outwitted," Barlow exclaimed.

> His statements that we lost no materials of war or ammunition are simply false—I believe that the Army properly handled could march into Richmond even now, but with our present Generals never—We are surprised to hear from the New York papers that we won a great victory—We thought that we had made a disastrous retreat leaving all our dead & wounded & many prisoners & material & munitions of war in the hands of the enemy—though it is true that the *men* by hard fighting often temporarily repulsed the enemy.[39]

Barlow's disgust at McClellan's leadership and the pro-McClellan propaganda published in northern papers intensified throughout the summer. He concluded a long anti-McClellan diatribe to his brothers with the wish that the "Young Napoleon" be removed.[40] Barlow was not the only one whose estimation of

McClellan had fallen. Finally convinced that nothing could make McClellan move, Lincoln ordered the Army of the Potomac off the Peninsula. The first elements departed on 14 August, and the last units reached the Washington defensive perimeter 12 days later.

Sumner's II Corps disembarked at Aquia Creek, and moved off to Arlington where Barlow found himself on his "old parade ground." Shortly afterward, the corps was dispatched to Centerville to cover the retreat of General John Pope's Army of Virginia after it had been thrashed by Lee and Jackson at Second Manasses.

Although Barlow's promotion had not yet been processed, he was put in charge of the consolidated 61st and 64th New York regiments. The merger of the units was necessitated by the heavy losses suffered by the two regiments, and New York State's practice of creating new regiments rather than replenishing existing ones. From what Barlow could see the prospects for the northern cause seemed grim. "People are dispirited and I don't wonder at it," he wrote.[41] But even though the military situation looked bleak, Barlow did not think Lee would follow up his victory at Manasses with a frontal assault on Washington. He foresaw Lee's move into Maryland, but assumed that would be preparatory for a strike against Washington from the west. As always, Barlow gave vent to his emotions, and, as ever, he raged pessimistically although his moods of gloom and doom always proved short-lived. "The affairs of this country are melancholy enough," he wrote home. "It is not worth while to make any predictions, but I think there is no prospect or hopes of success in this war. The Gov't is too rascally and corrupt besides being imbecile. I am in a state of chronic disgust."[42]

4

From Antietam to Gettysburg

GEORGE MCCLELLAN MAY HAVE CONCEIVED OF WAR AS A SERIES of sieges and slow, methodical, cautious advances, but Robert E. Lee had something else in mind. Satisfied that McClellan would not sally forth from his self-imposed confinement at Harrison's Landing, Lee moved decisively to deal with a Federal army advancing south from the Washington area. Commanded by General John Pope and christened the Army of Virginia, this force was composed of many of the units left to defend Washington, plus those regiments from the Peninsula which had already returned to northern Virginia. Disgusted with McClellan, Lincoln ordered Pope to take the offensive, a command which the vainglorious Pope enthusiastically accepted. After being pinned into position by Stonewall Jackson he was routed by Lee's combined army at Second Manasses on 30 August, 1862.

As Pope's broken army staggered back towards the safety of the fortifications surrounding the capital, McClellan's army continued to disembark. While Lincoln's confidence in McClellan had been largely exhausted during the Peninsula campaign, the president saw little choice but to turn to him to restore the army's confidence and organization. Pope was sent west to fight Indians. In the meantime, Lee, convinced that defensive victories in Virginia were sterile and that time worked against the Confederacy, prepared to cross the Potomac into the border state of Maryland.[1] Maryland, although it had remained in the Union, had a large population of southern sympathizers and many Marylanders were marching homeward in the Army of Northern Virginia. Lee hoped that the appearance of his army in Maryland would lead more to join the Confederate colors. But his major goal remained unchanged. He intended to threaten both Washington and Baltimore and force the Army of the Potomac into a battle in which it would be disastrously defeated, crushing popular support for the war in the North.[2]

Once his men were across the Potomac, Lee divided his army

into two main parts. Longstreet's corps dispersed into smaller units and began scouring the Maryland countryside for supplies while scaring away small Federal detachments. In the meantime, most of Stonewall Jackson's corps invested the Federal garrison at Harpers Ferry which lay at the rear of Lee's army and which could prove dangerous if not destroyed. His experience with McClellan in Virginia led the Confederate chieftain to believe that he had the time to carry out his initial objectives, and then reunite his units when McClellan finally worked up the nerve to move against him.[3]

On 3 September, the II Corps joined the rest of the Army of the Potomac as it moved off into western Maryland in its pursuit of Lee. With both the 61st and 64th New York under his command, Barlow crossed the Chain Bridge and passed through the District of Columbia and into Maryland. The regiments were posted at Tenallytown for a few days, and Arabella, who had followed Francis from Alexandria, joined him there, but was soon obliged to leave for a trip to Baltimore, probably on Sanitary Commission business. Barlow seemed to think the Army would remain in the vicinity for a while and sent word to his mother asking her to meet him, an invitation that he was soon forced to rescind. Additionally, he still wanted his brother Edward to come and "follow us about in the field."[4]

But the Corps soon pulled out of Tenallytown and continued northwest to Rockville and then west towards Frederick. By 13 September, the Army of the Potomac was rapidly approaching Frederick and closing in on Lee's dispersed army. McClellan's sudden aggressiveness surprised and alarmed Lee. Unbeknownst to the southern commander, a copy of his orders, which outlined the division of his army, had fallen into McClellan's hands. Armed with this unexpected great luck McClellan became jubilant and ordered his forces ahead at uncustomary speed.[5] Lee realized that he was in danger of being defeated piecemeal while in hostile territory and quickly began to reconcentrate his forces. A delaying action at the South Mountain passes bought some time, but when Lee turned to face McClellan behind the banks of Antietam Creek near the town of Sharpsburg, not all of Stonewall Jackson's Corps had arrived from Harpers Ferry, leaving him at a greater numerical disadvantage than usual.

On 17 September 1862, the Army of the Potomac opened battle against Lee. The Federal commander fielded 75,316 men to Lee's 51,844, some of whom were still on the road from Harper's Ferry. But McClellan's newfound boldness faded as he drew closer to Lee and as the battle began he reverted to his usual mode of leaving his corps and division commanders to manage the fighting themselves. Rather than a coordinated attack by the entire Federal force against Lee's positions, which the Confederates could not have withstood, McClellan watched passively as his corps attacked one at a time. The Union commander's disjointed attacks allowed Lee to use his internal lines to shift his men from one position to another which helped offset the Union army's significant advantage in manpower.

The battle opened with Joseph Hooker's Corps assaulting Lee's left. Hooker took part of the Confederate line and inflicted heavy casualties on the rebels before his assault was played out due to its own heavy losses. By mid-morning, Sumner's II Corps had begun its attack. Barlow entered the fighting with two badly understrength units. The 61st New York had about 105 men divided into three companies of about 35 men each. The 64th New York was slightly larger with approximately 200 men. The combined total left Barlow with 350 men, a little more than one-third of a full-size regiment.[6] Caldwell's Brigade, to which Barlow's regiments still belonged, advanced to the front on the left and slightly behind the Irish Brigade. As they moved forward into their jumping-off position, two snipers in a tree shot some of the advancing northerners. Barlow sent six marksmen to clear them out and within minutes two southern soldiers fell from the branches. In the meantime, the Irish Brigade attacked the rebels who were well ensconced behind a farmer's road that had been worn down below the ground level. The Irish charged forward gallantly, but massed musket fire ripped their attack apart and brought them to a standstill. Watching helplessly as his men were chewed up by the Confederates in their superb defensive position, the Irish Brigade's commander, John Meagher, called out to Barlow, "Colonel for God's sake come and help me." Barlow replied that he was under orders, but would join the attack as soon as he could.[7] As the New Yorkers waited in their position they saw the firing slacken as the Irish Brigade's line— the men were still standing in accordance to prescribed infantry tactics which had been made obsolete by the use of rifled muskets—was decimated by fire from the well-protected southerners.[8] The Irishmen's flag would fall only to be brought up, then fall and rise again.

Although it hardly looked that way to the attacking Yankees, Confederate strength in the road was being drained by both casualties and misunderstood orders which led some units to pull out of the line. When the orders finally came for the 61st/64th New York to attack, Barlow led his men from the front, sword held high in the air. Shortly after the battle, Ezra Ripley of the 29th Massachusetts wrote a vivid account of the transformation that came over Barlow as he entered the fighting:

> When our brigade passed Caldwell's brigade, to which Barlow belonged, just at the ford, he was sitting on his horse at the head of his regiment waiting to go into the fight. He had on an old linen coat and an old hat. We exchanged pleasant greetings with each other . . . and when he came up leading the way to our relief, it seemed as if a fairy had transformed him. He was on foot. Instead of the linen coat, he had a splendid uniform on, which seemed to shine in its newness—pants inside high-topped boots, and army hat and yellow regulation gloves. . . . It seemed as if a new suit must have dropped on him from the skies. And then he rushed up the hill at the head of his little regiment, looking so handsome, facing his men to cheer them, moving with such grace and elasticity, that it seemed as if he were dancing with delight. I have seen brave men and brave officers; I saw that day colonels coolly [sic] and bravely lead their regiments; but I never saw such a sight as Barlow's advance, and never expect to again. It was a picture—it was poetry.[9]

Exhilarated by the fighting, his natural combativeness unleashed, Barlow soon broke the stalemate at the sunken road. He led his men from behind Meagher's brigade and crossed in front of the beleaguered Irish. When his two regiments closed to within half the distance of the southern line they opened fire so effectively that the Confederates were forced to keep their heads down and hug the rear wall of the sunken road. Barlow quickly sized up the terrain and relative positions of the contending forces. Rather than simply reinforce the Irish Brigade's line and engage in a long distance firefight he saw that if he moved his men forward and to the left he would gain a slight rise from which the regiments could rake the Confederates in the sunken road. Putting theory into practice, Barlow's troops rolled forward and struck the Confederate's on their extreme right where the road was shallowest. What had been a formidable defensive position now become a death trap as the Yankee musketry spat vengeance on the southerners who had torn apart the previous assaults. As Charles A. Fuller later remembered:

> The result was terrible to the enemy. They could do us little harm, and we were shooting them like sheep in a pen. If a bullet missed the mark at the first it was liable to strike the further bank, and angle back

and take them secondarily, so to speak. In a few minutes white rags were hoisted along the rebel line.[10]

Miles called out for the Confederates to surrender and as they threw down their arms, Barlow ordered his men to cease firing.[11] Unable to rein in their fury many of Barlow's men kept firing into the surrendering rebels and the officers were forced to step in front of them and knock their muskets in the air.[12] Approximately 300 prisoners were taken and three colors captured, two by the 61st and one by the 64th.[13] After sending the prisoners to the rear, Barlow moved his men forward into a cornfield where soldiers of several regiments were mingled together. No enemy troops were visible from that position, but Barlow soon spied a Confederate force approaching his right. He called out "right shoulder shift arms" and the troops hurried off on the right oblique to the crest of a hill and commenced firing at the oncoming southerners.[14] After taking about twenty rounds from Barlow's men, the rebels broke and ran. Another Confederate force now reappeared on what had been the II Corps central front towards which Barlow was originally advancing.

The young colonel again swung his men back into the cornfield and beyond that towards an orchard from which the Confederates were firing two brass cannon. Barlow had his men form on the right of the 57th New York and Brooke's brigade and was sitting on his horse by a rail fence preparing his next attack when a piece of rebel case shot hit him in the groin.[15] Miles assumed command as Barlow was carried unconscious from the field.[16] After ordering Caldwell to halt his advance, Israel Richardson, the division commander, fell mortally wounded. Winfield Scott Hancock, later to play a major role in Barlow's career, took over the division. With the quick loss of key leaders, the Federal attack stalled as officers attempted to redress their lines and bring order to confused commands.[17] After the capture of the sunken road and the subsequent actions, Barlow's original regiment, the 61st New York found itself reduced to about 100 men.[18]

The focus of combat now shifted to the Federal left where, in late afternoon, Ambrose Burnside finally forced his way across the bridge spanning Antietam Creek. Burnside's attack seemed poised to break Lee's line wide open and unravel the entire Confederate position, when a dramatic last-minute counterattack by A. P. Hill's division arriving from Harpers Ferry stopped it in its tracks. As the day's fighting sputtered out, Lee's army, with a major assist from flawed Union generalship, had survived. Even so, it had been a near thing. The Army of Northern Virginia, bled by heavy losses, had been stretched to the breaking point. Had McClellan ordered a general assault the next day, Lee would likely have suffered a catastrophic defeat, one which could have significantly altered the course of the war. Despite the risk, which might have been suicidal with a more aggressive opponent, Lee remained in his lines, convinced—correctly—that McClellan would not attack. Indeed, McClellan agreed to a truce to bury the dead, the day after the battle. Having demonstrated that he would not be forced to retreat until he was ready, Lee crossed his army back over the Potomac into Virginia. The Battle of Antietam, or Sharpsburg, the bloodiest day in the War, had ended Lee's penetration of the north and given Abraham Lincoln the opportunity to issue the Emancipation Proclamation. But George McClellan had again demonstrated a lack of competence as a field commander.

After his wounding, Barlow was carried off the field and taken to a hospital near Keedysville, Maryland. In his first letter home after the battle he described his wound as ugly, but not serious.[19] He praised the "splendid" conduct of his troops as well as that of his subordinate and friend, Nelson Miles. "We drove the enemy back at every point whipping them thoroughly" he reported happily.[20] He confidently predicted that the battle would be rejoined, a forecast in which he was mistaken.

Barlow's recovery, both physically and psychologically, owed a great deal to Arabella's skill and devotion. As McClellan and Lee prepared for battle, Arabella, who had learned a great deal about tending wounded men from her nursing experience in army hospitals, was frantic to get out of Baltimore and back to her husband whom she knew would soon be in battle.[21] She managed to get to Sharpsburg while the battle was still raging. As Arabella put it in a letter to her friend Maria Daly, she arrived on the battlefield "just in time to see Col. Barlow brought in . . . 'mortally wounded' . . ."[22]

Arabella's constant attention to her husband was witnessed by George Templeton Strong, who visited the Army of the Potomac after Sharpsburg. He was making his way through one of the tented camps, jostled by soldiers and civilians and dodging wagons and horses when

who should suddenly turn up but Mrs. Arabella Barlow, nee Griffith unattended, but serene and self-possessed as if walking down Broadway. She is nursing the colonel her husband (badly wounded), and never appeared so well. Talked like a sensible, practical, earnest, warm-hearted woman, without a phrase of hyperflutination. We went to McClellan's headquarters and to Fitz-John Porter's.[23]

As Barlow began his convalescence under his wife's supervision, Lee withdrew to Virginia. McClellan remained on the battlefield, basking in the glory of having forced Lee back across the Potomac and concocting reasons why he could not follow him. Lincoln visited McClellan at his headquarters, in an attempt to determine the general's intentions and prod him into action. McClellan temporized. Finally exasperated, Lincoln removed the "Young Napoleon," and sent him home to await orders which would never arrive. The president put the Army of the Potomac in the hands of a man who accurately protested he was not qualified to command it, Ambrose Burnside. On returning to Virginia, the Army of Northern Virginia returned to its default defensive line behind the Rapidan and Rappahannock Rivers. Burnside, whose generalship was characterized by lack of energy and aggressiveness, decided to force Lee back from his position on the high ground behind Fredericksburg. In December, he ordered his troops against Lee's well-entrenched soldiers and saw each charge disintegrate under heavy fire and appalling losses. Barlow's convalescence spared him from taking part in the doomed assault. In spring, Lincoln removed Burnside from command of the Army of the Potomac, but not from Federal service, and put Major General Joseph Hooker in his place. Hooker, a good divisional commander, drew up a plan to flank Lee by crossing the Rapidan to the north and west of Fredericksburg.

With Arabella acting as a private nurse, Barlow, who despite his own optimistic predictions was not expected to recover, went on to improve "miraculously." When he appeared well enough to be moved, Arabella removed him from the military hospital and secured lodgings in Samuel Deaner's house near Keedysville. Two days after Antietam, Henry Halleck, Lincoln's chief of staff, endorsed Barlow's appointment as brigadier general, which was dated from 19 September. With former New York governor Edwin D. Morgan now a senator sitting on the military committee, George Bliss, who kept tabs on Washington doings, told Barlow there was no danger that he would not be confirmed.[24] Nor was Morgan the young warrior's only advocate. On 2 October, 1862, Arabella wrote Judge Charles Daly, influential New York judge and patron of Barlow's, that they had just received Frank's appointment as brigadier. He was a few weeks shy of his twenty-eighth birthday. Arabella conveyed Frank's thanks for the judge's aid in his promotion, and forwarded a copy of Brigadier J. G. Caldwell's report on the battle, which included laudatory comments about her husband's actions. She also wrote that she expected to move Francis back to New York as soon as he could make the journey and hoped to see the judge and his wife, Maria, when they got back into town.[25]

Captain Isaac Plumb of the 61st New York was chosen to deliver the brigadier's commission to Barlow. Plumb secured a broken-down horse and rode out from the regiment's camp to the farm where Arabella was tending her husband. Plumb found Barlow looking better than he had expected, and Arabella showed him the piece of case shot which had been extracted by surgeons. She was keeping it as a souvenir.[26] To make sure her weakened husband and his guest had a hearty meal, Arabella had ridden to Boonsboro to pick up fresh food for a dinner for Plumb and Frank. Plumb reported that her appearance on horseback "created a sensation among the people."[27]

On 23 October, after Arabella had brought Frank home, she invited the Dalys for a visit. The judge and his wife found Frank still lying on the stretcher on which he was carried off the field at Sharpsburg. Frank repeated Arabella's written gratitude and earnestly thanked the judge for his promotion. For his part, the judge demurred, saying he had done very little.[28] Obviously, the Barlows thought otherwise. Perhaps to please Daly's ethnic sensibilities, Barlow gave a detailed description of the fighting done by the Irish Brigade complete with accounts of Meagher riding before his troops under fire. He also extolled the valor and tenacity of the rebels while expressing a lack of confidence in McClellan who was still in command of the army.[29] In April of the following year, when he was able to move about more, Arabella and Frank called on the Dalys at their New York City home. Maria Daly thought he still looked frail and was not fit to return to duty, but Barlow had already made preparations to rejoin the army.[30]

When Barlow returned to active duty on 17 April 1863, he was assigned command of the second brigade in the second division of Howard's XI Corps. Until he was put out of action at Fair Oaks, Howard had been Barlow's brigade commander on the Peninsula and he had been effusive in his praise of the young colonel's performance under fire. For his part, Barlow respected Howard. Nevertheless, Barlow was ill at ease in his new corps where he had to deal with new officers and unfamiliar regiments. Subsequent events magnified his dissatisfactions with the XI Corps to the point where he swore he would never serve in it again. Despite his initial misgivings, Barlow settled in with his staff and seemed to have fully recovered from his wound, although he complained that he still needed a "good deal of sleep."[31]

As he had with his II Corps regiments, Barlow quickly instituted his trademark style of command, consisting of strict discipline and thorough training. One commentator remarked that Barlow "was a newcomer to the Corps and was little known to its members. His ways were too abrupt and his views too much of a martinet to please his brigade, but they learned he was as intrepid as Decatur."[32] Barlow's positive qualities may have subsequently led to grudging respect among some of the troops he led in the XI Corps, but he never developed the level of rapport which he had achieved with many in the units he commanded from the Peninsula through Antietam. Perhaps more so than in any other unit he commanded, many of his XI Corps men actively disliked Barlow with an intensity which little abated. After the war, Colonel James Wood of the 136th New York wrote, "Gen Barlow had the *happy faculty* of making himself disagreeable to every officer and private of the brigade."[33] Barlow was well aware of the reaction his methods evoked in his new unit and wrote home that "There has been some murmur at my drawing the reins but I am told they are beginning to like me better—I have been very mild."[34]

The new commander of the Army of the Potomac, Joseph Hooker, opened the campaign season with a thrust across the Rappahannock, which threatened to turn Lee's left. Unfortunately, having made this bold move, Hooker then lost his nerve and held his troops in position near a cluster of buildings somewhat grandiloquently called Chancellorsville. Lee countered with perhaps the most audacious move in a career characterized by aggressive, dramatic maneuvers. With Longstreet's corps on detached duty south of the James, the Army of Northern Virginia was badly outnumbered by their opponents. Nevertheless, Lee dispatched Stonewall Jackson on a wide flanking movement to hit Hooker on his right flank while Lee, with a much smaller force, kept watch on Hooker's center and left as well as the Federal force threatening at Fredericksburg. The XI Corps held the extreme right of the Federal line, the exact target of Jackson's attack. Before the battle began on 2 May, however, Barlow's brigade was detached from Howard and sent to beef up the III Corps under Daniel Sickles.

As a result of being sent to Sickles, Barlow was not present when Jackson's men charged screaming out of the woods, smashed into the XI Corps and hurled it into headlong retreat. As darkness fell and the Confederate attack halted, Barlow was ordered to close up with Birney's division which prevented him from returning to the XI Corps. Though his brigade was not heavily engaged, Barlow's men were sometimes under both bombardment and threat of attack. At the front of his men as the shells came whizzing in, the young brigadier again managed to impress at least those men he had not totally alienated. "Our brigadier although strict in camp is as cool as a South Sea Islander," Edward L. Edes of the 33d Massachusetts discovered. "When the shells are flying, he walked up & down our lines & coolly said 'Lie down, lie down & take it easy' although he thought us to be surrounded & that we would have to make our way out on the point of a bayonet."[35] On 3 May, the brigade finally returned to its parent corps, and his men occupied the rifle pits guarding the new Federal left. Hooker, however, had had enough. On 6 May 1863, he withdrew to the north bank of the Rappahannock and the Chancellorsville campaign came to an end.

Immediately after the battle, Barlow sent word to his mother and brothers that he had come through the clash at Chancellorsville unscathed. Since his brigade was separated from the rest of the corps when it was shattered by Jackson's assault, Barlow's brigade suffered few casualties, one officer and eight enlisted men wounded, and fourteen enlisted men missing, believed captured.[36] Barlow's immediate concern was for his own and his troops' reputation, especially as it appeared in print. Throughout the war, Barlow maintained a strong interest in the way his exploits, and those of his men, were presented in the press. "You can imagine my indignation and disgust at the miserable behavior of the 11th Corps," he wrote home, going on to say, "It does not appear as plainly as I should desire in the [New York] Tribune letter of May 4th that my brigade was not with the rest of the Corps. I trust that it will be stated more clearly in the Tribune and other papers."[37]

While Barlow was satisfied with the conduct of his own brigade, his contempt for the XI Corps deepened. More than ever he thought, wrote, and acted as though he had been exiled from his proper home. Although he sympathized with Howard and did not want to leave him at such a critical time, he clearly ached to get out of the XI Corps. At the time, he considered two possibilities. One was to return to his old corps—the II. His desire to return to his former Corps no doubt intensified after hearing from Winfield Scott Hancock, now in permanent command of Richardson's old division, that he would be delighted to have him in his command. Barlow pursued his efforts to regain a spot in the II Corps, and in June went to Hancock's headquarters to see about getting a brigade commission. But his attempts to get back to his old corps came to naught, and Barlow was fated to fight with the XI Corps in one more battle.

Like many Civil War soldiers, officers, and men (and, contrary to twentieth-century assumptions), Barlow generally held German troops in low esteem.[38] Their reputation for incompetence and lack of resolve in combat preceded the rout of the XI Corps at Chancellorsville, but the presence of many heavily German units in that corps reinforced the negative image. Even so, Barlow, who was in a position to know, realized that the collapse of the XI Corps was not wholly a result of the German units breaking. "Some of the Yankee Regts behaved just as badly," he admitted privately "and I think Hooker's failure thus far has been solely from the bad fighting of the men."[39] After Chancellorsville, Howard, smarting from the rout of his corps, determined to improve the morale and capabilities of his men. One of his first moves in this direction was to make better use of Barlow's known abilities as a disciplinarian and drillmaster. The commander of the First Division, General Charles Devens, had been badly wounded in the battle, and Howard took advantage of his absence to place Barlow in command. As Barlow later put it, Howard "seduced" him into taking control of the first division and make it fit for combat.[40] Barlow, in turn, hoped to get Miles out of the II Corps and place him in command of Colonel von Gilsa's brigade which contained most of his German troops. He was unsuccessful.

Hoping to improve the quality of the German regiments, Barlow put his political connections to work. On 27 May, he wrote the new governor of New York, Horatio Seymour, regarding officer appointments in the 41st, 54th, and 68th New York Volunteers, "all German Regts."[41] In the letter, Barlow explained that he did not hold the enlisted men responsible for the rout at Chancellorsville. "Your Excellency," he wrote, "is aware of the part taken by the Corps in the late battles—In such cases I always suspect the officers of having been faithless & incompetent & in regard to some of the Regts in the Division I feel certain that a change ought to be made in some of their officers."[42] Barlow went on to explain that, having just recently taken over divisional command, he had not had the opportunity to satisfy himself about the situation, but requested that Seymour not make any field officer appointments in the regiments he listed until he could investigate the "character and capacity of the applicants." He added his belief that "if these Regts were well commanded they would be inferior to none in the service & I am exceedingly anxious that officers of great strictness & high character should be selected for them."[43] Barlow closed his letter with the comment that he looked forward to discussing the regiments and their officers with Seymour when he made an announced visit to the Army. Unfortunately, Barlow's continued experience with German troops made him more, rather than less, dissatisfied with them.

In the meantime, Barlow threw himself into the work of making his division combat efficient and found himself busy morning and night working on divisional programs. He believed that Adelbert Ames' brigade would improve with training and decided that he would "confine myself particularly to the German brigade. I am going to move their camp tomorrow so as to bring them all under my immediate eye."[44] Barlow found a great deal of dissention and mistrust in the division, a situation that had been exacerbated by the debacle at Chancellorsville. Using the then common misappellation "Dutch" for Germans, Barlow wrote, "The Corps is in a state of continual excitement and quarrelling—one Dutchman accuses another of misconduct in the late battle and the Dutch accuse the Americans and vice versa . . ."[45] In the end, Barlow would never be satisfied with "these miserable creatures" as he termed his German troops.[46] When they were temporarily detached from him on the eve of Gettysburg, he assumed he would get them back "in case of a battle but I don't very much care if I don't."[47]

On 2 June 1863, Barlow vented his feelings towards his division in a letter to his old friend Charles Henry Dalton who served on special assignments for Governor Andrew of Massachusetts:

> Now I have command of the Division lately commended by General Devens. It was the first to break on May 2nd and is in a most disgusting condition as to discipline and morale. But if hard knocks and a tight rein will make them fight they will have to do it. One of the Brigades is wholly German and is commanded by Colonel von Gilsa (or rather is now commanded by a Major as Colonel Gilsa is away and I have the next Colonel in rank in arrest). I expect to have to arrest them all the way down until I find some private soldier who will make them do things properly. . . . I have just come in command and am working hard.[48]

Barlow's disdain for the German units with which he came into contact, though he did recognize individual officers as courageous and capable, probably derived not only from the failures of such units in battle but from Yankee nativism which had been activated by the large-scale immigration of Germans and Irish to the United States after 1845. It is doubtful that Barlow was comfortable with people whose language, in the Germans' case, he could not understand, and whose customs and religions seemed suspect as well. Barlow was never one to disguise his feelings, and while there is no reason to doubt that he lent his best efforts to the task of improving his division, there is equally no reason to believe his men were unaware of his attitude towards them.

At least Barlow got to visit troops whose abilities he respected—after all, he had trained and led them. On 1 June, Barlow, accompanied by Arabella and his brother, Edward, took part in a commemoration of the Battle of Fair Oaks. Howard was the presiding officer at the ceremony and Hancock attended as well. Barlow's old regiments, the 61st and 64th New York, were on the field, as were units who had fought alongside them, such as the 81st Pennsylvania and the 5th New Hampshire. The sight of his old commands, which he found "very small looking," moved Barlow. His impressions were correct as the 61st New York totaled only about 75 men at the time.[49] After the formalities ended, Barlow toured the New Yorkers' camp and reported that "my old men . . . were very glad to see me."[50] This was apparently no egotistical boast. Charles Fuller, who had risen to lieutenant, remembered, "Barlow appeared and gave us a chance to grasp his hand. I am sure this great soldier always had a special affection for the men of the 61st New York. He had their entire confidence."[51] It is highly unlikely that the same could be said for von Gilsa's Brigade of the First Division, XI Corps.

Barlow also pursued another way out of his exile in the XI Corps after the Battle of Chancellorsville. Calls to arm free blacks and escaped slaves arose in some quarters early in the war, but the Lincoln administration did not officially endorse such efforts until after the Emancipation Proclamation was issued. By 1863, efforts to organize black regiments were gathering momentum on state and Federal levels. Most often, black troops, especially those made up of former slaves, were organized into regiments of United States Colored Troops. Some states, however, created their own regiments of black soldiers. Massachusetts, the abolitionist center of the United States, raised a regiment of black troops designated the 54th Massachusetts. The unit was made up primarily of free blacks living in the north augmented by escaped slaves. Determined to ensure that the experiment in using black troops was successful, both the Federal government and the states raising such units strove to place experienced, competent white officers at their heads. Barlow's friend and pupil, Robert Gould Shaw, who had been wounded at Antietam, was appointed colonel of the 54th Massachusetts. It seems likely that Barlow had discussed the possibility of joining a black outfit with Shaw and other interested parties while he was out on convalescent leave. As a battle-tested leader of proven experience, the new brigadier certainly seemed a superb choice to lead the yet untested black soldiers. On 17 March 1863, Shaw wrote home reporting Massachusetts was considering creating additional black regiments and that he hoped "Frank Barlow can get the command. He is just the man for it and I should like to be under him."[52] Apparently Barlow was willing. On 24 April, after he had arrived at his new assignment with the XI Corps, Barlow told his family that he had written to "Lowell" (James Russell Lowell, Boston poet and abolitionist and ardent supporter of the recruitment of black troops) that he was "still ready to take command of the Negro Brigade if it is desired."[53] For his part, Lowell organized a group of prominent Boston abolitionists to petition Secretary of War Edwin Stanton to appoint Barlow to the command of a new black brigade.[54]

Probably because raising the new regiments proved more time-consuming than anticipated, neither Barlow's stated interest nor the lobbying of friendly politicos bore immediate fruit. Another hitch involved the expectation that Barlow would recruit the brigade himself. Barlow had little interest in that part of the project, though he did his best to keep his opportunities alive. "I am anxious to take part in the black experiment," he wrote to abolitionists back home. "Will you state to Gov. [John J.] Andrew and to anyone else that is interested in this matter that my services are at their command wherever they can be used."[55] On 18 June, when the 54th Massachusetts was already posted in South Carolina, Shaw wrote his mother that Barlow was still interested in commanding a colored brigade and "it would be a great piece of good fortune if we could get him and for the cause as well."[56]

Yet the commission did not come and events in Virginia were beginning to heat up, making any transfer from the Army of the Potomac difficult. Two days after mentioning Barlow's interest in the black brigade to his mother, Shaw brought it up with Charley Lowell, Federal cavalryman, son of the abolitionist-poet, and friend of Barlow and Shaw, asking if he could "do something towards getting Barlow for us?" Shaw was convinced Barlow's abilities would ensure that the black brigades saw effective and successful service. "I have no doubt we should do something under him," Shaw opined.[57] Other prominent people were of the same mind. On 29 June 1863, Governor Andrew of Massachusetts wrote Secretary of War Edwin Stanton, supporting Barlow's appointment over that of Thomas W. Higginson, who was also a candidate to lead black troops. Higginson, Andrew wrote, had "never seen much service." The Bay State governor dismissed James Montgomery, who commanded a unit of freed slaves in South Carolina, as "very useful as a good bushwhacker," but the governor wanted a brigade commander who would do the newly forming black regiments "justice . . . and no harm."[58] Barlow was his man. But, even as Andrew wrote, the Gettysburg campaign was well underway, and, by the time it was over, the opportunity for Barlow to take command of a black brigade had passed.

Perhaps more intriguing than Barlow's near miss in officering a black unit was the possibility that he lead another organization comprised of former slaves. Plans were then underway to create an agency to deal with the special problems of emancipated slaves. The embryonic organization, tentatively named the American Freedmen's Inquiry and Commission—which later became the Freedmen's Bureau—needed a capable director and Barlow's name was put forward to head it. In early June, Samuel Gridley Howe, husband of Julia Ward Howe and a major player in the movement to create the organization, offered Barlow the position of "Superintendent of the American Freedmen's Bureau."

The particulars regarding the offer are sketchy partly because the new agency had not yet been officially created and partly because Barlow himself wanted no public discussion until everything was arranged. On several occasions, however, he wrote relatives about what he called his "Darkey Plan." Initially, Barlow was uncertain as to whether or not he should accept the offer and warned his correspondents not to mention it.[59] He thought the position would prove advantageous politically, but wondered if he was suited for the job. More importantly, he disliked the thought of leaving military service "for which I am well fitted."[60] Nevertheless, by 26 June, with the Lee across the Potomac and marching into Pennsylvania, Barlow had decided to accept the position after the campaign concluded—if the offer was still open.[61] However, he still wanted no public notice of his joining the new organization. *"Don't speak of my darkey plan,"* he admonished his brother Richard.[62]

Indeed, at this critical juncture in the war Barlow had every reason to believe that his appointment as "Superintendent of the Freedmen throughout the United States" was virtually within his grasp. He was carrying two letters about his Freedmen's Bureau commission when the battle of Gettysburg began, but when he fell into rebel hands he feared that the Confederates "might not be inclined to parole so important a functionary as the 'Superintendent of the Freedmen throughout the US' so I destroyed the letters together with all others in my pocket."[63] Along with the possibility of commanding a black regiment, Barlow's pending career as director of the Freedmen's Bureau became a casualty of the Battle of Gettysburg. Barlow, however, would continue to show interest in both enterprises for another year.

Having turned back Hooker's attempt to turn his flank at Chancellorsville, Lee undertook his second invasion of the north. Lee went north partly to draw the Federal forces out of Virginia, but his primary aim—as it had been since he took command of the Army of Northern Virginia—was to win a decisive victory which would shatter the northern will to continue the war and thus secure the independence of the southern Confederacy.[64] The Army of Northern Virginia began moving out of its Rappahannock position on 3 June 1863, marched over the Blue Ridge Mountains, rolled up the Federal garrison at Winchester on 15 June, and crossed the Potomac shortly after. This time Lee did not halt in Maryland, but using South Mountain as a shield, pushed forward into Pennsylvania. By 25 June, the Army of the Potomac was also north of the Potomac, closing in on Lee from the south. The southern cavalry, under J.E.B. Stuart, had left Lee's army to carry out a raid, and Lee was unsure of the Army of the Potomac's location until 29 June. It was then that he learned that he faced a new Federal commander, George Gordon Meade. Through a series of unplanned movements and countermovements, both armies began concentrating around the town of Gettysburg on 1 July 1863.

On 26 June, as the Army of the Potomac marched northward after Lee, Barlow found himself on the Burkittsville Road near South Mountain. Not knowing Lee was already in Pennsylvania, Barlow reported home that a large force of rebels was in Maryland, "and I hope we shall have a battle which will settle the matter one way or the other."[65] He would get his battle. The settlement would take longer.

The Battle of Gettysburg began partly by accident on 1 July when General John Buford, commanding the cavalry screen for the Army of the Potomac, deployed his men to delay the Confederates moving towards the village. Throughout the morning, elements of both of the Confederate and Union armies went into action almost as rapidly as they arrived in the village. The first Federal forces to come to Buford's aid were the I and XI Corps. The I Corps under Major John Reynolds, who was killed shortly after arriving on the field, took up a position on the western outskirts of Gettysburg while the XI went into action on their right, north of the town. Barlow and his men hurried northward from Emmitsburg, Maryland on the morning of the 1 July, and pressed on to Gettysburg, about 10 miles away, amid reports of skirmishing cavalry. Even in the act of rushing to the embattled crossroads town Barlow's impatience and disdain with his German units reared its head. Barlow had previously considered Colonel Leopold von Gilsa, a former Prussian army officer and commander of his "Dutch" brigade, as insufficiently strict with his men. When von Gilsa allowed more than one man to break ranks to fill his canteen on the march to Gettysburg, Barlow placed him under arrest. Shortly after, as the division marched through Gettysburg, Barlow, perhaps seeing few options, restored him to his command, a move that was greeted with cheers from his men—which probably says something about the soldiers' attitude towards both their brigade and their division commander.[66]

By the time the First Division arrived on the field, Howard had taken over the command of the two Federal Corps then on the field. Karl Schurz became acting commander of the XI Corps. Schurz ordered Barlow through Gettysburg to a position on the right of Schimmelfennig's division, the Third, which held the ground immediately next to the I Corps. Barlow directed his men forward to seize a rise called "Blocher's knoll," subsequently known as "Barlow's Knoll," which formed something of a defensive salient. Together the two XI Corps divisions had about 6,000 men between them.[67]

Schurz soon discovered that Barlow's forward thrust had caused him to lose contact with Schimmelfennig. This unusual lapse in Barlow's proven eye for terrain was probably due to the badly confused situation, and his desire to hold the high ground. Although Schurz advanced the Third Division to restore the defensive line, nothing he or Barlow did could have prevented the impending disaster.

About 11:00 A. M. an artillery battery was dispatched to Barlow at his position on the west side of the York Pike. Barlow's initial placement proved too close to rebel fire for the cannoneers' safety. The battery was shifted slightly and remained in action until the division was driven from the field. While Schurz had seen problems with the Second Division's deployment, Barlow later described his position as "admirable."[68] The open spaces allowed him to observe the Confederate infantry forming for the attack, but apparently he did not detect the massive blow which was coming. Confederate Lieutenant General Richard S. Ewell ordered Jubal Early's division, spearheaded by John Gordon's brigade, to smash the XI Corps lines. Barlow, who held the extreme right of the Federal defenses, was hit on front and flank His first brigade, von Gilsa's, broke and ran back into Adelbert Ames' brigade, throwing it into confusion as well.[69] Barlow later claimed that he had his men well-positioned and ready for action at the point where Early and Gordon struck and asserted his men ought to have held their lines. He might have been correct that his division could have put up more resistance, but a more determined defense would only have slowed the oncoming Confederates. Barlow's harsh evaluation of his command might have stemmed from the embarrassment of being routed, not to mention the pain from the wound he received that day. His own expectations and dislike of his German units might also have affected his assessment of the day's fighting. It never seems to have entered Barlow's mind that the behavior of the troops might have been partly due to his attitude towards them. In any event, the Confederates were more generous in their descriptions of the fight. Ewell reported an "obstinate contest"[70] before the First Division fled, and Early described the clash as short and hot.[71]

But even if Barlow was too quick to condemn, the fact remained his line was quickly overrun. As he remembered it, his men began to bolt as soon as the Confederate skirmishers advanced. "No fight at all was made," he recalled, going on to explain what happened as his position was overrun:

> Finding that they [his division] were going I started to get ahead of them to try to rally them and form another line in the rear. Before I could turn my horse I was shot in the left side about half way between the arm pit and the head of the thigh bone. I dismounted and tried to walk off the field. Everybody was then running to the rear and the enemy were approaching rapidly. One man took hold of one shoulder and another on the other side to help me. One of them was soon shot and fell. I then got a spent ball in my back which has made quite a bruise. Soon I got too faint to go any further and lay down. I lay in the midst of the fire some five minutes as the enemy were firing at our running men. I did not expect to get out alive. A ball went through my hat as I lay on the ground and another just grazed the forefinger of my right hand.[72]

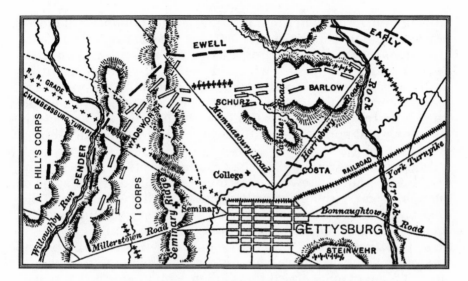

The First Day at Gettysburg. From *Campfire & Battlefield*, 1894.

What happened to Barlow, after the Confederates came upon him, became the subject of a romantic tale which enjoyed great popularity in the late nineteenth century. According to the widely circulated account, Gordon rode up with his men and spied Barlow lying on the ground, still alive. The Confederate dismounted and asked if he could aid his stricken opponent. Barlow asked Gordon to read his wife's letters which were in his pocket. After having done so, Barlow then asked Gordon to send word to Arabella, whom he believed was with the Sanitary Commission near Howard's headquarters, and tell her of his fate and that he had done his duty. Gordon said he would do so if he lived. Barlow recovered from his wound, and years later, upon hearing that a Confederate general named Gordon had been killed, assumed it was the Samaritan who had comforted him at Gettysburg. For his part, Gordon believed Barlow had died of his wound. In the late 1870s, Gordon and Barlow accidentally met at a dinner party and were stunned and delighted to find each other still alive. The two then began a friendship which lasted until Barlow's real death.[73]

The Gordon-Barlow story appealed to both late Victorian sentimentality and the prevailing desire to heal the wounds of the war. It was often repeated and found its way in many publications relating to both the War and Gettysburg (see chapter 9). The

moving tale of common humanity in the midst of national bloodletting originated with Gordon, who became a staunch advocate
of sectional reconciliation after the War. There is no evidence that
Barlow ever mentioned it, which has led to challenges about its
authenticity. A more direct source of the doubts cast on the encounter on Blocher's Knoll is the letter Barlow wrote from a military hospital outside Gettysburg on 7 July. This account of his
wounding and subsequent fate is dramatic enough, but Gordon
is not part of it.

As Barlow lay wounded on the ground, one of Early's staff officers, Major Andrew Lewis Pitzer, found him and directed some of
his men to carry the grievously wounded Yankee officer off the
field and into the woods. They left some water with Barlow and
then returned to the business of driving his men through the village of Gettysburg and onto the heights of Cemetery Hill. Somewhat later some prisoners from his division fashioned a stretcher
out of a blanket and carried their fallen commander into a house
on Joseph Bemer's farm.[74] Barlow's clothing was saturated with
blood and he was in great pain. A bed was found for him and as
night fell and the battle died down three Confederate surgeons
came to examine him. They knocked Barlow out with chloroform
and probed the wound. When he awoke, the southern doctors told
him that a minié ball had passed downward from the entry
wound, cut through the peritoneum and lodged in his pelvic cav-
ity. They told Barlow he had little chance to live, gave him some
morphine, and left.[75]

Barlow, the only Federal general captured that day, had become
something of a celebrity, and several Confederate officers visited
him that night. As was true of the other rebels with whom he had
come into contact, Barlow pronounced them "very kind."[76] Perhaps they knew Barlow from his reputation and gave him the respect due one warrior from another.

At any rate, on the morning of 2 July, a captured Federal surgeon examined Barlow along with the three southern doctors he
had seen the day before. Believing that Barlow's intestines had
been cut and that he would soon suffer from peritonitis, all the
phyicians concurred that there was nothing to be done. The young
general was then moved Miss Jane Smith's house in the village
of Gettysburg near the almshouse.[77] He remained there during
the remainder of the battle. Either because of the morphine he
was given for pain or the recognition that there was nothing he
could do, Barlow spent his time reading and talking as the battle

raged desperately through the Devil's Den, the Peach Orchard, the Wheat Field, and around the slopes of Little Round Top. The mother and daughter in the house, joined by some Union prisoners, attended to Barlow's wound, treating it with baths of cold water, which was prescribed as the only useful treatment.[78] Barlow took advantage of his situation to talk freely with the Confederate officers who came to visit him. Barlow did not mention Gordon, although he did write that he spoke with members of Early and Ewell's staffs. While Barlow despised the southern goal of rending the Union and devoted his energies to destroying the Confederacy, he was favorably impressed by both the manner and commitment of the Confederates he met while a prisoner:

> They were pleasant fellows. They despised our army and meant to fight to the last. I saw a good many of their men and was much pleased with them. They are more heroic, more modest and more in earnest than we are. Their whole tone is much finer than ours. Except among those who are fighting this war on antislavery grounds, there is not much earnestness nor are there many noble feelings and sentiments involved. I heard the battles of Thursday and Friday close to me. The enemy had no doubt of capturing or utterly destroying our army and I feared it would be so.[79]

Whether or not Gordon first told them of the wounded Yankee general's request, Early and Ewell sent word to Arabella Barlow informing her that her husband was seriously wounded and in their hands. Once again, Belle was on the field of battle working in the army hospitals, and ready to come to her husband's aid if need be. Arabella reached the battlefield with Major General Winfield Scott Hancock, the II Corps commander, who took over the Federal defenses on Cemetery Ridge before Meade arrived. On receiving the message that Francis was wounded, Arabella begged Hancock for a pass through the lines so that she could take care of him. Hancock, concerned that Arabella might inadvertently reveal information about Federal defenses to the Confederates, refused.[80] Undeterred and determined to get to Francis, Arabella made her way to Culp's Hill, where the lines were close together. From there, she made her way across no man's land into Confederate-held Gettysburg at daylight the next day. According to one account she ran from the Federal to the rebel lines under fire from both sides, but managed to avoid being hit.[81] This rendition of Arabella's crossing seems highly sensationalized. Her entry into the rebel-held village seems to have followed regular military procedure, which was daring enough in the middle of a battle. A Gettysburg civilian, David Skelley, left this account of Belle's presence in Gettysburg during the battle:

> On the evening of the 2nd on Chambersburg Street we were halted by two Confederate soldiers who had a lady in charge. She was on horseback and proved to be the wife of General Barlow who had come through the lines under a flag of truce looking for her husband who had been severely wounded on July 1.[82]

Once she found him, Arabella immediately took up the duties of a private nurse, a task she had performed so well after Frank's Antietam wounding. Under her tender and constant ministrations, Barlow proved the best medical experts of the Army of Northern Virginia and the Army of the Potomac wrong. Indeed, Barlow always credited his wife with saving his life after his wounding at Gettysburg.[83] Nor did the untiring Arabella rest when Frank was asleep or could otherwise be temporarily left alone. Instead, she worked alongside the other doctors and nurses tending to the thousands of wounded and dying soldiers crammed into temporary hospitals in and around Gettysburg.[84]

Barlow was still in the village of Gettysburg when Lee withdrew his forces from Cemetery Hill and into a straight-line formation in front of Seminary Ridge. Although he was barely ambulatory, Barlow believed that Lee's movement was a feint and sent word to the Federal command.[85] He was wrong. In their attempts to break through the Army of the Potomac's defenses, Lee's own troops suffered such fearful losses that the Confederate chieftain was forced to abandon the campaign in Pennsylvania and retreat back to Virginia. Following the Confederate evacuation of Gettysburg, Barlow was taken first to a small house outside of the village on the turnpike which led to Baltimore. This was probably an arrangement worked out by Arabella. In his first report home, Francis stated that he could sit up when he liked and could "hobble about easily." He predicted that the wound was less serious than the one he had suffered at Antietam and that he would be dressed in a week although several weeks of recuperation would be necessary before he could exert himself.[86]

Despite Barlow's optimistic prognosis, his recuperation proceeded slower than expected and included periods of regression. In early August, he was staying in Baltimore and wrote a friend that he was "still on my back . . . unable to be moved and suffering considerably from my wound which threatens to be more tedious than the former one in the groin."[87] Later in the month, Arabella transported him to her hometown of Somerville, New Jersey. At about this time, the minié ball was removed from Barlow's abdomen, and he complained of "violent pains when I stand or sit."[88] On 14 August, he revealed that he could not bear any weight on his legs or walk without suffering severe pain. Consequently, he was largely confined to a stretcher. Barlow's convalescence lasted until well into the fall with Arabella taking him to Boston, where they stayed with Julia Ward Howe. Howe attempted to arrange for Frank to visit his mother's old admirer, Nathaniel Hawthorne, but the somewhat reclusive author's wife sent word that the proposed meeting would not be convenient.[89] Barlow might have had better luck seeing Hawthorne if he had announced he was coming with Almira rather than Mrs. Howe. In any event Frank and Arabella returned briefly to New York before going back to Somerville again.[90]

Barlow's disgust at what he saw as the disgraceful behavior of his men on the first day of Gettysburg boiled over during the summer, fueled in part by the pain and stress of the slow recovery. The day after the battle ended, Barlow vowed to sever his connection with the XI Corps, though he enjoined those to whom he confided his feelings not to publicize them.[91] Barlow centered his criticism of the XI Corps on the German regiments. In a letter to a friend, Moses Blake Williams, Barlow explained that the desire to command a division led him to take over the unit "which was the first to begin the disgraceful performance at Chancellorsville" and that he had hoped "we might bring the Dutchmen up by strict discipline."[92] "But," he went on, "I am convinced that nothing can be done with the German Regts. They won't fight and the whole history of the war has shown it."[93] Barlow voiced approval at the rumors that the XI Corps was to be broken up or otherwise reorganized. Actually the XI and XII Corps of the Army of the Potomac were sent to the western theater after the Confederate victory at Chickamauga and became part of the force that Sherman led to Atlanta, the Sea, and ultimately North Carolina. Barlow was willing to exempt individual Germans from his overall condemnation of German military prowess, but otherwise he continued to vent his ire. "The Dutch won't fight. Their officers say so, and they say so themselves and they ruin all with whom they come into contact."[94]

Barlow's vow never to set foot in the XI Corps again went untested, as the formation went west while he slowly recovered from his wound. Certainly Barlow's commitment to the Union cause would have been severely tried if he had been ordered to return to his old division. His maneuvering to get back to the II Corps, which had begun before Gettysburg, continued during his months of convalescence. He kept in contact with Hancock, the II Corps commander, who was himself recovering from a serious wound received during the climactic attack by Pickett's and Pettigrew's divisions against the Union center on 3 July. He also had his old friend Miles keep his desires known to both corps and army leadership. On 12 December, Winfield Scott Hancock wrote Barlow informing him that he had advised Meade's staff that he would be glad to have Barlow as a division commander. Hancock explained that major changes in the Army's organization and leadership were in the works which would likely open the way for Barlow's return as a division leader. "I should always be pleased to have you in a command of mine," Hancock wrote.[95]

No doubt these words cheered the recovering general and Barlow looked forward to returning to the Corps in which he had begun the war and where he retained many friends. Although he could have had no knowledge of it, he would have probably approved the course of action, which was taking shape in the mind of the man who would direct the Army of the Potomac's actions during the rest of the war. These plans would have an indelible effect on Barlow and the men he would lead. From May 1864 until almost the end of the conflict, the II Corps would become the shock troops of the Army of the Potomac in the most intense, continuous, and bloody fighting the Civil War would see. Not surprisingly, Barlow would be right in the thick of it.

5

From the Rapidan to the Salient

WHEN HE REPORTED FIT FOR DUTY IN DECEMBER 1863, BARLOW was assigned to the Department of the South. The posting did not last long. Watching the war from a garrison outside Charleston or some other secondary objective was not his idea of soldiering. No doubt Barlow redoubled his efforts for reassignment to the II Corps utilizing every political connection he had with well-placed friends. Considering his known desire to secure Barlow for his Corps, Hancock was probably enlisted in the "Get Barlow" campaign as well. In any event, Barlow never left New York for the southern assignment, and on 26 January 1864, the orders sending him to the Department of the South were revoked, and he received the welcome news that he was appointed to a divisional command in the II Corps. Barlow's new orders directed him to report to Hancock, who was engaged in recruitment duty at Harrisburg, Pennsylvania.[1]

Barlow rejoined the II Corps at a time of major transformation, both for the Army of the Potomac and the entire Union war effort. On 29 February 1864, Lincoln appointed Ulysses S. Grant as Commanding General of all the Federal forces, the rank of lieutenant general, last held by Washington, being revived for him. Grant immediately began devising a northern offensive on all fronts with the objective of destroying the Confederacy in 1864.[2] Four major operations were envisioned. William T. Sherman, Grant's most trusted lieutenant, was to launch a deep, penetrating raid into the Confederate heartland of the Deep South. Nathaniel Banks was to take an amphibious force up the Red River in Louisiana and effectively end southern resistance in the Trans-Mississippi theater. Meade, who retained at least nominal control over the Army of the Potomac, was handed its traditional, and pivotal, assignment of defeating the Army of Northern Virginia, and capturing the Confederate capital at Richmond. For political as well as military reasons, Grant would accompany the Army of the Potomac.

Grant's decision to remain with the main eastern army was a response to the perceived failure of the Army's previous commanders to defeat Lee. As the Union's most successful general, the northern public expected Grant to take on the almost mythical southerner commander in a campaign which would pit champion against champion. Nevertheless, the arrangement proved awkward, and increasingly reduced Meade to the position of one of Grant's staff officers.[3] In the clumsy chain of command, Grant would issue orders to Meade, who would then issue them to his corps commanders and so on. The Army of the Potomac, and indeed all the Federal armies, faced another problem which was entirely of the United States government's own making. The unwillingness to create general officer rank above major general—Grant alone excepted—meant that the army was overstaffed with brigadier and major generals, whose ranking depended entirely on seniority. Major General Ambrose Burnside, who commanded the IX Corps, was senior to all the others of that rank in the Army of the Potomac, including Meade. Although Burnside had long since demonstrated an innate mediocrity in military leadership, political reasons prevented his removal. Consequently, to avoid violating Burnside's seniority, the IX Corps, part of the massive force Grant was concentrating against Lee, was theoretically independent of Meade's command. As a result, Grant had to issue special orders to Burnside explaining how he was to operate with the Army of the Potomac. The system was unwieldy and more than once impeded the effectiveness of the Federal forces.

The Army of the Potomac, strung out in its winter camps north of the Rapidan River, underwent major internal restructuring as well. On 25 March 1864, the army command announced its new organization. Due to severe losses at Gettysburg, the I and III Corps were disbanded and its divisions assigned to the II and V Corps, a move that was unpopular with the men of the defunct corps. The original regiments of the II Corps were consolidated in its first two divisions. Barlow was given command the First Division. At 29 he was the youngest of Hancock's divisional commanders and one of the youngest generals in the army. Already the nickname, "The Boy General," was applied to him, though those subject to his exacting standards of discipline and performance no doubt preferred other nicknames which have not been passed down through the records. His brigade commanders were his old friend Colonel Nelson Miles, leading the first brigade; Colonel Thomas A. Smyth heading the second, or Irish, Brigade; Colonel Paul Frank, commanding the third brigade; and Colonel

John R. Brooke, another old comrade of Barlow's, commanding the fourth brigade. Throughout the ensuing spring and summer campaign, Barlow, who felt Miles and Brooke were his best commanders, usually gave the first and fourth brigades the lethal honor of spearheading his assaults. The II Corps other divisional commanders were John Gibbon, Second Division; David Birney, Third Division; and J. B. Carr, who was soon replaced by Gershom Mott, leading the Fourth Division.

Hancock, Barlow, and the other officers of the Army of the Potomac had about six weeks to prepare their commands for the onset of the new campaigning season. As usual, Barlow imposed his demanding regimen of discipline and drill, measures which seemed especially necessary since there were many new recruits present in the army. Many of the new men were conscripts or bounty-jumpers, generally men of dubious character who often corrupted the units to which they were assigned and who required close supervision.[4] Barlow's insistence on tight discipline and training was well suited for the less motivated troops who made up a large number of the replacements for the Army of the Potomac in 1864.

As he had from his earliest days as an officer, Barlow instituted measures to make his division as combat ready as possible. He had long understood that effectiveness in battle required rapid marching and deployment without loss of unit cohesion. Striking quickly while retaining mass and firepower were usually the difference between success and failure—and, Barlow abhorred failure.

One example of Barlow's plan to create a lean fighting division was his order of 11 April 1864, directing that all unnecessary clothing be sent to the rear. Each soldier was allowed to retain a new uniform for the summer campaign, a change of underwear, a woolen and rubber blanket, an extra pair of shoes and a few light, personal items.[5] Barlow's concern for the amount of clothing and personal items stemmed from his belief that heavy knapsacks caused men to fall out of line from exhaustion during marches. He ordered his provost guard, the divisional military police who closed up lines and prevented straggling, to check the knapsacks of every soldier who dropped from the ranks "upon plea of exhaustion." Any extra or unauthorized articles were to be thrown away on the spot. Company officers were responsible for the surplus articles rule and their names were forwarded to brigade commanders if any men in their companies were found to have an overloaded knapsack. To ensure that no man could plead ignorance of the regulation, Barlow ordered that it be read out loud three times at the head of each company.[6] Observers agreed that Barlow's tried and tested techniques bore fruit. Samuel S. Parmalee, who first became acquainted with Barlow and his ways on the Peninsula reported, "Everything snaps in the Div[ision.]"[7]

Barlow made sure that he was supplied with what he regarded as an essential, almost totemic, piece of equipment—his cavalry saber. The saber, which seems to have been the only weapon he carried in battle, was used to drive the weakhearted back into line. But, more importantly, it seemed to function as a symbol of Barlow's warrior persona, and the young division commander did not want to begin the new campaign without his signature sidearm. He had lost the saber he carried at Gettysburg, and arrived at the Army of the Potomac in a swordless state. On 9 April 1864, apparently referring to a previous request, Barlow asked Brigadier General Alexander Webb, who commanded a brigade in the Second Division of the II Corps, if he had brought a sword for him from Washington. Hoping that Webb had accomplished the mission, Barlow requested that Webb send him the sword and "memorandum of price" directly by messenger.[8] Barlow certainly had his sword—presumably through Webb—before the campaign began and was photographed with it the following June.

Barlow spared neither himself (nor his men) to ensure that they were thoroughly prepared to meet Lee's men in battle. Even before he had seen combat Barlow had studied the tactical manuals of the day, and his personal experience in battle had given him a veteran's insight into what worked and what did not. During the ensuing spring and summer campaigns, Barlow demonstrated a willingness to deploy his men in a variety of formations depending on the situation facing him. Such maneuvers bespoke steady preparation during the spring. Like many combat-experienced officers, Barlow had moved away from deploying men in standing firing lines which presented clear and vulnerable targets to enemy rifles and artillery. Instead, he began to favor the skirmish line formation in which the men were spaced further apart presenting fewer clusters of men for southern infantry and gunners to mow down. Whether or not he experimented with drawing up his regiments by column rather than lines, a formation he used spectacularly on at least one occasion, is less certain. By the time Grant was ready to renew the struggle with Lee, Frank was generally satisfied with his efforts to make his division combat ready and believed that he had made a good impression on his men. He was particularly pleased that

he had not lost his temper or—at least according to his defini-
tion—spoken or acted harshly. "Though I am strict I think I am
well liked," he confided to Almira.[9]

One area of discipline which concerned Barlow was desertion.
The problem increased in severity with the changing nature of
many of the men coming into the army. Federal forces no longer
relied exclusively on volunteers. Conscription had been instituted
in 1863, and substitutes could be arranged for payment by those
who could afford it. Additionally, many states and localities offered bounties to those who enlisted. Unsurprisingly, many men
acquired through such methods felt little enthusiasm for the
soldier's life and the prospect of fighting. During 1864, admit-
tedly a year of unprecedented savage fighting in Virginia, desertions in the Army of the Potomac reached an average of 7,300 each
month.[10] This meant the army lost almost as many men through
desertion as through casualties. During the spring, even before
the campaign was underway, Barlow reported that three to four
men a day deserted his division.[11] For this reason, he thought it
was "mistaken humanity" for Lincoln to commute sentences of
death handed down by the Army's courts-martial since such re-
prieves inadvertently made desertion seem less perilous.

Barlow's heated intolerance of desertion, straggling, shirking
or any form of cowardice was rooted in his own set of values and
standards of personal behavior. Stringent discipline was a hall-
mark of his leadership from his earliest days as an officer, even
before he had met the enemy. Experience in battle only deepened
his abhorrence of skulking, deserting, or straggling, and he became convinced that such behavior impeded the Union war effort. Almost 30 years after Appomattox, during the debate on
granting pensions to all Union veterans, Barlow wrote a lengthy
public letter in which he declared that the large numbers of
troops who hung back or failed in their duty significantly length-
ened the course of the war.[12] "It was this want of bravery and
fidelity in many of our soldiers," he wrote, "which accounts for
the fact that it took the north with its greatly superior numbers,
its unlimited facilities for communication with Europe, and its
greatly superior resources in every respect, so long a time to put
down the rebellion."[13] Although Barlow extolled Lincoln, ranking him as co-equal with Washington in his importance to the
nation, he repeated his criticism that the president "inflicted a
great injury on the army by his pardon of deserters and general
leniency."[14] As for the course he would have taken, Barlow was
clear:

War is a savage business and it is idle to try to introduce tenderness
into it, except so far as relates to the care of soldiers and the treatment of the sick and wounded. If, after every action each regiment
should condemn to death every man who had fallen out without ur-
gent reasons, or who had flinched in battle . . . it would establish a
discipline and a spirit which would have saved thousands of lives.
Harsh as this may seem, it would in the end be the greatest humanity, for when cowards and stragglers are pardoned and honored, it is
at the expense of brave and faithful soldiers.[15]

Fortunately for the less committed, Barlow was not in charge
of military justice. It is highly unlikely the rigidly merciless
course he approved would have been tolerated by the North's
civilian population or, indeed, by many of the more stalwart men
in his own division. Lincoln understood the need for leniency and
flexibility in a civilian army. In the abstract, Barlow's preferred
response to shirking and desertion was logical. Realistically, it
would have provoked a backlash among the troops and the northern civilian population. In any event, Barlow could not impose
his wishes on the army. Nevertheless, within the parameters of
what was acceptable, Barlow implemented a notoriously tough
disciplinary code and meted out the harshest treatment of straggling, falling out, and desertion the system would allow.

More happily, Barlow's return to the II corps gave him the
chance to renew old relationships. His first regiment, the 61st
New York, was attached to Miles' brigade and Barlow visited
them in early April. Barlow found many of the old officers were
still with the regiment, but most of the enlisted men were new
recruits. "The 61st is almost an entirely new Reg't," Barlow discovered. Even so, "Now and then I see one [old] one and I always
shake him by the hand for I have real affection for the old fellows."[16] Barlow held great hopes that "the old ones will teach [the
new recruits] how to fight and become good soldiers."[17] His hopes
in this regard were generally fulfilled. The veterans absorbed and
taught those who had joined out of patriotism, and even extended
their influence over those draftees who were willing to do their
duty. Together, braced by Barlow's discipline and the example to
the leadership of the brigade and regimental commanders, the
veterans and better recruits were often able to offset the negative behavior and poor attitude of the bounty-jumpers, though
the latter caused continual problems.

Barlow made a positive impression on many of those meeting
him for the first time. Dr. William W. Potter, the First Division's
surgeon, thought he resembled Hancock in that he was "nervous,

impatient, wiry with a searching eye, and keeps himself at a distance. I believe in him and think the division has a competent commander who will make it do famous work."[18]

Potter soon found out that Barlow's "searching eye" extended to his hospitals as well as to his troops' training and discipline. On 7 April, the First Division's commander made a thorough inspection of the hospital, examining everything and finally pronouncing himself satisfied. He was surprised to find Cornelia Hancock on the hospital's staff as a nurse. Cornelia was a young Quaker woman who had served as an army nurse from the days immediately after Gettysburg. Barlow, apparently taken aback by her youth, bluntly asked Potter who she was and whether or not she did any good.[19] Potter assured him that the now veteran Miss Hancock was highly capable and Barlow left satisfied. For her part, Cornelia Hancock was surprised by Barlow's youthful appearance. "He is young to have such responsibility," she wrote, but admitted "there was not a spot in the hospital he did not look into."[20]

By the end of April, the new arrangements in the Army of the Potomac had proceeded well enough that major reviews of the divisions and corps were held. "Everything is ready for a move," Barlow wrote.[21] The First Division II Corps was reviewed on 19 April with Meade, Hancock and several other generals and colonels present. "It was a decided success," Barlow noted approvingly. Barlow celebrated the occasion by inviting all the officers back to his headquarters for a lunch which was arranged by his staff. "They stayed sometime and all went off very well," he declared. Theodore Lyman, Meade's volunteer aide and Barlow's Harvard classmate, was among the celebrants and Barlow noted, somewhat ambiguously, that he became "very jolly."[22]

Barlow attended a review of the entire VI Corps on 18 April, and on 22 April the entire II Corps turned out for a full review. "It was the best and most complete review of such a body of men that I ever saw and is so considered here. It beat the 6th Corps," Barlow boasted.[23] After the review the officers were invited back to Hancock's headquarters where Barlow was introduced to Grant.

The lengthening days and formal reviews signaled the onset of the spring campaign. Grant's plan was similar to that attempted by Hooker the year before. The Army of the Potomac would cross the Rapidan west of Chancellorsville and proceed as rapidly as possible through an area of tangled second-growth forest known locally as "the Wilderness." Once past that wooded area, the Army would enter more open country where Grant intended to get

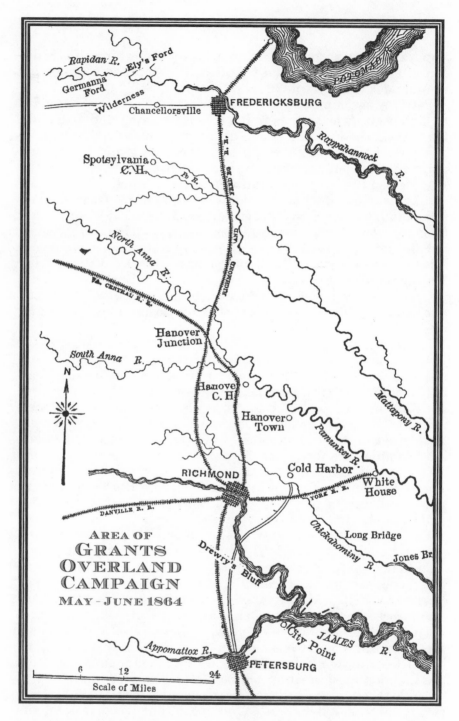

Area of Grant's Overland Campaign, May–June, 1864.

between Lee and the Confederate capital. Lee would then be forced to attack him, and Grant expected to use his superiority in men and equipment to destroy the Army of Northern Virginia as a fighting force. Lee had other plans. The Confederate chieftain had deployed his Army to the west of the Rapidan crossings, and he was kept apprised of Grant's movements from pickets along the river. Once Grant and Meade were completely across the river, Lee intended to attack the Army of the Potomac as it wended its way through the few roads which traversed the Wilderness.

The II Corps was stationed on the Army of the Potomac's right flank, and the First Division guarded the Corps on the right. With the army in such a deployment Barlow knew that he would lead the Federal host southward into enemy territory. To make the situation more appropriate, Barlow had placed Miles' brigade on the division's right, with the 61st New York occupying the extreme right of the line. Consequently, the units with the closest associations with Barlow would initiate the campaign. On 3 May 1864, Hancock verbally instructed Barlow to lead his units over the Rapidan at Ely's Ford at 6:00 A. M. on the following day. When the appointed hour struck, the First Division moved out leading the army into an unprecedented season of blood.

Marching in the van of the Army of the Potomac, Barlow and his division were furthest along the Brock Road when Lee hit Meade and Grant on their flank as they moved along the few roads which traversed the tangled woodlands. As the Federal army turned to face the southern assaults, Hancock reversed the II Corps and turned them north to face the rebels. Leaving Frank's brigade to hold the junction between the Brock Road and the road which cut off to the Catharpin Road, the remainder of the First Division was ordered to high ground behind the main Federal line on the left. This was practically the only cleared ground in the Wilderness and Barlow was assigned the task of protecting the II Corps artillery which was concentrated there. Barlow's deployment on the extreme left of the Army stemmed from fear that Longstreet, whose Corps was not in action on the first day, might attack the Federals from the south. Gibbon took temporary command of the First and Second Division on the field as Barlow had only been engaged partially. In order to meet A. P. Hill's assault two of Barlow's brigades, the Irish Brigade and Brooke's men, were detached from the division and sent into action. The fighting in the twisted brush and stunted trees raged on until nightfall rendered visibility in the ordinarily dim woods impossible. Conditions became even worse in the evening when

Barlow on horseback leads his division through the Wilderness. The First Division, II Corps flag, flies to his left. Drawing by Alfred R. Waud. *Library of Congress.*

fires broke out in the dry, tangled underbrush. The screams of the wounded unable to crawl away from the flames tormented the troops of both sides who girded themselves for the morning's battle. After the day's fighting began to flicker out, the second and fourth brigades were returned to Barlow, who remained in his position at the extreme left, or south, of the Federal line.

Reviewing the action after the first day at the Wilderness, Grant and Meade planned to launch a general assault against the Confederate lines on 6 May. In order to begin his assault with maximum strength, Hancock decided to pull Barlow from his far left position and place him in the center-left of his line, linking up with Mott. The redeployment was not made. Hancock always insisted he sent orders to Gibbon, who was in command of Hancock's left, to move Barlow forward. For his part, Gibbon was adamant that the order was not given.[24] As it was, only Frank's brigade joined Mott's men when they began their attack on the morning of the of the second day of the Wilderness along the north end of the left flank. With Barlow held back, Mott's men advanced into the rebel lines with their flank in the air.

Nevertheless, when the battle was renewed, the Federal line seemed to surge forward irresistibly as Hancock drove A. P. Hill's men back down the Orange Plank Road. Just as it seemed the northerners were poised to achieve Grant's objective of breaking Lee's line and smashing the Army of Northern Virginia, General James Longstreet, who had followed an unfinished railroad cut to reach the edge of the Federal lines undetected, hurled his men against Hancock's flank. Longstreet struck almost exactly at the point where Hancock had intended to place Barlow to bridge the gap between Birney and Mott.[25] Stunned by the unexpected southern assault, the II Corps fell back in confusion towards their original line along the Brock Road. "You rolled me up like a wet blanket, and it was some hours before I could reorganize for battle," Hancock confessed to Longstreet after the war.[26] Hancock rallied his men along the Brock Road, strengthening log earthworks built the night before and working furiously in the smoke produced by black powder weapons and burning woods to repel the increasingly powerful Confederate attacks.

The Confederates, whose momentum had slowed after Longstreet was wounded, roared out the woods towards the Federal lines whose wooden fortifications were blazing in places. The attacking rebels temporarily breached Hancock's defenses, but in the end were thrown back. At the end of two days' fighting, Grant's attempt to punch it out with Lee had failed and the Army of the Potomac bloodied. But, the Yankees remained unbowed and, unlike previous commanders, Grant refused to relinquish the initiative. Instead he immediately sought to move around Lee's right. For Barlow, the battle was likely a frustrating experience. Most of the time he was out of the fighting guarding the artillery. For a man who thrived on closing with the enemy, the role of an observer in a defensive position must have been maddening. Barlow left no record of his thoughts during the Wilderness. If he were disappointed at not getting into the thick of the action he would find his desire for action more than satisfied in the weeks ahead.

On the evening of 6 May, the two armies faced each other behind prepared positions, with Lee's being somewhat more formidable. Early the following morning, Grant sent Meade southeastward in another attempt to place his army between Lee and Richmond. The goal was the small hamlet of Spotsylvania Court House, ordinarily an insignificant country crossroads that had temporarily become crucially important to both armies.

The Army of the Potomac began its shift towards Spotsylvania during the night. Warren's V Corps, followed by Hancock's men, set out towards Spotsylvania along the Brock Road. Sedgwick's VI Corps and Burnside's IX were ordered to swing wide along the road to Fredericksburg marching southward to the courthouse to link up with Hancock and Warren. Lee, at first unsure of Grant's movements, realized that whether Grant moved south or retreated towards Fredericksburg, holding the crossroads at Spotsylvania would be crucial. Confederate cavalry were dispatched to slow Federals moving down the Brock Road, and Richard Anderson, who had assumed command of the Lee's First Corps after Longstreet's wounding, moved quickly behind the southern horsemen towards the hamlet. The race for the crossroads at Spotsylvania was a close-run affair, but in the end the Confederates reached Spotsylvania first. Desperate fighting by Fitzhugh Lee's troopers prevented their Federal counterparts from taking the vital village and the cavalrymen slowed Warren down just long enough for Anderson to arrive. The rebel infantry quickly thwarted the V Corps' efforts to take what became Lee's left flank at Laurel Hill.

While Warren was digging in at Laurel Hill, the II Corps, covering Grant's rear, had proceeded to a position west of Todd's tavern across Catharpin Road. Jubal Early, leading the Confederate Third Corps towards Spotsylvania, decided to test Hancock's lines. He gave the assignment to William ("Little Billy") Mahone. Mahone's attack ran into Barlow, who conducted a slow and grudging retirement to entrenchments dug near the tavern. Secure in his defensive lines, Barlow awaited Mahone's next move. Looking over the field, Early thought better of attacking the dug-in Yankees, and continued on his way to Lee. Barlow and his men held their lines until the next morning when they resumed their march to Spotsylvania.

The action on 8 May closed with an assault by Sedgwick and Warren's men against Confederate lines along Laurel Hill. By this time Ewell's Second Corps of the Army of Northern Virginia had moved into the Confederate front on Anderson's right, and the beefed up Confederate firepower blew apart the Federals' attempt to turn Anderson.[27] By the morning of 9 May, the basic configuration of the battle lines at Spotsylvania had begun to take shape. Lee's forces manned a line of entrenchments from the Po River north and east across the Brock Road and Laurel Hill. Just beyond the Laurel Hill sector, Lee extended his lines northward to encompass the high ground around the Harrison and

McCoull houses. This produced a salient the soldiers dubbed the "Mule Shoe" due to its shape. Federal lines paralleled the southern position and both sides quickly began constructing increasingly elaborate, and formidable, entrenchments. The Confederates, on the defensive from Grant's attacks, took special pains to make their lines as strong as possible. In addition to trenches protected by abatis, they laid in traverses, secondary lines at right angles from their trenches from which they could direct enfilading fire at any Yankees who might pierce their first trench system. Increasingly, the fighting in the Overland Campaign presaged the powerful and deadly defensive networks of the western front during the World War I.

9 May began badly for the Army of the Potomac. About 9:00 A. M., a Confederate sharpshooter placed a bullet directly under the left eye of Major General John Sedgwick, commander of the VI Corps, killing him instantly.[28] Meade appointed Horatio Wright to succeed him. Later in the day Hancock reported to Grant that Early had evacuated his position near Todd's Tavern. Grant was unsure about Lee's intentions. His cavalry chief, Phillip Sheridan, had been infuriated by Meade's criticism of the performance of the cavalry during the race for Spotsylvania, and had bragged he could defeat Jeb Stuart if the army commanders turned him loose. Meade and Grant assented, and Sheridan rode away towards Richmond seeking a decisive battle with the legendary rebel cavalryman. Sheridan's raid was partly successful. His men killed Stuart in an engagement at Yellow Tavern, but Lee had retained enough of his own horsemen to reconnoiter, scout, and picket, while Grant's intelligence regarding Confederate dispositions was weakened by the absence of almost all his horsemen.

Grant concluded that Early's withdrawal indicated Lee was shifting his forces eastward, possibly to launch a strike towards Fredericksburg. In reality Lee was strengthening his position just north of Spotsylvania Court House. More than willing to use his superior resources to break the southern lines, Grant devised a hammer-and-anvil operation using the IX and II Corps. The IX, under Burnside, would serve as the anvil, holding the Federal left along the Ny River while Hancock's corps would provide the hammer. Thrusting eastward towards the main Confederate line they would cross the little Po River and take the Confederate army in the rear. The V and VI Corps facing the rebels at Laurel Hill and the Mule Shoe would attack as the opportunity presented itself.

In late afternoon, Grant and Meade made a personal visit to

Hancock to explain the II Corps role in the plan. From their vantage point on the northern bank of the Po, the Federal generals could see Confederate wagons moving on the opposite shore of the river. Hancock's artillery began shelling the rebels and Grant ordered Hancock to push across the river and capture the train, initiating the drive around Lee's rear in the process. Barlow went over first, with Gibbon and Birney crossing above and below him. At 5:50 P. M. Hancock ordered Barlow to proceed as far as he could towards Spotsylvania Court House, but cautioned him to build good bridges over the Po to his rear. Apparently, Hancock was concerned that his men might be trapped against the river if something went awry in the assault. Some of the first units over the river were forced to cross on a fallen log, but Federal engineers soon had three pontoon bridges spanning the Po.

The weakness in Grant's plan was that a sharp bend in the river meant that Barlow and the other II Corps divisions would have to cross the Po twice in order to reach the Confederate rear. The second crossing was spanned by Block House Bridge which would have to be taken or bypassed for the corps to get behind Lee's lines. Hancock warned Barlow, who commanded the lead division in the operation, to expect rebels at Block House Bridge, but that the other divisions would soon arrive for support.[29] Having committed his divisions late in the day, and not sure of the strength of Confederate forces at Block House Bridge, Hancock decided to halt the II Corps short of the Block House crossing and wait until morning to resume his advance.

Grant's late-day determination to push Hancock towards Lee's rear and the II Corps commander's own decision to halt his troops in the evening gave time for Lee to discern Grant's intentions and launch a counterstroke. Seeing an opportunity to destroy all or part of a Federal Corps with its back against the northern bend of the Po, the southern commander stripped his right of all but one division and sent Early with Heth's and Mahone's division to the Po sector. Mahone was to push forward directly from Lee's left flank while Heth arced southward and then northward against the II Corps, which would be caught between the two turns of the Po.

Barlow's immediate concern was a stronghold the Confederates had erected directly behind the Block House Bridge, which promised to make any attempt to force the bridge extremely costly. On the morning of the 10 May Barlow sought to turn these works by fording the Po where Glady Run entered it, just to the south of the bridge. Brooke's brigade had already waded across when

Hancock received word to detach two divisions to the Laurel Hill front to reinforce yet another attack in that sector.[30] Hancock ordered Gibbon and Birney, who were not as far advanced as Barlow, to pull out of the Po position. This withdrawal left Barlow alone and vulnerable with a river at his back.

The unexpected change in plan was the result of Grant's reassessment of the battlefield situation. By the morning of the 10 May, he realized that not only was Lee not moving further east as he had thought, but that he had reinforced his lines near the Po. Grant then erroneously concluded that Lee had reduced his troops along the Laurel Hill line in order to attack to the south. He then planned to leave one of the II Corps divisions south of the Po to lure the Confederates into an attack, while Hancock's other divisions joined the V and VI Corps at Laurel Hill and the Mule Shoe. Here, the augmented northern forces would smash the presumably weakened Confederate lines exploiting whatever breakthroughs were made. Barlow was to play the decoy—or bait—on the Po. Hancock well understood the danger of leaving a single division in the stretch of land between the river's turns. Even as he moved his other two divisions back across the Po and prepared to send them to the northern sector of battlefield, he again instructed Barlow to be cautious. The First Division leader was directed to make no attack of his own, but have his men in readiness to move out when the order came.[31]

The fight on the Po was one of several engagements fought along virtually all sectors of the Spotsylvania area that day. Having seen Gibbon and Birney to their new positions, Hancock returned to the Po line about 2:00 P. M. He now had orders from Meade to withdraw Barlow, who then undertook the exceedingly difficult task of directing a fighting retreat as the Confederates opened their attack. Falling back before Heth, Barlow arranged his men in skirmish-line formation, a tactical deployment he had adopted as a result of his combat experience. The days of standing and firing by lines had long since passed. Francis A. Walker, Assistant Adjutant of the II Corps, who witnessed the First Division's withdrawal back across the Po, was struck by its expertise in utilizing skirmish-line tactics in the face of enemy attacks:

Most regiments in the service had as little idea of skirmishing as an elephant. But to Barlow's brigades the very life of military service was in a widely extended formation, flexible yet firm, where the soldiers were thrown largely on their individual resources but remained in a high degree of control of the resolute, sagacious, keen-eyed officers,

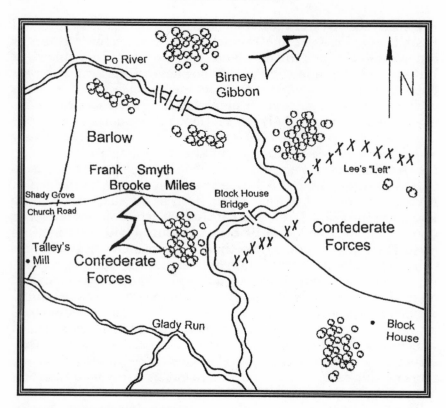

Barlow on the Po, May 10, 1864.

who urged them forward or drew them back as the exigency of the case required.[32]

Barlow pulled back towards the bridges in careful, grudging stages, as Heth's men, who had forded the river near Glady Run, pressed close behind them. Barlow, Hancock, and their staffs rode in front of the men, carefully supervising the withdrawal. Only two brigades at a time could be deployed against the oncoming rebels. Barlow formed Brooke's and Frank's brigades at the right of Miles and Smyth. The latter two units then withdrew to the last crest in front of the pontoon bridges where they quickly threw up fortifications made of rails and anything else they could lay their hands on.[33] Additionally, all the artillery except Arnold's battery was ordered back to the north bank from which they could sweep the surging southerners.

Sensing victory, Heth ordered an attack against Barlow's entrenchments along Shady Grove Church Road where Brooke and Frank had halted. Assistant Secretary of War C. A. Dana, observing the action, watched as Barlow allowed the southerners to come within easy rifle range and then saw the rebels "mowed down by Barlow's musketry."[34] Hancock himself later described the sharp action as "close and bloody." Heth's men were repulsed in what Hancock reported as "the wildest disorder, leaving the ground strewn with their dead and wounded."[35] In the meantime, the dry woods to the right and rear of the division caught fire, adding a further element of urgency to the retreat and confusion to the fighting. After the repulse of Heth's first attack, Barlow ordered Brooke and Frank to pull back and get ready to cross the Po. The Confederates with their superior numbers again tried to break Barlow's lines, but were stopped once more by First Division musketry.

The casualties were not one-sided, however, and the Confederate fire inflicted stinging losses on Brooke and Frank as they were forced to abandon their wooded position and cross open ground before finally crowding together to cross the narrow pontoon bridges. Once they had made it over, the troops on the north side, who had been joined by Birney's division which Hancock had called back to the Po, laid down a covering fire for those still moving out of the increasingly untenable position. Smyth crossed by the central pontoon bridge, the one on the right being already destroyed, leaving only Miles' brigade manning the hastily constructed fortifications. Confederate artillery opened up on Miles, providing cover for their infantry who were preparing to launch an attack against the one remaining brigade south of the Po. But massed northern artillery silenced the rebel batteries and the rebel infantry again made no progress in their assault.[36] Miles then hurried his men across the Po by the two remaining bridges. One of Miles' last units across the river was the 116th Pennsylvania, detached from the Irish Brigade, which had acted as a skirmishing screen for the retreating brigades. Once they had returned safely back on the north bank, Barlow personally thanked the regiment for its cool performance under difficult conditions.[37]

But, it was the 148th Pennsylvania of Brooke's Brigade that had the closest brush with disaster in getting back to safety. In the fury and confusion of battle and the difficulties of maneuvering through the burning woods, the 148th, under Colonel Beaver, never received the order to withdraw. Without fresh orders from Brooke, Beaver stayed in place for an hour while the other northerners withdrew. He then began to realize that he was isolated with woods burning on his left and no sign of Frank's brigade which had been on his right.[38] Although neither he nor the rebels knew it at the time, Beaver's lone regiment was facing two advancing Confederate divisions. Only the delay in reforming their ranks in the smoke and fire prevented the southerners from rolling up the isolated Keystone staters. Even so, the Confederates occupying the Irish Brigade's former rifle pits began to rake Beaver's exposed men with concentrated musket fire.

Beaver had already decided that his position was untenable when a scout he had sent to find the location of the third brigade rushed back with the news that the "Johnnies" were coming up against his flank. The Pennsylvanians fortunately discovered a small ravine which they were able to follow back to the bridges without being cut off or totally ground up.[39] As the regiment reached the Po, Beaver called for his men to turn and fire at the pursuing rebels. The volley temporarily stopped the southerners, and Beaver quickly hurried his men across by companies. By 5:10 P. M. the entire First Division was finally back on the north bank and the pontoon bridges were cut away and swept into the Po.

Reaching the safety of his own lines, Beaver collapsed exhausted on the ground. A passing colonel of artillery spied him lying there and offered him a flask of whiskey. Beaver admitted the alcohol revived him, although he claimed it was the only strong drink he took during the war. Regaining his composure, Beaver discovered that the rest of the brigade had been already withdrawn. He sought out Brooke and complained about his regiment's near abandonment. Brooke replied that he had sent several staff officers to order him back, but that they had been unable to find him in the smoke and fires from the burning woods.[40]

A fighting retreat ranks among the most difficult military operations to execute, and Barlow had carried out his superbly—although the near loss of the 148th Pennsylvania demonstrated just how close the engagement was. The only negatives were that he was forced to leave his wounded in rebel hands, and he lost one gun from 1st Rhode Island Light Artillery. In the opening stages of the withdrawal, Barlow had ordered the battery forward to his picket lines to buttress his defenses and to provide additional firepower against any rebel assaults. Pushing artillery into the front line during a withdrawal was a risky maneuver and the battery commander, Colonel Brown, protested the move. The loss of the gun, the first such from the II Corps, came about when the woods caught fire and the battery horses had become terrified and bolted. The panicked animals pulled the piece between two trees where it became wedged and could not be budged.[41]

Once back on the safety of the north bank, Barlow had one bit of unpleasantness to attend to—the removal of Colonel Frank, his third brigade commander. During Heth's first attempt to break Barlow's line, the third brigade was driven back on Smythe and Frank's officers complained that their commander was drunk. Barlow thought it ill-advised to remove Frank in the midst of battle, but as soon as his men had reached safety, he replaced Frank with Colonel Hiram L. Brown of the 145th Pennsylvania, widely known for his singing abilities and his dog "Spot."[42]

Although Barlow had good reason to be pleased with his division's performance, things looked different on the south side of the Po. Early believed his attacks had forced Barlow's withdrawal and he sent his compliments to Heth on his leadership during the battle. In reality, Barlow's retreat had been ordered by Meade as a consequence of Grant's change of plans. The withdrawal was generally orderly and coolly executed, with Barlow's men giving better than they got as they recrossed the Po to safety.

As Barlow and his men were catching their breath on the north side of the Po, the attacks on the Laurel Hill-Mule Shoe sectors began. Warren launched a precipitous and unprepared attack on Laurel Hill which was readily driven back, while Mott, who had been sent to the left of the VI Corps facing the apex of the Mule Shoe, also assaulted the Confederate line. Some of Mott's men temporarily breached the rebel position before they too were forced back.

The most effective attempt to break Lee's line was made by Emory Upton about 6:00 P. M. Upton prepared a special assault force of twelve handpicked regiments to pierce the Confederate lines on Laurel Hill. He ordered his men to charge without firing until the rebel line was breached and then fan out to the left and right to exploit their breakthrough.[43] Upton's men gained an initial breakthrough, but a combination of Confederate reinforcements and lack of support ultimately doomed it. While ultimately failing, Upton's tactics of massing troops in column to penetrate an enemy position were a portent of the future and anticipated the tactics successfully used by German storm trooper units during World War I.

The main lesson Grant took from the day's fighting was that Lee's lines were not unbreakable. A well-prepared, sledgehammer attack with the proper support might achieve what Upton had been unable to do. Summing up his overall plan, Grant said, "A brigade today—we'll try a corps tomorrow."[44]

THE SALIENT

To carry out his most audacious attack yet, Grant again turned to the II Corps. At 4:00 P. M. on 11 May, Hancock received orders to extract Barlow and Birney from their positions just north of the Po, and join Mott who was entrenched across from the tip of the Mule Shoe. Lt. Colonel C. H. Morgan, inspector general of the II Corps; Major William G. B. Mitchell of Hancock's staff; and Lt. Colonel Comstock of Grant's staff rode out to reconnoiter the rebel lines, but accomplished little since the exact point to be attacked was unclear. Additionally, the weather refused to cooperate. The dry, hot days, which had contributed to the fires at the Wilderness and the Po, had turned wet by the night of 11–12 May. A slow, steady rain, which later turned to fog, covered the field at Spotsylvania, making accurate reconnaissance virtually impossible. About the only useful thing accomplished by the scouting party was selecting the ground on which the divisions could form for the attack.

At 7:00 that night, Hancock called a council of war at his headquarters. Barlow, Gibbon, and Birney were present. Mott, who had made the unsuccessful attack earlier that day, did not attend. Hancock informed his division commanders that the corps was to assault the Confederate position at daybreak. No further information regarding the Confederate works and the strength of the units therein was available. Barlow was told to lead the movement of the three II Corps divisions from their position on the Federal right to a point immediately facing the rebel salient. Once all the troops had arrived on the field across from the Salient, the division commanders would meet the staff and engineering officers who were to conduct the storming units to their jumping-off places and supposedly provide all necessary information.[45]

The slow, wet, tiresome march around the V and VI Corps to the field opposite the Salient put Barlow in a bitter and cynical mood. He rode at the head of the column with his personal friends and favorites, Miles and Brooke. Soon their party was joined by Morgan and Lieutenant Colonel G. H. Mendell of the engineers who had been sent to guide them to their new position. The uncomfortable weather and mounting anxiety resulting from an obvious dearth of any real intelligence regarding the enemy's dispositions, or even the terrain over which they would have to charge, induced a facetious mood in the officers. All five officers tore into the plan—such as it was—leavening their criticism with some degree of vulgarity and probably with a heavy dose of gallows humor. As Barlow later recounted in his 1879 memoir on the Salient:

> As we staggered and stumbled along in the mud and intense darkness, and I vainly sought for information, the absurdity of our position—that we were proceeding to attack the enemy when no one even knew his direction, and we could hardly keep on our own legs—appealed to me very strongly as I listened to the conversation of Colonel Morgan (who was what might be called a profane swearer) and his criticisms on the "conduct of the war."[46]

The acerbic condemnations of the plan's (and probably the Army's) stupidity, provided some relief from the tensions and apprehensions the officers undoubtably felt. Barlow remembered that the remarks were so caustically humorous that he could barely sit on his horse from laughing. He finally turned to Morgan and said "For Heaven's sake, at least, face us in the right direction, so that we shall not march away from the enemy, and have to go round the world and come up in their rear."[47] Miles and Brooke continued to rip into the inanity of the projected assault with such vehemence that Barlow finally felt he had to tell them to shut up.[48]

The II Corps' march took about two hours. It was a little past midnight when Barlow, his staff, and his guides reached the spot from which he was to launch his assault. Peering through the darkness, drizzle, and fog, Barlow could see very little of the Confederate lines and neither corps nor army staff could tell him much about the southern works. Upon learning that Mott had made an attempt on the rebel lines the previous afternoon, he rode over to Mott's headquarters at the Brown House.

The preparations for the assault were laid out at a council of war held at the Brown House. It may have occurred when Barlow went to see Mott, or perhaps when Barlow was first told of the projected assault earlier in the evening. Probably, it occurred at the former time as Barlow, in his memoir of the Mule Shoe attack, states that he did not see Mott at the first meeting. Whatever the time, the exchanges at the meeting are significant since they reveal Barlow's own state of mind before the attack, and shed some light on how he determined the dispositions he made for battle.

All the leading participants in the forthcoming attack were present—Hancock, Barlow, Gibbon, Birney, Mott, and Lieutenant Colonel Morgan, of the II Corps staff. Members of Barlow's staff and probably the staffs of the other divisional officers were there as well. Again Barlow asked about the nature of the ground over which his men would attack. Again he was told, "We do not know."[49] Barlow then asked the distance to the Confederate lines. He was told it was something less than a mile. He asked about the type and degree of southern obstructions such as abatis and slashings to which his respondents again confessed ignorance. Exasperated, Barlow exclaimed, "Well, have I a gully a thousand feet deep to cross?" Honestly, if unhelpfully, the staff and reconnaissance officers replied, "We do not know."[50]

At this point Barlow stated, "Then I assume the authority to form my division as I please, and that I will do it in two lines of masses." Some protested that such a formation would not be effective if Confederate artillery were present in strength. Barlow brushed the objections aside stating, "If I am to lead this assault I propose to have men enough, when I reach the objective point, to charge through Hell itself and capture all the artillery they can mass in my front."[51]

With little in the way of hard information to go on, the direction of the attack was fixed by a line determined by a compass on a map from the Brown House projected outward in the direction of a large white house, the McCoull House, which was known to be inside the Confederate entrenchments.[52] Barlow and Birney were to spearhead the assault, Barlow attacking the right of the salient, Birney the left. Mott formed behind Birney and Gibbon's men made up the reserve. Approximately 20,000 men were to be involved in the II Corps attack. Additionally, Grant intended for Burnside to assault the Salient from his position on the Confederate right, while Wright and Warren would attack from the left. But the storming of the Mule Shoe's apex, and securing the breakthrough, was the task of the II Corps.

Barlow's deployment into double columns was reminiscent of Upton's formation earlier in the day. Possibly Barlow had received some intelligence about Upton's assault, though he left no record of it. More likely, drawing on his experience in attacking entrenched positions, he hit upon the method of a tightly concentrated storming force independently. Nevertheless, it took some argument at the council before Hancock acceded to Barlow's decision. Although he had gained approval for his formations, Barlow remained despondent about the prospects for the attack. The near total lack of accurate intelligence regarding the Confederate line weighed heavily upon him. His staff officers noted that he acted depressed, as if weighted down by what was a veritable leap into the darkness.

Whatever his private feelings, Barlow went about the necessary business of preparing his men for battle, although in an uncharacteristically subdued and gentle manner. His officers were struck that he did not issue the exhortation he usually voiced when preparing for action. In previous, and perhaps later, fights, Barlow would call his staff and brigade commanders together and announce "Make your peace with God and mount gentlemen. I have a hot place picked out for you today."[53] But there was no devil-may-care levity before the Mule Shoe assault. Missing too was the remark that Barlow had often made to buoy the nerves of his staff and subordinates. "Well, gentlemen, it beats Hell that none of my staff get killed or wounded,"[54] he would exclaim on hearing reports of losses among members of other staffs. Although he may never have lost the unquestioning faith in his own survival, Barlow seemed genuinely worn down by fears of disaster for his men. And, who knows, perhaps his belief in his own invincibility was—at least temporarily—shaken for he handed over his valuables to a friend for safekeeping, something he had never done before and seems never to have repeated.[55]

However apprehensive he felt, Barlow busied himself seeking more information about the Mule Shoe. At the Brown House he found Lieutenant Colonel Merriam of the 16th Massachusetts who had taken part in Mott's attack of the 11 May. While the attack failed, Merriam had gotten close enough to the Confederate works to get some impression of their structure and the ground which lay between the two armies. Responding to Barlow's questions, Merriam drew a sketch of the Confederate works on a wall in the Brown House. Merriam's impromptu drawing and impressions provided the only solid information Barlow received regarding the rebel lines. In addition to getting some idea of the shape of the rebel entrenchments, Barlow received the welcome intelligence that the ground over which he would charge was open and relatively free of obstructions. Merriam's information gave Barlow enough to go on that he was able to strike almost exactly at the angle formed by the refusal (reverse bend) of the Confederate lines.

Barlow relayed what he had discovered to Gibbon and Birney, who were organizing their troops in conventional formations. He then called his brigade commanders together. Gathering in a clearing lit only by a lantern, Barlow drew a map of the Confederate position in the dirt using Merriam's drawing as his source. When the brief council was over, each brigade leader understood his role in the morning's attack.[56] To shorten the distance his men would need to cover before reaching the Mule Shoe, Barlow placed his division as close to the Union picket line as possible. Having done all he could, the young general returned to Mott's headquarters where he caught two hours of sleep.

Inside the Mule Shoe, the Confederates were suffering anxieties of their own.[57] Lee and most of his officers understood that the salient, exposed as it was on three sides, made an inviting target. Lieutenant General Richard Ewell was in overall command of the Salient, which was manned by Major General Edward "Allegheny" Johnson's division. Having received the erroneous intelligence that Grant might be preparing to retire towards Fredericksburg, Lee wanted to be able to move quickly. Since withdrawing from the Salient would take time and slow the army's movements, Lee ordered the artillery removed from the position, thus depriving the Salient's defenders of the one element which might have given them a decisive advantage over any potential attackers. During the night, however, as Barlow and Birney slogged to their new positions, the Confederates heard rumblings and creaking of wagons and the sloshing of thousands of shoes in the mud. Although the troops had secured their canteens and accouterments to reduce all noise to a minimum, there were simply too many men in motion for the march to remain totally undetected.[58] What it all meant, however, was something else and the southerners were uncertain as to whether the Union troops were moving out or preparing for an attack. But by midnight, about the time Barlow arrived at the Brown house, Johnson's concerns led him to send word to Ewell, asking the artillery be returned. Ewell turned down the request and Johnson rode over to Corps headquarters to press the case himself. After a face-to-face meeting, Ewell concluded Johnson might be correct and sent word to have the artillery turned around and redeployed in the Salient. For whatever reason, his orders did not reach the gunners until 3:30 A. M.

The Federal attack was originally scheduled for 4:00 A. M. Shortly before 4:00 A. M. the men were roused from their sleep by their officers, and the regimental leaders began calling their company commanders together, telling them, what they had probably already surmised, that they were about to storm the Confederate lines. Orders were issued forbidding firing until the Confederate works were breached.[59] Despite the poor visibility and clinging mist, Barlow had his men up and ready in 15 or 20 minutes. However, the weather remained so dank and foggy that Hancock postponed the assault for another half hour to 4:30 A. M.

Barlow's final dispositions had been made earlier in the early morning, shortly after his conversation with Merriam. As was his preference, Barlow placed Miles and Brooke, his first and fourth brigades, in his first line, with the second (Irish) and third brigades, in the second line. The regiments were formed in the cleared land between the Brown and Landrum House which ran south and then west towards the Mule Shoe. The units were doubled on the center and closed en masse, creating the double-column fist that Barlow had successfully argued for at the council at the Brown House. Five paces were ordered between regiments, and ten paces between brigades.[60] During the assault the spacing dissolved, which had the effect of turning the First Division into an even denser mass of soldiery than Barlow had envisioned. The officers, including Barlow himself, were dismounted, and marched between the first and second lines from where they rasped their orders.[61] Altogether, 23 regiments rushed forward in an almost solid square. Screening the main column, Barlow's skirmishers moved forward at one-pace intervals, with orders not to fire when they reached the rebel pickets, but to take them in a rush before they could sound the alarm.[62]

When the order to advance was given, the First Division swept over the intervening ground in about five minutes. At one point, the troops saw the ground swell up in front of them, and thinking it was the rebel position, some units, probably the Irish Brigade, sent up a cheer only to climb the rise and find the actual Confederate lines still facing them.[63] A few rebel pickets fired on Barlow's left flank mortally wounding Lieutenant Colonel Stricker of the 2nd Delaware. But the rebel pickets scattered before the surging blue columns who quickly brushed aside the felled trees the southerners had placed before their entrenchments. Inexorably Barlow's men closed in on the Salient. "Forward, double-quick. Charge," Barlow barked as small arms and some cannon began to open fire on the advancing Yankees.[64] He later remembered that as his men came into sight of the works they "instinctively swayed off to our left," which insured they would strike the angle dead on.[65] A vision of the day to come flashed across the mind of one rebel defender as the northern troops came pouring over the Confederate earthworks. "Look out boys!" he yelled. "We will have blood for supper."[66]

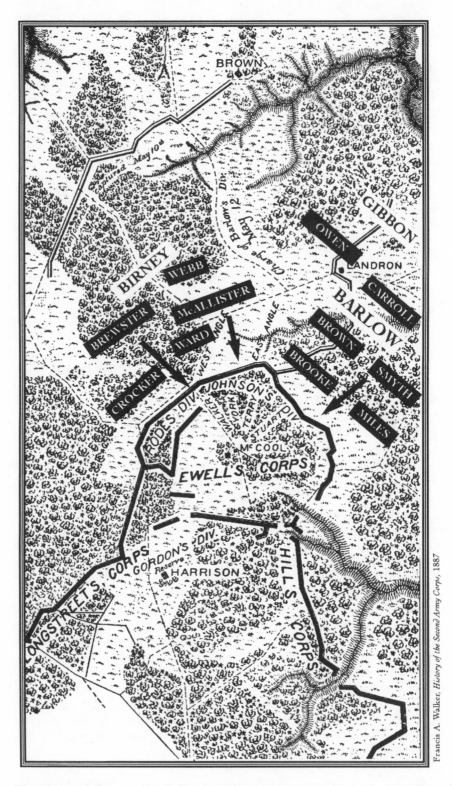

The II Corps Storms the Salient, 12 May 1864. From Francis A. Walker,
History of the Second Army Corps, **1887.**

Barlow and Birney smashed into the Mule Shoe at about the same time, though Barlow always held that his men reached it first, as they had charged across a generally clear field, and his more solid formation allowed for a more rapid passage. Johnson's concerns about the vulnerability of his position had not been transmitted to his men, nor had the premature cheer from the assaulting columns done much to forewarn them. On the contrary, the Confederates were stunned by the ferocity and momentum of the attack and Barlow later remembered "their bewildered look." While Barlow believed initial resistance was light, Nelson Miles, who was in the first wave, described it as heavy.[67] Whatever the situation, resistance was relatively brief, as the II Corps men ripped the abatis aside and rolled over the Confederate works bayoneting and clubbing the dazed defenders. Barlow himself mounted the captured entrenchments shortly after Miles and Brooke had punched their way through it. Brooke's men, who smashed through the right side of the Angle, ended up sweeping down along its left, driving the disorganized Confederates before them, and using the bayonet liberally in the tight confines of the Mule Shoe.[68] The success of the initial assault was clear enough. Together, the First and Second Divisions had captured almost 3000 prisoners, including Johnson and his senior subordinate George H. "Maryland" Steuart. Thirty Confederate flags and 18 field pieces, which had returned to the Mule Shoe in time to be captured, were added to the Federal spoils.

The breakthrough at the Mule Shoe was everything Grant had hoped. But, the rupture of the Confederate defenses did not guarantee Grant's major objective—the splitting of Lee's army. Barlow later pointed out that while the initial attack was "undoubtedly the most brilliant thing of its kind during the war," it was also a "lucky accident."[69] The lack of thorough planning, which had characterized the operation from the beginning, now worked against its complete success. Cohesion had been replaced by chaos as the Federal troops poured into the salient and pursued the retreating Confederates. Barlow struggled to reform his brigades, and began to fear for his flank, causing him to direct Miles to guard against a counterattack. The problem now facing him was that the Federal troops were almost as confused in victory as the Confederates were in defeat. Barlow and Birney's men were confined and intermingled in the narrow space of the Angle, rounding up and hurrying away prisoners and searching for guns and colors.The officers found their efforts to reorganize their units tough going. To make matters worse, Hancock continued to send fresh units into the position. In some places the Union troops were 40 deep and all but totally disorganized.

Barlow became increasingly agitated by the inability to restore order and keep the momentum going. When another brigade was sent pell-mell into his position he rode back to Hancock, who was at the Landrum House and, dispensing with military protocol, called out "For God's sake, Hancock, do not send any more troops in here."[70] Barlow quickly told Hancock that they needed to re-form the men already in the salient and that fresh troops should then advance down along the enemy's flanks.

By 6:00 A. M., the Federal assault had stalled. Barlow believed that an hour or so went by during which the surviving Confederates had fallen back, unpressed, to a second line which Lee was feverishly throwing up across the base of the Salient. Realizing that the Union breakthrough imperiled his entire position and possibly his Army, Lee reacted with the dash and determination that characterized his leadership throughout the war. His own desperate aggressiveness was matched by that of John Gordon, Barlow's erstwhile Samaritan at Gettysburg, who quickly and effectively organized Confederate counterattacks. The men of the Army of Northern Virginia, as they had done so often before and would again in the future, rose to crisis and struck ferociously at the numerous but disorganized Federals.

The Confederates soon discovered that the II Corps had not pushed far from the outer line of the Salient's entrenchments nor had they moved down along the southern flanks. Their backs to the wall, Gordon and his men slammed into the milling Federals and slowly pushed them back towards the outer works of the Salient. Brooke's brigade, which may have advanced further than any of Barlow's units, had reached a second line of southern works with a marsh in front of it. Unable to reorganize his troops, Brooke found it impossible to mount a determined attack on the rebel line and instead found himself being forced back with the rest of the division.[71] But at least he was able to withdraw his men and avoid the fate of Colonel Hiram Brown. Barlow lost the recently appointed commander of the third brigade when he was captured trying to attack Gordon's lines. As Brooke struggled to create an effective defensive line on the outer side of the Mule Shoe entrenchments he encountered what he described as a large number of Birney's men "who seemed to be engaged in gathering spoils and who could not be made available for the defense of this line."[72]

As Barlow's second, third, and fourth brigades were pushed

back, he became concerned for his own left flank and sent John D. Black of his staff to Hancock, this time seeking reinforcements. Black found the action increasingly hot. As he rode off looking for Hancock, he passed an officer who seemed about to speak with him when a shell surgically took off the man's head directly above the jaw. The officer fell backwards and in passing him Black saw the tongue moving as if speaking.[73] On receiving Barlow's request, Hancock told Black that he would dispatch reinforcements as soon as he could get them from the VI Corps. He further asked Black to let Barlow know he had done splendidly and that Brooke and Miles should "consider themselves brigadier generals from today." More to the point, he instructed Black to tell Barlow to hold what he had captured at all hazards, and protect his flank as best he could until help could arrive.[74]

The Confederate attackers succeeded in reaching the inner line of the Mule Shoe's entrenchments, but now it was the Yankees who were determined not to give an inch more. Thus began a daylong contest in which the two armies fought each other to a frenzied stalemate along the line of the Angle. In many cases, especially along the Federal right, the troops struggled within a few feet of each other, ramming muskets through felled logs and firing, thrusting bayonets forwards, and using the bodies of fallen soldiers as protection. The intermittent rain, occasionally heavy, contributed to the misery of the fighting, bleeding, and dying men. John D. Black recalled a young recruit hurling his bayoneted rifle into the chest of a southern soldier, who had killed an officer of the 64th New York. With the muzzle of the gun rammed into his body, the rebel "uttered the most unearthly yell I have ever heard from human lips as he fell over backward with the gun sticking in him."[75] The concentrated volume of musketry was such that trees were felled and bodies shredded by minié balls and shrapnel. The carnage, which Barlow likened to the sunken road at Antietam, gave rise to the term "Bloody Angle."

Barlow's immediate problem, in the face of the Confederate counterattack, was his left flank, which was now "in the air." Ambrose Burnside, whose corps operated still independently of the Army of the Potomac and whose operations were directly under Grant's control, had been ordered to cooperate in the assault on the Mule Shoe by attacking the Confederates on their right flank. Burnside launched his attack on time, but was soon checkmated by Confederates and the unimaginative IX Corps commander did little else to threaten the Confederates on his front. When Black reported back that Hancock had no immediate reinforcements,

Barlow immediately sent him to Burnside's headquarters to request that the IX Corps quickly extend its lines to connect with his left. As Black prepared to leave, Barlow told him to take care, but admitted it was likely that he would be captured. "If you are," Barlow said gravely, "it is by my order."[76] The odd remark may have been intended to relieve Black of the onus of incompetence should he be snared by the rebels. Out of Barlow's earshot, Black's tent mate and fellow staff officer, Major Marlin, remarked that "that order will be cold comfort for you in the Old Libby," a reference to the Confederate prisoner of war facility in Richmond,[77] a possibility which had probably already occurred to Black. Nevertheless, Black's mission was successful and Burnside extended his line to effect the link with Barlow. Black did, however, come near capture, almost blundering into the Confederate lines in the confused fighting and escaping as a rebel yelled out, "Come in you Yankee son of a bitch."[78]

With his left flank secure, Barlow himself spent most of the rest of the day with Hancock at the Landrum House, which was in plain sight and musket shot of the outer wall of the works he had taken. There was little for a division commander to do in a struggle fought by troops pressed against each other muzzle to muzzle with neither side willing to give way. From this vantage point he watched the savage fighting rage along the lines of the Angle. As the day went on, the bloody frenzy reached its crescendo along the Federal right where the VI Corps was engaged. Indeed, rather than receiving reinforcements from Wright, Brooke's Brigade was detached from Barlow and sent to bolster the VI Corps as the remorseless, hand-to-hand combat sucked more and more troops into the earthen amphitheater of death. Hancock added to the maelstrom of death and misery by ordering up artillery on the high ground around the Landrum House. With a clear view of the bloody struggle along the works of the Mule Shoe, the Yankee cannoneers hurled canister over the Union lines and into the swarming rebels. At one point, Hancock's artillery rolled right up to the breastworks with the muzzles of the guns pushed into the faces of the Confederates. From the almost point-bank range the cannons spewed more flesh rending canister into the Confederates before them as well as those massing in the woods. The relentless bloodletting continued into the night and only ended about 4:00 A. M. on the 13th—almost exactly 24 hours after Barlow and Birney launched their attack—when Lee withdrew his men to the new line south of the Salient.

The day after the battle, with the Confederate's glaring at them from behind Lee's new line, the northern troops crawled over the earthen defenses and picked their way over the blood-soaked ground of the Angle, shaken by the wastage of men that met their eyes. Barlow reported that only at the sunken road (Antietam) had he seen such a mass of dead and wounded. Miles later wrote that it was impossible to walk over the line of earthworks without stepping on fallen soldiers.[79] On the other side of the line, General John Gordon likened the scene to "a slaughter pen . . . a sight to make one sick of war."[80] John D. Black declared that the "men [were] lying six and eight feet deep, almost to the top of the works, and, sloping back, hiding the earth from sight ten to fifteen rods."[81] Black and an officer from the 26th Michigan, part of Miles' brigade, scoured the battlefield seeking the body of a young soldier so it could be shipped home for burial. Friends of the soldier told the officers where he had fallen, and Black and his companion went to retrieve the dead man's watch for return to the family as verification. When they found the dead man Black was appalled by the sight. "There was no semblance of humanity about the mass that was lying before us," he wrote. "The only thing I could liken it to was a sponge, I presume five thousand bullets had passed through it. And after a careful search the largest piece [of the watch] we could find was three links of the chain. No more than ¼ inch."[82]

With thousands of men wounded and dying, Barlow's medical units were working full time. The still primitive nature of medical knowledge made the amputation of limbs a common occurrence, and disease was spread through imperfect notions of the use of antiseptics. The First Division's medical service consisted of 22 hospital tents, which were supplied and transported by 18 wagons. Four of the wagons were reserved solely for medical supplies. Each brigade was assigned its own operating table and its own medicine wagon. During an engagement, troops from Barlow's notoriously tough provost guard remained at the hospital to prevent "malingerers," shirkers, and the fainthearted to escape their duty there.[83] The scenes such men would have witnessed at the hospitals might have led them to run further or take their chances on the line. Going into battle, each regiment was accompanied by a medical officer. Other surgeons set up operations at an "advanced ambulance depot," which were usually stationed about 500 yards behind the front lines. Additional surgeons worked at the division hospital, which was located further back from the fighting. If the wounded were numerous, medical officers in the "advance ambulance depot" might be sent to the division hospital to act as dressers. Grant's strategy of almost continuous attack ensured the medical corps was constantly in operation.

The struggle for the Salient cost Barlow's division 221 killed in action, 999 wounded, and 210 missing for a total of 1430 casualties.[84] The Second and Third Division lost 519 and 726 in all categories, with the artillery brigade suffering another thirty men killed, wounded, or missing.[85] In fact, Mott's division was so used up by casualties and expired enlistments it was reduced to a brigade and assigned to Birney on 13 May.

The heavy losses suffered by the II and VI Corps at the Angle had brought a brief moment of unexpected and stunning success. In his appraisal of the contest, Hancock praised both Barlow and Birney stating, "they are entitled to high commendation for the valor, ability and promptness displayed by them [at the Salient]. The magnificent charge made by their divisions, side by side, at Spotsylvania, on the 13 May, stands unsurpassed for its daring, courage and brilliant success."[86] The day after the assault, Barlow recommended Miles and Brooke for promotion to brigadiers for their roles in the attack.[87] Barlow's omission of Smyth and Brown from his request for promotion may have stemmed from the fact that they were placed in the second line of the assault. In Brown's case he had only recently been named leader of the third brigade. Yet, especially in Smyth's case, Barlow may have been playing favorites and, considering his ethnic prejudices concerning the Germans, he might well have harbored some biases regarding the Irish Brigade. Such a possibility is suggested by his alleged behavior at the Second Deep Bottom action later in the summer.

Barlow confidently expected a promotion to major general as a result of his performance at the Mule Shoe. In fact, Hancock had included his name in a list of officers deserving higher rank, which he forwarded to Meade. The lack of vacancies at the time made it impossible for Meade to grant every request. Deciding that he could advance only one brigadier, he gave the promotion to Gibbon, who was in reserve during the attack on the Salient, as he was senior among Hancock's divisional generals. When word of Meade's action leaked out Barlow was outraged and Gibbon was surprised, writing that Barlow "to whom of all others, the success of our assault was due received no promotion."[88]

Promotions or no, the ultimate objective of the assault on the Mule Shoe had not been achieved. Lee's lines had not been severed and the combination of Union confusion and Confederate determination resulted in stalemate. Barlow himself stated that after the initial breakthrough his division accomplished little. He had demonstrated, as did Upton, the advantages of the tightly massed column formation as a means of punching through a defensive position, a tactic that would be increasingly refined in future wars. For the Confederates, the battle had been a nightmare. Alone of all the contests in the Overland Campaign, the fight at the Angle cost Lee more than Grant. Lee's heavier losses were due to the extremely high number of men captured. Johnson's old division, including the famed "Stonewall Brigade," was virtually annihilated, which was surely a blow to the Army of Northern Virginia. Yet, while such attrition in men and experienced officers eroded the efficiency of Lee's force, the Army of the Potomac was being ground up as well. And the battle of Spotsylvania was not over.

Like two punch-drunk fighters, the Confederate and Union armies watched each other warily. Grant still sought a weak spot where a decisive breakthrough could be made. Lee continued to refine the Confederate defenses and his men were becoming increasingly adept at rendering their works murderous for any opponent to assault. On the night of 13–14 May, it was the turn of the V and VI Corps to make a night march in the torrential spring rains and pass behind Hancock and Burnside in an attempt to outflank Lee from the east. But rain, mud, and the fatigue of the fighting made it impossible for Meade to organize a major assault and small, inconclusive skirmishes ensued. Grant wired Washington that the weather was a major factor in hampering operations. "We have had five days of almost constant rain without any prospect yet of its clearing up. All offensive operations necessarily cease until we can have twenty-four hours of dry weather."[89]

During the weather-determined pause in the fighting, Barlow had allowed himself to unwind, journeying over to Army headquarters where he found his friend Lyman. He told his old classmate that the "Headquarters are a good place [because] you can get victuals and stationery there."[90] Lyman and the other staff officers were anxious to hear Barlow's descriptions of the fighting in the Mule Shoe. The staff officer was most impressed by Barlow's anecdotes detailing how he had enforced discipline on his own officers. The young general, according to Lyman, "whacked one officer with his saber for being in a hole. . . . [and] compelled two others to resign, and had endorsed that they were 'cowards' on their applications."[91] As for the tactics of the attack, Lyman found that his friend "believes greatly in the close column of attack."[92]

When the rain finally broke and the sun reappeared, Grant decided that Lee's movements to meet him northeast of Spotsylvania Court House must have led him to shift men from the old front near the Mule Shoe.[93] Grant's conclusion was based almost entirely on instinct and supposition, as he had no hard evidence that such was the case. Sheridan's cavalry was away on a raid, and little scouting and reconnoitering had been carried out along the front, which Grant presumed to be weakly held. Indeed, Grant's major defect as supreme commander during the Overland Campaign lay in making assaults against Confederate positions without any serious attempts to ascertain their strength. The policy had resulted in a growing butcher's bill of heavy casualties suffered by the Army of the Potomac with little to show for it.

Although Grant's attacks, including that on the Mule Shoe, had not achieved their intended objectives the northern commander was undaunted. On 16 May, Grant had received replacements for his losses. Restoring his own numbers and convinced that Lee, with his smaller army, was weaker than ever, Grant searched for another promising spot in the Confederate lines. But Lee too had received fresh troops while he had been busily strengthening his lines. Consequently, his army was not as weak as Grant had presumed and his works were even stronger. Once again, when Grant ordered a new assault by Hancock and Wright across part of the 12 May battlefield neither he, Meade, nor the corps and divisional commanders had any accurate understanding of the nature and strength of the Confederate lines. In fact, the major portion of the line, still manned by Ewell's Corps, consisted of a formidable network of entrenchments fronted by tree slashings which acted much as barbed wire would in World War I. Additionally, Confederate artillery was well positioned to sweep the ground over which the Union troops would cross.

The deployments for the 17 May attack mirrored those at the Mule Shoe five days before. The II Corps moved by night to their old jumping-off position in front of the Landrum House. The VI Corps again formed on its right while Burnside, who was to storm the Confederate right, massed his troops on Barlow's left. Barlow altered his formations again and both he and Gibbon, who together spearheaded the II Corps attack, organized their men in lines of brigades. The Federal units had to pass through the old Salient to reach Ewell's lines which had been pulled back to an almost straight-line formation to the south. Most of the dead from the pitiless fighting in the Mule Shoe had remained unburied, and Colonel Mitchell remembered, "The stench that arose from the [dead] was so sickening and terrible that many of the men and officers became deathly sick from it. The appearance of the dead who had been exposed to the sun so long was horrible in the extreme as we marched past and over them—a sight never to be forgotten by those who witnessed it."[94]

Unlike the situation on the 12 May, Ewell was well prepared to meet the attack, and his men waited confidently as the Federals charged out of the wooded area in the Mule Shoe and into the cleared land that stretched before their works. None of the attacking Federals breached the Confederate line. Barlow's men became entangled in the slashings fronting Ewell's trenches and Confederate artillery tore into them unmercifully. Tersely summing up his repulse, Barlow wrote, "We struck upon an abatis [sic] and were stopped."[95] Hancock informed Meade that there was little chance of breaking the rebel line. The attack was called off and Hancock returned to now familiar lines north of the Angle.

Grant had finally had enough and concluded that there was little remaining chance of finding an opening at Spotsylvania. Once again he prepared to swing southward around Lee's right sending the II Corps towards the rail line between Richmond and Fredericksburg. A reconnaissance in force by Ewell caused a postponement of this maneuver, but after Ewell's repulse at Harris Farm, Grant once again prepared to sidle around Lee's right and, by getting himself between the Army of Northern Virginia and Richmond, force Lee to attack him in open terrain where Grant's superior numbers would crush the Army of Northern Virginia. Lee for his part was determined to be uncooperative and anxiously looked for a chance to rip off a piece of the Army of the Potomac and, at least temporarily, deprive it of its offensive punch.

Both armies had been mauled by the twelve days of relentless combat at Spotsylvania. The assault in the salient had been a close run fight for Lee and he had suffered heavily, particularly in prisoners taken by Barlow and Birney. Total losses in the Army of Northern Virginia during the battle were close to 8000.[96] But, if Lee was hurt, the Army of the Potomac was hemorrhaging. Grant's reliance on frontal assaults to break the Confederate lines resulted in enormous casualties. The northern home front was appalled by the lists of killed, wounded, and missing, while the attrition of seasoned officers and men soon began to tell in the army's performance. During the fighting at Spotsylvania, Barlow's division suffered 346 men killed, 1684 wounded, and 357 missing or captured.[97] This contrasted with the 253 men killed,

1285 wounded, and 294 missing at the Wilderness where the
First Division was not fully engaged.[98] The heaviest casualties
were in the first and fourth brigades which had spearheaded the
First Division's assault on the Salient. Losses for the II Corps at
Spotsylvania amounted to 1188 killed, 6,135 wounded, and 801
missing or captured.[99] The entire bill for the ultimately unsuccessful attempt to turn or break Lee's lines between 10 May,
when the action at the Po began, and 18 May, when the II Corps
made a vain attempt to pierce Lee's last defensive position south
of the Angle, came to 18,399.[100]

For Barlow, and for most of the officers and men of the Army of
the Potomac, the continual fighting and marching left little time
for correspondence. Indeed, Barlow's letters to his family grew
noticeably thin during the Overland Campaign. On 20 May, as
the Union and Confederate forces maneuvered for advantage,
Barlow finally got a chance to send a missive to his brother,
Richard, in which he reported that all his leisure time was taken
up by eating and sleeping. Arabella was near, only about 10 miles
away, nursing the wounded at military hospitals in Fredericksburg, but she might as well have been in Boston, as the unceasing fighting made it impossible for Frank to take any leave.

The little town on the Rappahannock, which had already seen
its share of war, had been temporarily transformed into a major
junction center for the Federal forces. Confederate prisoners were
herded to nearby Belle Plain to await transport to northern prison,
while reinforcements for the army arrived from the north. More
significantly, Fredericksburg had been selected to become the
receiving station for the wounded from the Army of the Potomac.
Numerous hospitals were hastily constructed or improvised to
serve the needs of the unprecedented number of casualties who
were brought in daily from the killing fields of the Wilderness
and Spotsylvania. Doctors from both the army and the Sanitary
Commission worked around the clock to provide aid and succor
to the ocean of bleeding, broken, and dying men. Arabella, who
arrived shortly after the fighting in the Wilderness, was one of
775 medical students and nurses, who supported the 142 "con-
tract" doctors and 194 "reserve surgeons" employed by the Sanitary Commission. Working under Clara Barton, Arabella augmented her the usual nursing duties with the supervision of the
"special diet kitchens" at her hospital.[101]

Arabella's reputation as a nurse of unusual energy and initiative was secured during the Overland Campaign. One fellow
medical staffer remembered that she was called "The Raider" due

to "her great activity and inexhaustible activity . . . in a sort of roving work, in seizing upon and gathering up such things as her quick eye saw were needed."[102] While serving at Fredericksburg, Arabella acquired a small farmer's wagon pulled by "a wretched-looking pony" with which she scoured the area seeking straw for bedding and other supplies which would meet the needs of the army of wounded which soon flooded the town.[103]

Though she herself was heavily involved in her duties, she managed to write her husband, and presumably he wrote back, but the swirl and confusion of the campaign made it impossible for the couple to meet.[104] Consequently, when it came to his own needs, Frank had to satisfy himself with letters to and from his wife, plus the comradeship of his favored officers. Not that he was granted much time to ruminate on his personal life as Grant and Meade were already planning a new movement against the Army of the Potomac's time-honored opponent.

6

To Cold Harbor and Across the James

MISFIRES

IT WAS ON THE BLOODY TRAIL FROM THE RAPIDAN TO THE JAMES that Barlow's reputation as a commander of exceptional resoluteness and ferocity was sealed. Soldiering under Grant, he found all the fighting he had bargained for—and more. And, exhausted and fatigued as he, and the entire Army of the Potomac, undoubtedly was, the "Boy General" thrived in it. After all, his belief that he would not be killed in the war had been vindicated by his surviving serious wounds at Antietam and Gettysburg. And yet, his behavior did not arise from complacency or lack of imagination. Indeed, he was surprised that he had come through the savage fighting in the Wilderness and at Spotsylvania without being hit again. "I am looking for a wound, but it has not come," he wrote back to his friend Charles Dalton.[1]

Throughout the desperate struggle between the Armies of the Potomac and Northern Virginia, Barlow repeatedly demonstrated that he was one of those soldiers who reveled in combat, although anyone who gave him no more than cursory notice would hardly have guessed it. Theodore Lyman, Meade's aide and a former classmate of Barlow's, left an indelible portrait of his combative classmate on the battlefields that lay between Grant and Richmond. "He looked like a highly independent mounted schoolboy," Lyman observed. "He was attired in a flannel checked shirt; a threadbare pair of trousers, and an old blue kepi." Nor had Barlow discarded his now signature sidearm. "From his waist," Lyman noted, "hung a big cavalry sabre [while] his features wore a familiar sarcastic smile."[2]

Barlow's appearance was caught by Mathew Brady at Cold Harbor shortly after the battle. The famous photographer took advantage of the break in the action to photograph a number of leading Federal officers and their staffs or major subordinates. On 11 or 12 June 1864, Brady photographed Hancock alongside his divisional commanders, Barlow, Birney, and Gibbon. In the most famous of the photographs, a close-up of the Corps commander surrounded by his division leaders, Hancock sits jauntily on a stool trying to hide the near constant pain his old Gettysburg wound was giving him. Barlow stands out, not only from his fellow divisional commanders, but also from the general officers in the other Corps whom Brady photographed at the time. It is easy to see why he was dubbed the "Boy General." Twenty-nine years old, yet a battle-tested leader, his clean-shaven appearance (a distinct rarity among Civil War officers) and his lithe (five foot eleven) boyish figure make him instantly recognizable among the bearded, older officers.

In the close-up of the II Corps leaders, Barlow's gray eyes gaze evenly at the camera, the checked shirt and cavalry sabre clearly visible.[3] The "sarcastic smile" mentioned by Lyman is clearly in evidence and his expression goes beyond self-confidence into an almost belligerent insolence. It is difficult to look at the picture and miss the lethal determination scarcely hidden by the young face. The one element in the photographs missing from Lyman's description is the kepi. Barlow seems to be holding a slouch hat, perhaps the unusual headgear that Winslow Homer placed atop his head in his painting *Prisoners from the Front* which depicted Barlow a month later at Petersburg. In his drawing of the action at Spotsylvania, combat artist Alfred Waud depicts a beardless officer in a checked shirt seated on a chair in front of the Landrum House watching the struggle at the Angle. This is apparently another view of Barlow in his battle dress.

That Barlow's mien reflected his character was well attested by all who knew him throughout the war. Lyman provides yet another account of Barlow's disdain for danger, this time during the first days before Petersburg in June, 1864:

> Barlow was so brave, that he made a joke of danger. Once he and General Humphreys, who was just such another man, rode towards the enemy on a reconnaissance. Neither of them was willing to face about, and they nearly went over the rebel skirmish line, when a shower of bullets persuaded them to retreat, both laughing heartily at the peril.[4]

Moving his Army east and south around Lee's right, Grant sought an opportunity to attack Lee successfully. Lee, who if anything was becoming more adept at responding to Grant's maneuvers, repeatedly blocked his way in strongly defended, well-designed entrenchments. On 20 May, the II Corps led the Army

The Boy General. The leaders of the II Corps enjoying a respite after Cold Harbor. Winfield Scott Hancock takes a seat surrounded by his division commanders. Barlow is to his right wearing his signature combat garb. Birney is to Barlow's left and Gibbon stands at his far left. Mathew Brady photograph. *Massachusetts Commandery of the Military Order of the Loyal Legion of the United States and the U.S. Army Military History Institute.*

of the Potomac away from the killing grounds of Spotsylvania towards Guinea Station. The next day, the Army of Northern Virginia began its countermove. Two days later, Lee had his men in position on the south bank of the North Anna River, where his engineers were preparing the defensive works which were making frontal assaults horrendously costly and unlikely to succeed.[5] Grant had moved the Army of the Potomac in a wide arc hoping to entice Lee into an attack in open terrain where northern numbers could be effectively deployed. Again Lee did not bite, and skillfully placed himself in a position where he could do the biting.

The Federal V and VI Corps, situated on the right of the Army of the Potomac, crossed the North Anna near Jericho Mill. They were soon attacked by A. P. Hill's Corps, but the Confederates were turned back by artillery, after which they dug in on a line straddling the Virginia Central Rail Road. Burnside's IX Corps, which was officially absorbed into the Army of the Potomac's command structure the following day, held the Union center at Ox Ford. Hancock's men had pushed down the Telegraph Road on the Army's left. After Birney's division cleared out a Confederate advance redoubt on the north side of the river at Chesterfield Bridge, Hancock threw the rest of his divisions across the river where they quickly entrenched.

The North Anna proved the battle that never was. Many of the northern officers fully expected another sanguinary encounter, and Lee was prepared to give them just that. The southern commander anchored his line on the high ground that comprised his center at Ox Ford. Facing the Confederates' "inverted V" formation, Grant could advance men across the North Anna on either of Lee's flanks, but they would soon came up against formidable earthworks. More importantly, Lee's position provided him with exceptionally efficient interior lines. If Grant assaulted either wing of the Confederate Army, Lee could easily shift men from one flank to the other. Grant and Meade, in contrast, could only reinforce either of their flanks by sending troops on a long march behind their lines on the north bank of the river. Having received too painful an education in the danger of attacking well-entrenched Confederates, Grant decided to call off any major attacks, including a proposed assault by Barlow on the Confederate position on the south bank of the North Anna below Chesterfield Bridge.

Lee's forbidding entrenchments on the North Anna, and Grant's reluctance to charge them, highlighted the increasing importance of fortified positions during the campaign. Indeed, it had become the norm that as soon as both armies halted, they immediately began to dig in. Since the Army of the Potomac was usually the one doing the assaulting, Lee had his men take special care to construct deadly defenses. Theodore Lyman considered the "extraordinary use of earthworks" one of the salient features of the campaign. "The Rebels form a line of battle," he reported:

> They then collect rails from fences, stones, logs and all other materials, and pile them along the line; bayonets with a few picks and shovels soon suffice to cover this frame with earth and sods, and within one hour, there is a shelter against bullets, high enough to cover a man kneeling, and extending often for a mile or two. When

our line advances there is the line of the enemy, nothing showing but the bayonets, and the battle flags stuck on top of the work. It is a rule that, when the Rebels halt, the first day gives them a good rifle pit; the second, a regular infantry parapet with artillery in position; and the third a parapet with an abates [sic] in front and entrenched batteries behind. Sometimes they put three days work into the first twenty-four hours.[6]

If Grant was frustrated by his inability to find a weak link in Lee's armor, the southern commander was more so. Lee saw the isolated pocket south of the North Anna of II Corps as a prime opportunity to destroy a significant portion of Grant's army. Hancock's men were confined in a relatively small bridgehead with its back against the river. Only a few narrow bridges provided an escape route back to the north bank. Lee hoped for a replay of his attack of 10 May on Barlow's division as it lay isolated south of the Po. This time the prize was even greater, a larger Federal force in a vulnerable position. A well-coordinated attack against the North Anna bridgehead had a genuine chance of destroying a large part of the II Corps. Such a defeat would be a major blow to the Army of the Potomac's offensive capability, and, if nothing else, would buy the Confederacy some badly needed breathing space.

Yet Lee did not move. While the II Corps remained vulnerable south of the North Anna, Lee lay in his cot sapped by an attack of severe dysentery. While the Confederate commander raged helplessly at the need to hit Grant, he was incapable of providing the essential leadership.[7] And he had no one he felt he could entrust with the responsibility. Jackson was dead a year. Longstreet was convalescing from his Wilderness wound. A. P. Hill had proven unreliable in command and Ewell seemed to be losing his grip. While Lee lay in his tent unable to direct his army offensively, Grant, deciding he could not successfully assault the southern position, pulled away seeking more promising circumstances.[8]

But, the federal commanding general too was feeling the pressure, and his frustration seemed to make him more reckless in his efforts to smash Lee's lines, break the rebel army, and clear the way to Richmond. By late May, it was clear the Federal campaign to destroy the rebellion was unraveling.[9] Although Sherman had drawn closer to Atlanta he had neither destroyed the Confederate army opposing him nor taken the city. Banks's foray up the Red River in Louisiana had been turned back, and the

Federal army charged with clearing the Shenandoah Valley was routed. Of more immediate concern, Grant's attempt at a pincer movement on Richmond had come to naught. Grant had appointed General Benjamin Butler commander of the newly designated Army of the James, consisting of the X and XVIII Corps brought up from the South. Butler was assigned the task of taking the rail center of Petersburg, south of the James, from which he would advance on the Confederate capital, drawing off units from Lee's army, while Grant battered down the door to Richmond from the north and east. Butler, as incompetent as he was provocative, was defeated by a much smaller Confederate force at Drewry's Bluff on May 16. General P. G. T. Beauregard, the Confederate commander below the James, then proceeded to bottle him up on the Bermuda Hundred peninsula. Deciding he could put Butler's troops to better use, Grant ordered the XVIII Corps under General William F. "Baldy" Smith to White House Landing, the Federal supply depot on the Pamunkey. From there it was to march to the vicinity of Hanovertown where it would link up with the Army of the Potomac, giving Grant an immediate infusion of troops to supplement those which were continually funneled southward to replace the staggering losses incurred in the ongoing slug out with Lee.

Even before Smith disembarked on 30 May, the Army of the Potomac had already commenced another sidling movement south and east hoping the Confederate leader would commit an exploitable blunder. The two armies faced off on Totopotomoy Creek, a tributary of the Pamunkey, with the VI Corps on the Federal right, II Corps on the center, V Corps on the left, and Burnside in reserve. Lee's men had gone over the ground at the Totopotomoy on 28 May and extensive defensive works had already been prepared. Probing for a weak spot in the rebel lines, Grant attempted to feel out the Confederate position. The result was number of small, short, but hot firefights. Around noon on 29 May, Barlow conducted a reconnaissance in force against the rebel lines. He drove off a light southern cavalry screen but halted before rebel breastworks along Swift Run, a small creek that ran into the Totopotomoy.

On the following morning, Barlow and Hancock had another brush with fate and emerged unscathed. The II Corps commander accompanied Barlow and their respective staffs to the lines held by Miles' brigade where they paused to watch coehorn mortars in action. The small, easily movable guns were used against Confederate lines in places where artillery batteries could not deploy or could not do so without being lacerated by counter-fire and sharpshooters. The cluster of Federal officers was soon detected by southern artillerists who opened fire. One shell exploded so near that shell splinters went whizzing about the group who were covered with dirt thrown up by the burst. Thinking better of remaining in such an exposed position, Hancock, Barlow, and the rest of the officers moved off to a site less enticing to enemy cannoneers.[10]

At about 7:00 P. M. on 30 May, Hancock received orders to attack the Confederate position as soon as he found a weak spot in the line. Hancock's assault was intended to relieve pressure on Warren who was hotly engaged with Jubal Early's Confederates near Bethesda Church. Hancock later wrote that there was really "no point on my line where an assault could be made with success at short notice, but I at once gave the order to General Barlow's division to attack. He moved as usual with most commendable promptness."[11] Brooke led the assault against the rebel lines and succeeded in carrying the advanced Confederates' rifle pits. As was becoming the norm, the main Confederate position proved quite strong, with its front covered by the Totopotomoy and a marsh.[12] Recognizing that prospects for a successful attack were slim, Meade and Grant called off further operations that day.

The next morning, Hancock resumed probing for a spot where he might force a crossing of the small waterway. Barlow continued extending his skirmish lines trying to get a better picture of the Confederate position on the Totopotomoy. He believed the southerners were in a strong position, but admitted he could not tell how strong without an assault.[13] When a report reached the Federal command that the rebels had left part of their works, Barlow ordered Miles to take the supposedly weakened line. The newly arrived 2nd New York Heavy Artillery was chosen spearhead of the attack. As was true of most of the heavy artillery regiments drawn from the Washington defenses, it was much larger than the units which had been worn down by months if not years of fighting. In fact, the 2nd "Heavies" was so large it was broken up into three battalions for easier maneuverability.[14] The New Yorkers, joined by the 183d Pennsylvania, were ordered to storm the Confederate lines head on, while the rest of the brigade charged obliquely to the right so the two lines would diverge, hitting the rebel works at either end of a presumably weak position. Captain Robert S. Robertson, one of Miles's staff officers, was selected to guide the green "Heavies" into action.

The troops clambered down the high ground and into the

marshes which bordered Swift Run. Unfortunately, the Confederate breastworks looking down on the stream from the south bank were manned by seasoned troops who instantly laid down an effective fire. Miles's men were quickly mired in the swampy valley. "The marsh and stream were between us and the enemy's position," Robertson later recollected, "and while the men, sinking to their middles in the oozy mud, were doing their best to push through it, a galling . . . fire was directed on them from the rebel line. It was more than new troops could stand."[15] The 2nd New York Heavy Artillery's Colonel, J. N. G. Whistler, ordered his men to get down and cover themselves as best they could. He entreated Robertson to report to Miles that an attack through such a morass was impossible under rebel fire.

Robertson remounted his steed, and rode back up the slope where he found Miles and Barlow watching the attack. Robertson quickly explained Whistler's predicament, but Barlow was in no mood to stop the attack. "Go back to Colonel Whistler," he ordered Robertson, "and tell him there must be no more impossibilities; that his regiment must charge the works in his front at once, and to do it with a yell." Robertson was about to remonstrate when Barlow cut him short. "You are losing valuable time; they must push forward at once." he declared sharply.[16] Although he believed Barlow was demanding an "impossibility," Robertson reined his mount around and headed for the marsh. However, before he could reach the 2nd New York Heavy Artillery's position, he was hit by Confederate fire and thrown from his horse. Barlow's message was never conveyed and the attack stalled. Robertson himself joined the long wagon trains of wounded rolling from the battlefields to the Federal base at White House Landing on the Pamunkey. He was then placed aboard one of the many steamers conveying the seriously wounded to the hospitals surrounding Washington.

Whatever the cause of Barlow's obstinate refusal to admit that his men had no chance to reach the Confederate lines, let alone breach them, he had had enough. Later in the morning he sent his negative assessment of the situation to Meade. "I do not believe," he informed his commander, "that these assaults upon intrenched [lines] through thick woods, where we do not know the ground, are likely to be successful where the enemy hold their line in force." Nevertheless he wrote, possibly facetiously and certainly hyperbolically, "we will cheerfully try if ordered."[17] How cheerfully the 2nd New York "Heavies" would have returned to the offensive is not difficult to surmise.

Grant and Meade had already written off an assault as impracticable and a battle on the Totopotomoy, like that on the North Anna, was not in the offing. Despite the lack of a major collision between the armies, II Corps lost 1,651 men in total casualties from the North Anna to the Totopotomoy. Barlow reported 456 in total losses from his division in these small indecisive operations.[18] As the II Corps prepared for its next inevitable rendezvous with its old foe, it listed an effective strength of 1,292 officers and 25,608 men. This was about fifty per cent of the corps' paper strength.[19] Barlow's First Division, which had been the largest in the Army when the campaign began, was now the smallest in the Corps, 15,807, compared to 16,046 for the Second Division and 18,769 in Birney's Third Division.[20] The prestige of spearheading the army's most vaunted corps bore an increasingly heavy cost.

Barlow was acutely aware of the wastage of his men. Neither his uncompromising zeal for discipline nor zest for combat prevented his being moved by the heaps of broken bodies his division left along Grant's path from the Rapidan. Nor did his unshakable determination that his division succeed in executing their battlefield assignments indicate unquestioning approval of the overall conduct of the campaign. "I am not much delighted with the performance here," he wrote Charles Henry Dalton from the North Anna, though he quickly added, "this is in the strictest confidence."[21] Barlow's critical remark seems aimed at Grant and Meade and probably reflected his evaluation of the many poorly coordinated attacks and his memory of the near total lack of intelligence provided before the assault on the Mule Shoe.

As was the case when he was frustrated and dissatisfied with his command in the XI Corps, Barlow again turned his thoughts towards the Freedmen's Bureau or a black regiment. "What is the state of the Darkey Bureau question?" he asked Dalton, indicating that he still harbored hopes of such a position. "When this campaign is over I think I should like it unless I can get an independent command."[22] Independent command would, of course, free him from control by commanders whose leadership he found flawed. While Grant continued to press southward, Barlow was no more convinced of his invincibility than he had been with the previous commanders of the Army of the Potomac. Not knowing of Lee's physical frailties, Barlow had been confident that the rebels would attack at the North Anna, "as they did in 1862 and I always doubt the result of these great battles."[23] From what he had seen, Barlow believed that Grant's drive on Richmond was no more assured of success than that of McClellan two years earlier.

On 31 May, Sheridan's cavalry ran across Confederates at a small crossroads named Cold Harbor. Torbert's cavalry division drove the defenders west of the crossroads and began to dig in. Grant, sensing an opportunity to take Lee on what he believed was a thinly held southern right flank, ordered VI Corps to move around the Totopotomoy line and, after linking up with "Baldy" Smith's XVIII Corps, attack the rebels at Cold Harbor. The execution of the plan proved more difficult in practice than it appeared on paper and the Federals were not in position for an attack until 6 P. M. on 1 June. The Union troops on the field drove the southerners from their forward lines, but Confederate resistance stiffened and the advance ground to a halt. Grant, impatient to hit Lee before the Army of Northern Virginia could reinforce his right, directed Meade to send Hancock to Wright's left on the Cold Harbor line. The V Corps was formed up on Smith's right and Burnside was lined up to Warren's right and rear. With his army thus deployed Grant expected to storm the Confederate position on 2 June.

What the commanding general had overlooked, or underestimated, was the debilitating effect of body-numbing fatigue caused by the near incessant fighting. To make matters worse, the territory was unfamiliar, the few roads were of poor quality, and the maps were deficient. Lyman recalled the Army's move to Cold Harbor as another of "those infernal night marches" which were difficult to conduct, and characterized by heavy straggling and exhaustion.[24] Worse, Captain William H. Paine, an engineering officer sent by Meade to guide the II Corps, attempted to take a presumed shortcut, which narrowed to a passage so tight the guns could not negotiate, costing Hancock additional time.[25] Moreover, losses among officers resulted in many green or inexperienced men in command of units which themselves included many replacements who were novices in military maneuvers. While Grant had hoped to wear Lee out, he had yet to accurately appreciate the debilitating effect of his tactics on his own forces.

After the grueling march through the darkness, the lead units of the II Corps reached Cold Harbor about 6:30 A. M on 2 June. Although Grant chaffed at the delays, Hancock reported his men were in "exhausted condition" and the attack projected for 7:30 A. M. was postponed until 5:00 P. M. and finally put off until 4:30 the following morning. As the jump-off time for the attack was pushed back, the First Division suffered a reverse. When

Barlow first arrived on the field, he sent Miles' brigade to occupy
a rise in front of the Federal lines known as Turkey Hill. A low
ridge rather than a hill, the elevation commanded a view of both
the northern lines as well as the Chickahominy, which lay to the
south and rear of Lee's position. Realizing the advantage of possessing the ridge, the Confederates attacked Miles' men and drove
them off, regaining control of Turkey Hill.

At about 5:00 P. M. Barlow sent word to Hancock that the rebel
skirmish line on the ridge was strong and "much higher and more
commanding than ours."[26] Barlow also mentioned the Confederate artillery which had begun to lob shells into his lines. He
thought that southerners might have had two guns operating
against him. This was a woeful underestimate. By the following
morning the Confederates would have about sixty cannon on
hand to meet any Federal attack.[27] On the other hand, Barlow's
assessment of the strength of the rebel line was totally accurate.
Upon reconnoitering the rebel position he informed Corps headquarters that "I can not move my line farther forward."[28] Gibbon
sent a similar assessment back to Grant and Meade.

If Grant saw the reports they made little impression on him
and the plans to assault the Confederate lines in the morning
stood unchanged. Grant's impatient belligerence derived from
his own faulty assumptions regarding the relative strengths and
weaknesses of the Confederate and Union forces. Lee's defensive
stance since the Wilderness led the lieutenant general to conclude that Lee's army was near its breaking point and one more
punch would finish it.[29] Indeed, Lee was concerned about his
numerical disadvantage and was reluctant to expend his men in
an assault unless the possibility of success was clear. Nevertheless, neither he nor his men had lost their resolve to hurl back
the Yankee host. On the other hand, it had not yet occurred to
Grant that his own losses, and the physical and emotional drain
of the relentless fighting, had diminished the efficiency of the
Army of the Potomac as much as the Army of Northern Virginia.

The fragmented Federal command compounded the problem.
Grant handed responsibility for the assault to the disaffected
Meade who did little more than announce the time of the attack.
Coordination was left to the corps commanders who did little or
nothing in this regard.

Barlow and Gibbon were given the honor of leading the attack
while Birney was held in reserve. As had been the case too often
throughout the campaign, Grant's offensive was ordered with
little or no reconnaissance. Again, the Federal commander made

assumptions about the disposition of the Confederates which had little relationship to the actual situation on the field. Grant, for example, had convinced himself that Lee had been hurt so badly he was incapable of repelling a determined Union attack. In reality, Lee's men were dug into an extremely strong, elevated, slightly crescent-shaped position, which gave them superb opportunity for bringing enfilading fire against any approaching forces. Despite the horrendous losses which each side had suffered in the previous battles, Lee, having received reinforcements from North Carolina and Bermuda Hundred, had about 70,000 men, while Grant, with the arrival of the XVIII Corps had 113, 875 men ready for action.[30] Despite their numerical inferiority, on the morning of 3 June, the Confederates enjoyed the decisive advantage in their defensive deployment, while Hancock and the other Federal Corps commanders had barely gotten their men into position for a brief respite before the renewing the offensive.

Barlow did not repeat the column formation he used at Spotsylvania, and arranged his lines by brigade, Miles and Brooke again in the lead. The Irish Brigade and the third brigade, now under Colonel Clinton D. McDougall after Brown's capture at Spotsylvania, constituted the second wave. At 4:30 on the morning of 3 June the II, VI, and XVIII Corps rolled forward against the Confederate line. On the II Corps front, Gibbon's men made almost no progress in the face of withering Confederate fire. The rebel defenders also mowed down the XVIII Corps before they even reached the Confederate trenches. The VI Corps barely moved forward and the IX and V corps on the northernmost part of the union positions did nothing until the afternoon. Consequently, the proposed massive stroke against the Army of Northern Virginia fell apart before it even began. Barlow, however, gained an early and deceptive success. Brooke's brigade captured a protruding salient in the rebel lines and about 200 prisoners and a stand of colors were taken by the attackers.

But Barlow paid a heavy price for his fleeting success as two more experienced officers were cut down. Colonel Brooke was badly wounded as he was preparing his second line to move forward. Command of the brigade devolved upon Colonel Orlando H. Morris of the 66th New York, who barely had time to acknowledge it before he fell mortally wounded. Colonel L. O. Morris of the 7th New York Heavy Artillery, which comprised Brooke's first line, took effective command and attempted to turn the captured Confederate guns towards their former owners, while the remainder of his troops were at work clearing out the "rat holes,"

The 7th New York Heavy Artillery of Barlow's division in brief control of the captured Confederate salient, Cold Harbor, June 3, 1864. Drawing by Alfred R. Waud. *Library of Congress.*

where the surviving Confederate defenders of the sunken road were lurking. In the melee of smoke, blood, and screaming men, the New Yorkers could not find the cannon's friction primers without which the guns were useless.[31] Meanwhile rebel reinforcements moved quickly to seal the breach and the Confederate 2nd Maryland Battalion and Finnegan's Floridians slammed into Barlow's dearly bought toehold. The heavy fire from the main Confederate line had already chewed up many of the Yankees in the captured works and the screaming counterattack proved too much to bear. In the face of the murderous rebel fire, the 7th New York Heavy Artillery fled the oncoming Confederates.[32] With the men in headlong retreat, Barlow abandoned any thought of sending MacDougall's men into action. How long Barlow's men held in the captured position under the heavy fire is not clear. Barlow tersely stated that his men were "driven out" and exposed to severe artillery fire without any possibility of Federal artillery being deployed in support.[33]

Barlow's other lead brigade (Miles's) had made even less headway and the first brigade's assault was smashed before it even reached the rebel lines. As Miles's troops dug in, Byrnes raced to his support with the Irish Brigade, but he was shot dead and his men joined Miles's troops in trying to gouge out some shelter where they were stopped. The third brigade, which had been held in readiness to brace Brooke's men, was broken up by the withering Confederate fire as well as the stampede of the men from the sunken road. They too attempted to dig in where they stood, but Rebel shell and canister ripped them mercilessly and the endurance level was breached. McDougall reported that his men finally broke and fell back in confusion, only reforming when they reached the Federal breastworks.[34]

Bloodily repulsed, the First Division withdrew to about 30 to 50 yards from the Confederate lines where the soldiers frantically used bayonets, plates, and hands to gouge out some shelter for themselves.[35] The attack was repulsed so swiftly that Barlow was forced to leave behind his wounded, whose bodies, along with those from Gibbon's failed attack, lay strewn across the field. Their numbers were continuously augmented by fresh victims of the incessant southern fire. Confederate General Iver Law, watching from the other side of the battlefield, described the carnage inflicted on the First Division as worse than Marye's Heights at Fredericksburg. "It was not war. It was murder," he wrote grimly.[36]

Perhaps because of Barlow's brief success and the prisoners sent to the Federal rear, Grant and Meade, who were not present on Hancock's front, seemed unaware of the severity of the repulse. At 8:45 A. M., Meade directed Hancock to support an attack by Wright and Smith. Hancock, affecting to believe that he had some discretion in the matter, declined. For his part, Grant continued to believe the situation was not so desperate that the offensive had to be abandoned, and he directed Meade to order an attack as soon as the troops' condition warranted. He gave the nominal army commander the option of halting operations if it were clear they would fail, but told him to pile on the troops anywhere a penetration was made.[37]

Attempts to get the troops to advance were met by passive resistance. When ordered to charge, the soldiers would increase their rate of fire and sometimes cheer in what southerners called "the Yankee manner," actions which led the Confederates to expect another assault. But none came. The troops, the divisional commanders, and the corps commanders had had enough of charging well-prepared entrenchments manned by an experienced and well-led enemy. As McDougall put it, "All efforts to rally [the men] were without effect, that is the large proportion of them."[38]

Hancock, for his part, made no effort to seriously renew the attack. At 11:00 A. M., Grant rode over to Hancock's line where the II Corps commander told him bluntly the Confederate line could not be taken.

Barlow, Hancock, and Grant thought that the failure of the attack lay in the lack of speedy reinforcements and the early loss of key officers. Barlow felt that Brooke's wounding and the failure of his replacement, Colonel Lewis O. Morris, to immediately prepare for Confederate countermeasures, cost him the sunken road.[39] A larger issue was the failure of Birney's division to move up in support of Barlow and Gibbon. Hancock was convinced Birney's laggard support doomed the assault. This latter interpretation found its way into the II Corps daily memorandum which states, "We might have held on in Barlow's front had Birney's division moved promptly to its support which was not done—great delay occurring on Birney's part or that of his subordinates."[40] Considering all the evidence, it is doubtful that the attack at Cold Harbor could have achieved any measurable success to compensate for the heavy losses. Emory Upton, one of the Army of the Potomac's rising stars and a perceptive observer, condemned the attack as "murderous. . . . because we were recklessly ordered to assault to enemy's intrenchments knowing neither their strength nor position. . . . I am disgusted with the generalship displayed."[41]

From where he stood, Barlow too, had concluded that it was unwise to resume the attack. He confessed to Hancock, probably with some relief, that he had been ready to make the attempt before receiving Hancock's order to desist.[42] He did not use the word "cheerfully" in describing his plans for the aborted assault. Searching for some means to improve the desperate situation, Barlow called for coehorn mortars, small portable artillery weighing about 294 pounds, which could be moved by four men.[43] The mortars were about the only guns he could deploy in his open position, and Barlow anticipated using them to lob shells into the Confederate line at its angle, perhaps providing a weak point for the northern troops to attack. Hancock confided to Humphreys that he would be "gratified" if Barlow could do anything with the mortars, but he doubted their efficacy, having become convinced that further attempts on the southern lines had little chance of success.[44] "My loss has already been pretty heavy," Hancock wrote Humphreys, "and I am losing men all the time, owing to the exposed condition of my men, and the constant skirmishing resulting from it."[45]

In truth Hancock was stunned by the losses at Cold Harbor,

which, along with the casualties in the earlier battles, led him later to remark bitterly that the II Corps lay "buried between the Rapidan and the James." Morgan, Hancock's Chief of Staff, believed the II Corps received a "mortal blow" at Cold Harbor "and never again was the same body of men."[46] Although Hancock himself was not quite that pessimistic, he conceded that the disastrous assault was "a blow to the corps from which it did not soon recover."[47] Events were to prove him right, though the evaluation could be largely applied to the entire Army of the Potomac.

The losses were particularly heavy in experienced officers, the men, in Morgan's words, "whose presence and example were worth many thousand [enlisted] men.[48] Six colonels and 46 other commissioned officers fell before Confederate muskets and artillery at Cold Harbor. In addition to Brooke, who would be out for many months with a serious wound, Byrnes had been killed, and Colonel Haskell of Gettysburg fame was shot down along with Colonels McKeen and McMahon. Colonel Morris, who briefly took command of Brooke's brigade when Colonel James A. Beaver of the 148th Pennsylvania deferred to his rank, was shot dead the following day. Beaver then took his place.

The totals for Cold Harbor were appalling. Losses incurred in the initial assault on June 3 were about 3500. Official casualty returns for the Army of the Potomac include those suffered through the entire time the army remained at Cold Harbor, from 3 June to 15 June. They tell their own story. The II Corps suffered 3510 casualties, 494 killed, 2,442 wounded and 574 missing or captured.[50] Barlow's First Division lost 1561 men. Of these 190 were killed, 1108 wounded, and 263 missing or captured.[51] Most of these losses occurred in a single day. In contrast, the II Corps suffered 4194 casualties in three days of fighting at Gettysburg.[52] In the army, and among the northern civilian population who read the casualty lists in the newspapers, Grant's reputation had reached its nadir. The U. S. in his name was no longer boastfully celebrated as "Unconditional Surrender"; in the popular mind it now stood for "Unceasing Slaughter." Grant, whose willingness to exploit northern population advantage to ensure victory was well established, admitted the enormity of his blunder at a meeting of his staff on the evening of 3 June. "I regret this assault more than any one I have ever ordered," he confessed. "I regarded it as a stern necessity, and believed that it would bring compensating results, but as it has proved, no advantages have been gained sufficient to justify the heavy losses suffered."[53]

Though the intense combat had ended, the agony of the II Corps

continued. Between the two lines lay hundreds of wounded northerners, mostly from Barlow's division. They shrieked and cried
out for water and aid, but nothing could be done for them without a truce. Both turkey vultures and black-headed vultures
cruised the ground between lines seeking to feed upon the pu-
trefying dead.[54] Any attempts to reach the wounded men without a cease-fire were suicidal. Hancock asked Grant to arrange a
truce so some of the men could be collected before they expired
in the baking Virginia sun. Grant, however, was loath to concede
he had been beaten and his attempts to arrange a truce with Lee
foundered on this point. The Confederate leader, whose losses
compared to Grant's had been negligible, refused to enter a truce
of "mutual accommodation" for both sides to gather their wounded
as few of his men lay in the open. In the meantime the number
and strength of calls from the wounded diminished. Those who
were able crawled back to the Federal lines on 4 and 5 June.
Many, however, still lay in front of the rebel positions and it was
certain death to raise one's head.[55] When Grant finally arranged
a truce for two hours on the evening of 7 June, few of the wounded
remained alive and those searching for the wounded found mostly
dead soldiers rotting beneath the sinking June sun.

In the meantime, Barlow extended his lines in hopes of achiev-
ing some advantage in the event the fighting was renewed. He
even anticipated one of the most dramatic gambits of the Petersburg Campaign by planning to run a mine underneath the Confederate works. Explosives would then be placed in the mine, and
detonated, tearing a gap in the rebel position for his men to exploit. On the morning of 4 June Barlow arrived at the bombproof
shelter which Colonel Lewis O. Morris, commander of the fourth
brigade, was using as his quarters. Together the two officers inspected the advanced trenches fronting the First Division's lines.
Barlow was particularly interested in the section called the "angle"
where the Union and Confederate lines were closest together. He
and Morris were discussing the construction of the tunnel when
they reached a point in the lines where the Union trench became
shallow. Rebel snipers were at work in the area, and Barlow and
Morris were warned to take care. Refusing to show fear, neither
of them wanted to return the way they had come and the only al-
ternative was to cross an exposed area before reaching the shelter of a deeper trench beyond. Although Barlow had convinced
himself he would not be killed in the war, he was not foolish. He
crouched down to present as small a target as possible and dashed
across the death strip without drawing fire. In a gesture possibly

intended to one-up his superior, Morris calmly walked into the gap and was shot through the shoulder, spine, and left lung. He was carried off to the division hospital where he died.[56]

Whether he really believed his tunnelling efforts would be successful seems unlikely. On 6 June, three days after his first attack, two of his brigades were removed to relieve Birney's men who had been supporting Gibbon. The detachment of his reserve brigades left him with a single line, far too few men to renew any assault, as he informed headquarters. As aggressive as any man in the Army of the Potomac, Barlow's hard-earned battlefield acumen led him to recognize the impossibility of renewing the offensive against Lee's position. In a later letter on 6 June, to Lieutenant Colonel Francis A. Walker, Assistant Adjutant of the II Corps, Barlow offered a candid assessment of his situation:

I have the honor to report that I do not think we should succeed in an assault in my front. We might perhaps carry the first weak line, but I am of opinion that their second line is very strong and that in passing from the first to the second line of the enemy's works we should encounter a fire of artillery and infantry from all sides which we could not go through. We could not hold the outer side of the enemy's first line, because it is in like manner swept from all sides. If we carried this first line, which could only be with loss, we could not hold it. And even this success would be very doubtful. There is no ground where troops could be formed for attack, and even when formed they would be broken up in passing over our own intrenchments. I do not think it expedient to assault again at present. The men feel just at present a great horror and dread of attacking earthworks again, and the unusual loss of officers, which leaves regiments in command of lieutenants, and brigades in command of inexperienced officers, leaves us in a very unfavorable condition for such enterprises. If the attack had been made on the evening of the 2nd as first ordered, I think we should have found the enemy unprepared; but having had four days for preparation, I think it would be hazardous to attack.
PS—I think the men are so wearied and worn out by the harassing labors of the past week that they are wanting in the spirit and dash necessary for successful assaults.[57]

The bloody repulse at Cold Harbor forced Barlow to concede that Lee had again barred the door to Richmond. Reluctantly, Grant was coming to the same conclusion. After a month's fighting and an astronomical expenditure of blood, Grant was no closer to Richmond than McClellan had been two years before with far fewer casualties. While he had attempted to find Lee's weak spots, Grant's desire for quick decisive results had all too

often led him to hurl his men at Lee's positions with little preparation or forethought. The result had been bloody stalemate. Lee
too, had been hurt and also suffered heavy casualties in both experienced troops and officers. Drawing on the north's greater resources Grant could more easily make up the losses in troops and
material. What he could not instantly order up were competent,
experienced officers or dedicated soldiers. For some time, at least,
the Army of the Potomac's ability to exploit their initiative would
be hobbled by the bloodletting of the Overland Campaign.

The indifferent quality of many of the new recruits was becoming a serious problem, and even veterans were so worn down by
the fighting that straggling became a major concern. Barlow, with
his hypersensitivity towards disciplinary and protocol infractions,
took energetic steps to suppress and punish such violations in his
division. On 26 May, after the army moved away from the North
Anna, Barlow had shirkers tied up and thrashed for what Lyman
called "the great benefit of the service."[58] A few days after the
Cold Harbor attack, Lyman found him "in a merry state for he
put some hundreds of stragglers in an open field and left them
there while the shells were flying, and one got hit."[59] Lyman may
well have been writing facetiously when he described Barlow's
mood as "merry." Infuriated and stressed might have been closer
to Barlow's genuine feelings. But, despite the ferocity of punish-
ments, straggling and shirking increased with the arrival of more
bounty men and draftees, while veterans began to calculate their
odds of surviving frontal assaults on entrenchments.

As the armies, and the fighting, shifted southeast, so did the
medical units who labored among those who had fallen. The great
chain of makeshift hospitals in Fredericksburg was gone, and the
surgeons and nurses now worked feverishly behind the lines at
Cold Harbor. The medical personnel labored continuously in the
hospitals amputating torn limbs, dressing wounds, comforting
the dying, and sending the wounded who could be moved to White
House, where they were transferred to the network of hospitals
in Washington. Arabella too had left Fredericksburg and arrived
at White House shortly after the battle. Francis received word
she was nearby and he sent his headquarters ambulance to convey her and Cornelia Hancock from the Pamunkey to the Tyler
House behind the Cold Harbor lines. Arabella and Cornelia had
originally hoped to set up a sort of halfway station to serve troops
moving from the field hospitals to White House. The medical
corps, however, decided that the wounded should be moved directly
to the rear hospitals and the two nurses found only light duty at
the Tyler House.[60]

Arabella and Cornelia remained at the Tyler House until 11 June. Arabella busied herself dispensing milk punch to wounded soldiers and helped get them ready for the journey to White House. The Barlows' proximity to each other made visits possible: Arabella sometimes joined Francis at his Cold Harbor headquarters, and he was occasionally able to slip away and join her at the Tyler House.[61]

Despite the carnage and battlefield failure Grant held fast to the strategic initiative. Lee could stymie him but he lacked the offensive punch to drive him away from Richmond, let alone defeat him in the field as he had Hooker in 1863. Conceding his inability to batter Lee back into Richmond Grant took another tack. He decided to change fronts by sending the Army of the Potomac south of the James before Lee could detect his movements. His target was the city of Petersburg, about 30 miles south of Richmond, the strategic rail hub for the Confederate capital and Lee's army. With Petersburg in his control, he could isolate Lee and Richmond from the rest of the south and either starve it into submission, as he did at Vicksburg, or force Lee to come out in the open and assault him. If the latter occurred, Grant would use his superior numbers to crush the Army of Northern Virginia. The James River crossing required secrecy, speed, and boldness. Grant was successful with the first and partially with the second, while the third element eluded him.

To mask his river crossing, Grant sent the V Corps on a feint towards Richmond. Lee positioned himself to block what seemed like another attempt by Grant to batter his way into the Confederate capital. Instead, most of the northern host marched across the James on 2000-foot long pontoon bridges, which Union engineers had constructed in ten hours although some units were ferried over the water in transports. Speed was of the essence if Lee was to remain deceived, and the Federal forces moved swiftly towards the river. Barlow moved his division so rapidly that Theodore Lyman was ordered to catch up with him and tell him to slow down lest he lose contact with the other divisions. When Lyman finally found Barlow, he was surprised to find the First Division's commander seated on the limbs of a cherry tree. Barlow greeted Lyman by remarking he knew he wouldn't be able to enjoy his cherry picking for long before a staff officer interrupted his respite. Just the same, he invited Lyman to climb up and pluck some cherries for himself. Lyman declined and chalked up Barlow's cherry tree interlude to his eccentricity.[62]

Barlow's division was noted for its rapid marching, an accomplishment which its commander had instilled through hard and thorough training. Watching the First Division's rapid march to the James, an admiring Lyman credited its speed to high morale coupled with the terror evoked by Barlow's provost guard. These watchdogs followed the men with bayoneted rifles and, according to Lyman, drove up "the loiterers with small ceremony, of course their [the provost guards] tempers do not improve with hard marching."[63] Indeed, Barlow's provost guards felt little compunction about insulting laggards and threatening bodily harm to those who did not follow orders quickly enough. Barlow, who instilled and encouraged such practices, was no doubt highly satisfied with the results. His disciplinary methods, which he rarely relaxed, were hard, but they bore fruit when the time came to pit his men against the enemy.

However skillfully Barlow, and the other divisional commanders, withdrew their divisions from Cold Harbor and crossed the Chickahominy on their route towards the James, many soldiers felt a sense that an era was passing with each southward step. Francis Walker captured the mood and summed up the effects of the campaign when he wrote that

> in the long column which wound its way, in the darkness, out of the intrenchements at Cold Harbor, on the 12th of June, 1864, and took the road to the Chickahominy, little remained of the divisions that had crossed that river on the 31st of May, 1862 to the rescue of the broken left wing. And the historian feels that, as he concludes the story of Cold Harbor, he is, in a sense, writing the epitaph of the Second Corps.[64]

South of the James

At 5:30 P. M. on 13 June, the II Corps began to cross the James at Wilcox's Landing with Barlow's division bringing up the rear. Grant's thrust across the James succeeded in confusing Lee, who had no clear idea of his opponent's intentions. From the 12 June, when most of the Army crossed the Chickahominy, to 15 June, when the II and XVIII Corps were slipped over the James, the Confederate chieftain anxiously sought accurate information as to the location of the Army of the Potomac. In the meantime, Petersburg was thinly defended by an array of home guard units, as most of the rebel forces in the area were engaged in keeping Butler bottled up at Bermuda Hundred. Nevertheless, the Confederate commander south of the James, P. G. T. Beauregard, became increasingly aware of the Federal buildup in front of him. Although the Louisianan wired Lee warning him that Grant had slipped across the river and was beginning to mass against Petersburg, his messages sometimes seemed unclear and contradictory. Lee remained unsure whether the buildup of Federals at Petersburg was a feint intended to draw southern strength, while Grant prepared a new blow against Richmond from the east. Consequently, for three days the strategic railroad center of Petersburg might have been taken in a walk. Yet, it did not fall.

To a large measure, the failure to take the poorly defended rail center stemmed from the difficulties in coordinating the complex movements of a large army after they were across the James. Once on the southern shore, the corps and divisions had to be deployed for the advance on Petersburg which took time. Equally important, both officers and men were physically drained by the near continuous heavy fighting. The replacements continuously sent to the army lacked the experience of the thousands whose moldering corpses marked Grant's path southward. The hot, humid Virginia summer increasingly further enervated the men and depressed morale. Indeed, at one point during the crossing of the James, Hancock went looking for Barlow and found him asleep.[65] During the ferocious and exhausting campaign, officers and men had to take their rest where they found it and there was no fault in Barlow catching a nap as long as his men were properly organized and deployed. Nevertheless, Hancock would remember Barlow's nap and it would play a role in a later controversy.

On the morning of 15 June, Hancock, now south of the James at Windmill Point, prepared to move towards Petersburg to cooperate with Smith's XVIII Corps, which was leading the Federal advance. Unfortunately, Grant had neglected to inform either Meade or Hancock of his plans to take Petersburg on the 15 June, nor had he told Hancock that he was expected to support Smith in an assault.[66] As a result, Hancock began his march towards Petersburg at 9 A. M., an hour late, having halted for rations which did not arrive. The march was hot and dusty and the map, which had been issued to Hancock, was defective. Birney led the Corps' march towards Petersburg, which may have been a good thing since Barlow was given a faulty map as well. Indeed, he took the wrong road and turned east away from Petersburg and had gone almost to City Point before he realized his error and backtracked. Hancock reached Smith at 6:30 P. M. and relieved the XVIII Corps troops in their entrenchments, an action which would later cause controversy and bruised pride. Nevertheless, the decision not to

attack proved a major blunder as Smith had already broken the
northern sector of the rebel works and seized part of the Dimmock line, the defensive system which encircled Petersburg and
which Beauregard strove to man with only 2,200 infantry and
artillerymen.[67]

When Barlow's division finally trudged into the Petersburg
lines, he sent a member of his staff, Major Marlin, to report to
Hancock and ask where he should place his troops. Hancock,
clearly under a great deal of stress and plagued by recurrent pain
from his Gettysburg wound, pointed to the left and told Marlin
they should go there. Marlin turned to pass on the order to the
fourth brigade commander, Colonel James A. Beaver. At that
point Hancock, who had been speaking facetiously, quickly inter-
jected "Yes, put 'em there, if you want every one of them killed."
Then he went on impatiently, "Where's General Barlow?" Marlin
replied that his commander had stopped a small distance back
to bathe his feet. Hancock immediately became agitated, dropped
his reins and began wringing his hands "as if in agony."[68] "That's
it; that's it," he exclaimed, "always asleep or washing his feet."[69]
Marlin and Beaver were unsure how to take Hancock's outburst
and began to laugh nervously, treating it as a ludicrous jest.
Hancock turned his horse and rode away. Clearly, finding Barlow
asleep had rankled him, whatever the rationale, and Barlow's
delayed appearance and use of a staff officer to report aggravated
him more. The wrong turn on the road to Petersburg would soon
become a matter of contention between Barlow and his superior.

When the Union forces launched their first major assault
against Petersburg the next day the situation had changed. Beauregard had moved most of his men from Bermuda Hundred to
the city's defenses and had fashioned a new set of works to compensate for those taken by Smith the previous day. Nevertheless,
Petersburg's commander remained badly outnumbered. He had
received no troops from Lee, who remained uncertain if Grant
had indeed crossed the river in force. Together, Hancock and Smith
had about 30,000 men on hand and the IX and V Corps were on
their way.[70] The Federals spent most of the morning reconnoitering the Confederate position seeking a vulnerable spot to attack.
At 9:30 A. M., Barlow sent word to Hancock, then in command of
all northern troops at Petersburg, that the rebel right was weakly
held and "another division around our left flank would be well
[past] the enemy's right flank."[71] Despite this inviting prospect,
nothing was done to exploit the exposed flank. After the Federals
had completed their reconnaissance Grant wired Meade that he

wanted a general assault about 6 P. M. By this time, the IX Corps had arrived and began to fill in the front south and south west of Barlow who manned the II Corps' extreme left.

The assault, which began about 6:00 P. M., was primarily a II Corps operation, with a brigade each from the IX and XVIII Corps on their left and right flanks respectively. Unfortunately, the ferocious heat—which played an important role in sluggish troop performance all summer—and the long march from the James had drained the strength of the newly arrived IX Corps men and they provided little aid in the attack. Gibbon remained primarily in reserve, leaving Birney and Barlow to take the brunt of the action.

In order to reach the entanglement-fronted rebel lines, Barlow's men were forced to storm across an open field near the Shand House. As they charged into the open they came under fire from Confederate riflemen and gunners in rebel-held Dimmock line redoubts as well as from Beauregard's secondary line. Bitter experience had taught the men the hazards of charging entrenchments under such conditions and growing apprehension spread among the ranks before the assault. Gilbert D. Frederick of the 57th New York in Barlow's third brigade wrote, "the boys dreaded this charge as it seemed a hopeless one. After forming lines they waited quite awhile before advancing and this led to a calculation of chances for life and a consequent loss of nerve."[72] Attired in his checkered combat shirt, trousers tucked into boots, and waving his hat in the air, Barlow tried to fire his troops' martial ardor by personally leading the forward. "Come on boys" he yelled as the men pressed onward, the Division color guard at his right. After blasts from Confederate cannon levelled the color guard, Barlow, having done what he could, fell back into a gap in the lines from which he could oversee the action.[73] But his best efforts bore little fruit. The men in his third brigade, under Colonel Clinton D. MacDougall, charged in close column formation, and quickly reached a fence fronting the Confederate rifle pits. Here they halted and hunkered down until the color bearer of the 57th New York, Charles Van Hise, carried the flag over the fence, inspiring—or shaming—the rest of the men to follow.

But the Confederate line was not seriously breeched, with the rebels yielding only their advance rifle pits.[74] Colonel Beaver of the fourth brigade temporarily succeeded in leading his men into one of the forts which studded the Petersburg defenses, but a rebel shell burst at his feet and tossed him into the air, leaving his men temporarily leaderless. Beaver was carried to the rear as his men were driven out of the rebel bastion. The Federals managed to stand fast in the captured outer works and drove off Confederate attempts to retake these positions. Miles's brigade, which attacked on the right, did no better, capturing only a few rifle pits and forward trenches. But these small gains were offset by the loss, 2000 men and more of Barlow's experienced officers.[75] Colonel Patrick Kelly of the Irish Brigade was killed and Beaver became the third commander of the fourth brigade to fall in three weeks. Moreover, it was increasingly obvious that the men were played out. Captain James Kelly of the 28th Massachusetts of the Irish Brigade remarked, "The men were utterly used up, and dropped asleep in the pits. The utmost exertions of the officers were almost ineffectual in keeping them in a wakeful condition."[76]

The failure of three Federal corps, now numbering about 50,000 men, to take the Petersburg defenses which were manned by only 14,000 defenders[77] stemmed from several causes—all of which would combine to frustrate Federal efforts to capture the "Cockade City" when it was most vulnerable. A major problem was poor leadership. Meade failed to attack the Confederate right flank earlier in the day when Barlow reported it open, and then ordered an attack where Beauregard was strongest. Grant himself remained strangely detached at his headquarters at City Point several miles away. Additionally, neither Meade nor his corps commanders succeeded in coordinating their attacks. Instead of falling upon the rebels with all the power available to them, only two depleted divisions made the assault. Lastly, Beauregard and his men played a masterful game with a weak hand.

And yet, the men were soon called upon to make further "exertions." Three attacks were made on the Confederate lines on 17 June. At 3:00 A. M. Potter's IX Corps division attacked south of Barlow who was to have supported him. Whether due to misplaced or misunderstood orders, the First Division, II Corps was mostly asleep when Potter began his attack and this time it was Barlow's turn to provide tepid assistance.[78] Physical exhaustion probably played a major role in Barlow's weak showing as it had with Burnside's men the day before. About 2:00 P. M., the IX Corps began another attack, this time led by Orlando Wilcox's division. Miles's brigade was assigned to support him on his right. Miles's regiments, especially the 5th New Hampshire, performed their part well. The Granite State men seized some high ground from which they poured such accurate fire into the Confederate entrenchments that the rebels could not raise their heads above the breastworks. The New Hampshiremen reported that each man fired over 160 rounds at the southerners.[79] Beauregard's second line, quickly constructed after the Dimmock line was largely abandoned, seemed on the verge of cracking when one of Wilcox's brigades became confused, veered away from the Confederates and turned to their right, totally exposing their other flank. The surprised and delighted Confederates unleashed volley after volley into the disoriented Yankees, who finally broke in disorder colliding with their second line which then collapsed as well. Many of the men were so panicked they did not stop running until they reached the safety of Barlow's lines.[80] This debacle effectively ended the mid-afternoon attack.

The last major attack on 17 June was made around 6:00 P. M. as Barlow and Burnside tried again for a decisive breakthrough near the Shand House. Again, Barlow personally led his men and his lines held steady until they reached the rebel earthworks manned by Colquitt's southerners. Once again the men became caught up in the abatis where they became easy targets for Confederate artillery and infantry. Those who were not shot down were forced to retreat or surrender. Only the 66th New York in the fourth brigade managed to hold on to a chunk of the southern position, but was forced to fall back at 9:00 P. M. when their ammunition ran out.[81] Barlow's regiments suffered heavily in killed, wounded, and especially prisoners. The IX Corps also carved out a temporary salient in the rebel lines but it too was lost to Confederate counterattacks. Barlow reported to corps headquarters that he could have hung on to the advanced position the 66th New York had won if the IX Corps had not fallen back under Confederate pressure.[82]

Hancock had not been able to provide much direction to the attacks on 16–17 June. Although he put a brave face on it, his once indomitable energy was being drained by his Gettysburg wound which had been suppurating throughout the campaign, causing him great pain. On 17 June he formally turned his command over to his senior division leader, David Birney, who then led the II Corps until Hancock reported himself back to duty on 27 June. Shortly before he reported himself sick, Hancock requested that his division commanders forward a report on the strength and condition of the troops. The response was not encouraging. Gibbon replied that he could supply only two brigades as the Overland Campaign had gutted his division.[83] Barlow was similarly pessimistic. If he were ordered to attack again, he informed headquarters, he would have to call up his second and third brigades who were recovering from the effects of the first day's fighting in his second line. He made it clear that the lack of officers in those brigades made any prospect of success unlikely in the extreme.[84] While the II Corps occupied a strong position close to Beauregard's line, as an offensive force it was a ghost of its former self, and in the words of a later historian, "comparatively few in number and physically spent."[85]

As Hancock took himself out of action, Meade grew desperate to smash the Confederate lines and seize Petersburg. He was certain that the lines before him were held solely by Beauregard's understrength force, and he was convinced the rebel positions could be broken and the city taken if the attacks were pressed hard. Moreover, the situation at the front was changing rapidly. Meade knew that Lee was now fully alerted to the threat at Petersburg and the seasoned veterans of the Army of Northern Virginia were on their way. The wonderful window of opportunity which had been open for three days was beginning to close and Meade was frantic to seize the city before it shut. He now had the V Corps totally in line on Burnside's left and the VI Corps was just beginning to reach the field which gave the Federal commander somewhere between 70–80,000 men.[86] While Kershaw's division had arrived from Lee, Beauregard had received no other reinforcements, and Meade retained an overwhelming numerical advantage. Continuing to make the best of the resources at his disposal, the Creole made another adjustment in his lines, carefully pulling back to a new line of entrenchments laid out to provide his men excellent fields of fire while any attackers would have to advance through with ravines and railroad embankments before reaching him.

Meade called for a dawn attack by the II, V, and IX corps supported by the XVIII and part of the VI Corps. The attack was immediately thrown off track by Beauregard's tactical withdrawal during the early morning. The Yankees charged into abandoned works and then had to reform while they sought to determine the new rebel lines. From that point on, Federal cohesion virtually disintegrated. Birney informed Meade that the new southern position was strong and it would be difficult to bring artillery to bear on it. Nevertheless, he declared he was prepared to attack as soon as the XVIII Corps was ready on his right.[87] Barlow sent a cryptic report stating that his division was not well positioned for an attack.[88] Birney ordered Gibbon's division forward at noon only to see it quickly driven back. The IX Corps also joined in the assault and apparently expected Barlow to support them. Barlow, behaving with uncharacteristic caution, had already informed

Wilcox that he had no orders to attack and when the IX Corps brigades went forward Barlow did little.[89] Barlow's peculiar passivity may have stemmed partly from a lack of clear orders from Meade or Birney as he said. But it might also have risen from a growing conviction that the attacks were doomed and he saw no point in bleeding his depleted regiments further. He might also have become uncertain how his division would respond to orders to make another frontal assault. If so, his instincts were born out by what happened in Mott's (Birney's) Division later in the day.

Birney, however, proposed to try again and Meade, still believing that Petersburg was within his grasp, ordered him to "select your own point of attack, but do not lose any time in examination."[90] Before Birney could prepare another assault, he received further orders from Meade informing him that both Burnside and Warren were to join his attack. Unfortunately, Meade found it impossible to get his corps commanders to advance in any sort of coordinated fashion. In fact, he was forced to send a thinly veiled threat to Warren to move as directed. The Army of the Potomac's commander became increasingly impatient and pressed his officers to attack wherever possible, apparently hoping that the sheer weight of numbers would carry the day. "You have a large corps, powerful and numerous," he wrote Birney, "I beg you will at once, as soon as possible, assault in strong column. The day is fast going, and I wish the practicability of carrying the enemy's line settled before dark."[91]

Birney dutifully followed Meade's instructions and attacked the Confederate lines with Mott's division in the van supported by Barlow and a brigade from Gibbon's division on the left. When they learned that they were to make another attack many of Mott's men balked and the relatively fresh 1st Maine Heavy Artillery was chosen to storm the Confederate lines near the Hare House. The attack was a complete and bloody failure. By 6:30 P. M. Meade conceded he could not carry the line. The II Corps was then pulled back behind the left-center of the front and temporarily placed in reserve.

The door to Petersburg, which had been virtually open for over two days, had been slammed shut. The soldiers understood the situation before Meade did. Indeed, the troops had gone through a major mood swing in their four days before Petersburg. The shift of the theater of war had a tonic effect on many soldiers, and spirits and morale improved as the men left the blood-soaked fields at Cold Harbor and crossed the James. When the II Corps came up next to Smith on 15 June, the men sensed that they had finally stolen a march on Lee and that they were finally going to have the chance to strike a successful blow and end the war in Virginia. The fire of combativeness, smothered by the bloodlettings between the Rapidan and Cold Harbor, flickered up again. Many of the men wanted to attack on the night of 15 June, when Hancock deferred to Smith and simply ordered them into Federal entrenchments.[92] The uncoordinated and unsuccessful attacks of the next three days proved that the opportunity had been squandered, and the soldiers began to make their own adjustments.

Generally, the men fought well on 16 and 17 June, but when the sun rose on the last day's fighting in the opening round at Petersburg everything had changed. By the time the II Corps made its last doomed attack on 18 June, one veteran watching newly arrived heavy artillery regiments prepare to charge yelled out, "Lie down you damn fools, you can't take those forts."[93] A Massachusetts regiment heeded the advice and held back. The 1st Maine Heavy Artillery disregarded the warning. The regiments supporting the "Heavies" quickly fell back as they neared the rebel works; but the Maine unit went on with 632 of its 900 members falling before Confederate fire. This was the single highest casualty rate suffered by any regiment during the Civil War.[94] Heat, exhaustion, and casualties had dulled the fighting abilities of the Army of the Potomac. Aloof, passive, and sometimes atrocious leadership doomed the great opportunity to take Petersburg and shorten the war. With Lee's men filing into the Petersburg lines, Grant suspended frontal assaults and settled on a campaign to cut the city's communications.

For his own part, Barlow was to find the summer before Petersburg the most trying time of the war.

7

Stalemate

On 19 June, with the initial round of fighting at Petersburg flickering out, Barlow finally found enough time to send a letter home. His brother, Richard, had been serving with him for some time at the front, presumably as a volunteer aide, similar to the position his elder brother, Edward, had held the year before. Richard left for Boston on 20 June, covered with fleabites and dirt. Barlow warned his mother that Richard was "disgusted with the life of a soldier," but he had little sympathy for his sibling as he himself was "so much dirtier I don't appreciate his filthiness."[1] And, of course, Francis had been in almost continual combat, which, he informed his mother, meant he had to take advantage of every chance he had to get some sleep. Barlow reported that the Army of the Potomac had attacked the city at various times and had pushed back the enemy's lines. Nevertheless, he admitted that they had not been able to penetrate the southern defensive line, and that no Federal soldier, other than a prisoner, had yet set foot in Petersburg.[2]

While Hancock rested up trying to restore his strength, he found time to read over the newspaper accounts of the opening of the Petersburg campaign. He was incensed by what he read. According to the newspaper accounts, the northern failure to take Petersburg on June 15th, when it was barely defended, was the fault of the II Corps. Telegrams written by Secretary of War Edwin Stanton faulting the II Corps for its alleged lack of celerity that day found their way into newspapers. Articles also appeared in the *New York Times,* charging the II Corps with a lack of drive on that pivotal day.[3] In a letter of protest to Meade and Grant, Hancock stated that if Petersburg were so lightly garrisoned, as seemed the case after the fact, Smith could have taken the place himself. "And certainly," the ruffled II Corps commander argued, he could have done so "with the assistance of the two divisions of the Second Corps which I offered to General Smith just after dark on the 15th."[4] Hancock maintained that had he been present before nightfall he would have taken "decisive actions." Instead, he deferred to Smith who had seen the Confederate lines in daylight and relied upon Smith's "judgment and desiring not to interfere with his honors, as he was directed to take the place." Consequently, Hancock made his offer of troops to Smith. Rather than order an attack, Smith simply asked Hancock to relieve his men and prepare to defend against a Confederate counterattack.

Hancock did concede that the orders he had given for the assaults on the 16 June were botched, which he attributed to overall confusion and his own failing ability to oversee operations. Nevertheless, Hancock proclaimed that his corps made every attempt to carry out Grant and Meade's directives, but since he now saw evidence of "an improper attempt to place the failure to capture Petersburg on the 15th on my command I respectfully ask for an investigation on the subject."[5]

The last thing the Army of the Potomac needed was an investigation or court of inquiry into the alleged failings of the corps, which had been its shock troops during the Overland Campaign. Besides, an impartial inquiry would reveal that the performance of many officers, including Meade and Grant, was less than stellar. Meade responded with a brief reply which concluded that he could not see "how any censure can be attached to General Hancock or his corps."[6] On 28 June, Grant squashed the whole idea of an investigation with a note designed to assuage Hancock's, and probably the whole corps' feelings. "No investigation can now be had without some great prejudice to the service," Grant began,

> nor do I think an investigation necessary at any time. The reputation of the Second Corps and its commander is so high, both with the public and in the army, that an investigation would not add to it. It can not be tarnished by newspaper articles or scribblers. No official dispatch has ever been sent from these headquarters which, by any construction, could cast blame on the Second Corps or its commander for the part they have played in this campaign.[7]

Grant did mention the delay on 15 June, when Hancock halted for rations, but admitted that the delay amounted to only an hour or two and was not critical to the unfolding of subsequent events. Apparently, Hancock was satisfied by the outcome of his written protest.

In his concern to demonstrate that the failure to take Petersburg on 15 June could be laid neither on his corps nor himself personally, Hancock reviewed the actions of his divisional commanders, and asked for copies of their orders. Not surprisingly, he focused on Barlow's actions on that day, particularly the reasons for his detour away from Petersburg which resulted in his late arrival on the battlefield. Hancock's inquiry led to an exchange of memoranda and letters which continued from 26 June to 4 July, resulting in indignant protests and injured pride— mostly Barlow's. On receiving Hancock's request for copies of the orders he had been sent from corps, or from Meade and Grant, Barlow initially replied that he had only two at hand since, as he put it pointedly, "until lately I have not been in the habit of keeping orders received longer than the period to which they relate."[8] He then summarized the crossing of the river on 15 June, the wait for rations and then the order to move, his division following behind Gibbon and Birney. He recollected that he had his men on the march around 1:00 P. M. He claimed his delay was caused by confusion in the verbal orders given to him by Colonel Morgan of Hancock's staff, which was transmitted to him by his chief of pioneers, Captain Bird. It was difficult to decide which roads to take, he went on, since the map he possessed did not even have Petersburg on it. This led to his erroneous choice of the road away from Petersburg towards City Point. Consequently, Barlow did not reach the Petersburg lines until 10:00 P. M. He deployed his men on Birney's left at 5:00 A. M. the next morning and his division was fully entrenched in his assigned position on the II Corps line at 10:00 A. M. Barlow argued that even had he not made his time-consuming detour he could not have been deployed at Petersburg before 9:30 on the night of the 15 June "too late for the operations of the day."[9]

Barlow closed his missive with the request that he be informed if any blame were to be "attributed to me for delay in the march of the 15 June." Two days later, on 28 June, Barlow received a response from Hancock's adjutant, Francis Walker, stating that Hancock's letter was not directed at Barlow, but was a circular sent to all division commanders. Despite this, Walker admitted that Hancock expected an explanation for the First Division's delay and would have asked for it sooner if the pace of the fighting had allowed it.

All the correspondence on the issue was sent to the participants so they could respond and add their comments. Morgan, Hancock's Chief of Staff, sensed Barlow was setting him up as the scapegoat for his detour. Even before Walker's somewhat soothing letter had been sent to Barlow, Morgan submitted his account of the day in which he contended that Bird knew exactly what route he needed to take, and that Barlow's staff officers had been up the road to Petersburg and had reported their findings to Barlow himself. Morgan also mentioned a dispatch from Grant ordering Barlow to proceed to the sound of the firing, "whereas he marched directly away from it. There seems to be a disposition to father most of the mistakes of that day on me," Morgan concluded, making it clear he wasn't having any of it.[10]

On reading Morgan's account of 15 June, Barlow wrote a more heated report denying responsibility for the uncertainty caused by orders, which he maintained he did not receive firsthand. He also scoffed at Morgan's claim that the staff officer had only advised Barlow how to proceed. The disagreement between the two officers reached the point that Hancock, through Walker, directed Morgan to supply copies of all orders issued to Barlow. Morgan did so and reiterated his contention that he pointed out to Bird the road which Barlow should take to reach the Petersburg lines. He explained that after leaving the First Division he returned to Corps headquarters and finding the Second and Third Division in place, rode back to the First Division and found the rear of their column at Old Prince George Court House with their columns marching away from the fighting and towards City Point. Morgan rode up to Barlow and got him turned him around in the right direction, riding with him to Petersburg. According to Morgan, Barlow even stated that he thought the road to the left out of Old Prince George Court House, which Morgan had indicated was his assigned route, was the correct road, but he did not take it for fear it would cause a traffic jam with the Second and Third Divisions.[11] Barlow's response rebutted Morgan in all essentials with, of course, "all due deference." He continued to insist that his staff members had moved down the correct road but he had altered the route due to Morgan's orders. He went on to say that he was so close to Petersburg that staff officers who knew the country should have been sent to guide him.[12]

Hancock's evaluation and conclusion, written by Walker on his orders, reached Barlow on 3 July. The letter was highly critical of Barlow's actions and defense. Barlow had no reason to halt at Old Court House, the letter began. Captain Bird, Barlow's chief of Pioneers (Engineers) and a member of his staff, knew that the Second and Third Division were approaching Petersburg on Grant's orders. Additionally, Grant sent Barlow an order directing him straight to Petersburg. "That order," Hancock stated, "ought to have been sufficient to take him there and it was not necessary that staff officers should be sent to conduct him, for his own staff officers knew the road as well as any that the Corps commander could send him."[13] "The firing was a good guide," Hancock observed pointedly. Most telling in Hancock's eyes, "Each division commander had the same means of ascertaining the road to Petersburg and they all found their way there sufficiently except General Barlow." Hancock went on to give Barlow a little piece of elementary military science reminding him that "Division commanders must not expect at every turn of the road to find a staff officer from corps headquarters to indicate the direction when they have written orders indicating their march." The II Corps commander concluded his inquiry in the matter by laying the fault for Barlow's wrong turn on Barlow himself, effectively exonerating Morgan. "It appears," he had Walker write, "that General Barlow got an order from General Grant before reaching Old Court-House to march to Petersburg at once, which he did not obey. He clearly committed an error of judgment in taking the wrong road, for which he is certainly responsible, so far as any responsibility may attach to it."[14]

Barlow's response seemed almost perfunctory, suggesting he knew the truth of Hancock's evaluation. He maintained that he not actually halted at Old Prince George Court House while determining which route to take, and again tried to lay the blame on faulty orders from Morgan. He also repeated his contention that even had he not lost time on the road to City Point he could not have reached the field in time to take part of the day's combat. He dissented, respectfully, but "very firmly" from Hancock's assigning of responsibility to him. Furthermore, he requested that if any sort of official inquiry were to be made that he might "have a opportunity to make a more full and connected explanation than I have been able to do in these hasty indorsements."[15]

But Hancock had done all he intended. He had been mollified by Grant's letter and understood that there was little benefit in searching for a scapegoat for the bungled attempt to take Petersburg on 15 June. He was probably also satisfied that he had done all he could to discover what had happened on that day, and had chastised the commander whom he felt had not performed up to par. Hancock's subsequent actions and correspondence demonstrate that the high esteem in which he held Barlow remained generally intact. He was certainly in no mind to lose or demoralize him. But the fact remained that Barlow had not performed up to his standard on 15 June, and Hancock believed a reprimand was necessary. It is also likely that Hancock was further annoyed by Barlow's attempt to push his failures off on the II Corps Chief of Staff. As far as Hancock was concerned, that was the end of it.

Of course, Barlow might have been right in his assertion that he could not have reached the field until after nightfall. Then again, knowing his ability to drive his men, that too is uncertain. On the other hand, since Hancock and Smith had already decided against a night attack, Barlow's earlier arrival would have made little difference in the events and dispositions of 15 June. Whatever might have happened on 15 June, Barlow's mistaken route on the approach to Petersburg, and his subsequent campaign to absolve himself from blame did him no credit, and showed him at his worst—at least in terms of personal shortcomings. His uncritical assumption of his own intellectual and moral superiority, important ingredients in his aggressive battlefield demeanor, contributed to his substandard performance during the bungled march to Petersburg. Worse, they led him into the unethical situation of trying to lay the blame for his shortcomings at the feet of another officer. His peculiar, obstinate movement away from Petersburg certainly seems to have been a fluke—certainly, he never committed another blunder like it during his military career. But, his actions during the march provide further evidence that he was not immune from the effects of the fatigue that was wearing down the men of the Army of the Potomac. Barlow savored his reputation as a fighter. He gloried in it, and he tried to avoid tarnishing it. Yet, his stubborn attempts to maintain his name had the opposite effect of leaving a blemish, however small, on his fame.

Grant's strategy at Petersburg was to cut the rail lines into the city which supplied Lee's army and the Confederate capital. Throughout the summer and fall of the Petersburg campaign, Meade and Grant pushed the Army of the Potomac south and west, endeavoring to sever the rail lines and roads which would force Lee to stretch his numerically inferior force to block them. Grant might still have hoped to lure Lee into the open where he might be decisively defeated, but failing that he hoped to reduce the Army of Northern Virginia to such a condition that it could no longer give effective resistance. Of equal importance, Grant kept Lee pinned in his Petersburg lines, unable to move southward with either his entire army or any considerable force thereof in order to reinforce Joseph Johnston, who had fallen back towards Atlanta in the face of Sherman's superior force. As long as he had to defend the Confederate capital Lee had no option but to remain in place, parrying Grant's attempts to pierce or turn his line. Lee well understood the end result of a protracted siege at Petersburg. Should such an event occur, he told subordinates, "it would be only a matter of time."

Conducting a war on the Richmond-Petersburg front was arduous enough even without Confederate opposition. Although some sections of the Richmond-Petersburg front were bare and open, often the result of troops cutting down trees for wood or to create fields of fire, much of it was heavily wooded which rendered visual contact difficult. The forested, rolling terrain, cut by creeks and ravines, tended to break formations and disrupt cohesion. "The divisions have lost connection," Lyman observed in mid-June, describing the attempts of the Army to extend its lines westward. "They can not cover the ground designated, their wing is in the air, their skirmish line has lost its direction."[16] And Lee, as always, refused to cooperate.

Grant's soothing letter to Hancock, which was designed to mollify the veteran Corps commander's wounded feelings at the public criticism of his corps during the opening day's assaults at Petersburg, justifiably extolled the record of the II Corps throughout the war. However, between the time Hancock sent off his letter of outrage and Grant's reassuring reply of praise, the II Corps was involved in an operation which raised the question of whether or not the Corps was the same body which had elicited Grant's encomium.

On 21 June, with Birney still commanding the corps, Meade and Grant ordered a westward advance by the II and VI Corps designed to cut the Weldon Railroad which brought supplies from further south into Petersburg. When the operation commenced, the II Corps numbered 21,190 men, of whom 5,570 marched under Barlow in the First Division.[17] The Corps proceeded westward to Warren's left crossing both the Norfolk & Petersburg Railroad and the Jerusalem Plank Road. Barlow, on the left of the corps, came within two miles of the Weldon Railroad. During the early morning of 22 June, the VI Corps took up a position close, but not connected, to the II Corps' left. Both corps were to advance against the southern lines the following morning. The II Corps was also ordered to extend its lines parallel with the VI Corps, plugging the gap between Wright and the rest of the army.

Barlow was assigned the pivotal role of holding the left flank of the II Corps. On the morning of 22 June, he received three sets of orders which created consternation and confusion. The first, reaching him at 4:50 A. M., instructed him to synchronize his movements with Wright to ensure a link-up of the separated

Federal forces. At 7:30 A. M., he was told to close with both Wright
on his left and Mott's division on his right, a more difficult feat
which required coordination with the formations on either side
of his own. Once completed, however, the Federal line would be
restored. Shortly afterward the plan was drastically—disastrously—altered. Wright had difficulty making headway against
the Confederates and the VI Corps was unable to close up with
Barlow. The II Corps had pushed forward considerably beyond
Wright's men and much closer to the rebel lines. At 10:00 A. M.,
Barlow received fresh orders from Meade telling him he "will not
be dependent on any movement of the Sixth Corps."[18] In effect,
this meant Barlow was to advance against the enemy with his
left flank in the air and open to attack.

Hancock's chief of staff, Morgan, met Barlow shortly after he
had received the new orders. Morgan thought that a mistake had
been made, as it seemed obvious to him that such a move would
"imperil much of the command." Morgan rode back to Corps
headquarters where Birney confirmed that the II Corps was to
press forward without regard to the progress of the VI Corps.
While Morgan was conferring with Birney, Meade made a personal visit to Barlow. Barlow told the army commander that there
was some misunderstanding as to whether he should link up with
his right or left. Meade replied "You can not connect with both;
keep your connection to the right; each corps must look out for
itself."[19] On Morgan's return to Barlow's headquarters the two
men discussed the dangers in the ensuing operations. Barlow
was worried about leaving his left flank in such an exposed state.
He informed II Corps headquarters that his only connection with
the VI Corps consisted solely of a good skirmish line, which could
not "resist an attack of any force."[20]

Barlow led his men forward from their entrenchments into
the thickly wooded terrain that concealed whatever Confederate
forces lay in front of him. He executed a right wheeling movement
in an attempt to keep his link with Mott's division on his right,
but the maneuver thrust his division out so far in front of Wright
and the rest of the II Corps that it now became vulnerable to attacks from two sides. To protect his vulnerable left flank, he
placed his two reserve brigades on a right angle to his main line
hoping they would detect and repulse any attempt to take him
from that direction. Neither Barlow nor any other Federal officer
seemed aware that Lee and A. P. Hill had been monitoring the
clumsy Union advance and had discovered the gap in the Yankee
lines. While Wright probed slowly forward and Barlow attempted

to get his division in a suitable defensive position, Mahone and Wilcox's divisions slipped through the dense woods and made ready to strike the unwary Yankee troops.

Having completed the right wheel, Barlow's men rested in the woods where the heavy greenery made it impossible to see from one end of a company to another. Some of the men were, in the words of a regimental chronicler, "monkeying around," others were filling canteens when the rebels came screaming out of the woods at them.[21] St. Clair Mulholland, colonel and historian of the 116th Pennsylvania, described the rebel attack as "more than a surprise. It was an astonishment."[22] Barlow, anxious about his exposed position, was reconnoitering on horseback in front of his advanced line when firing broke out between Hill's advance elements and his own skirmishers. Although First Division pickets briefly drove off the rebel skirmishers, they could not see the size of the main force moving against them. Sensing trouble, Barlow ordered changes in the disposition of his forward lines, and rode back to Miles in order to pull him back to the rifle pits which were dug the night before and where he now intended to reestablish a common front with the VI Corps. But before he could change his deployments, Hill's veterans struck in force. Mahone and Wilcox crashed into Barlow's lead brigades almost simultaneously, and their men, who seemed to be everywhere, unleashed devastating fire into the stunned Yankees. Some northerners remembered the rebels breaking through on the left and then the right. Others believed the real collapse occurred when Confederates got around Barlow's right and even towards his rear. Whichever direction the Confederates came from—and it was probably both, the Yankees "skedaddled" and fled back towards their rifle pits in confusion.

The soldiers' panic was heightened by their inability to see what was coming at them. Barlow was himself unsure of how many rebels were assaulting him. "The bullets now came fast and our men began to fire, although no foeman could be seen in the hazy woods," was the way one participant described it.[23] Though he later discounted reports of a sizable body of Confederates, Barlow admitted, "In the thick woods it was impossible to tell what the force of the enemy was unless you were among them."[24]

Undoubtedly, the difficulty in making out the enemy, who seemed to be firing on them from all sides, stampeded Barlow's men and the Confederates captured large numbers of those who tried to flee as well as those who stood and made a fight if it. The exposed position and forward thrusting alignment of the northern regiments meant that as each body fell back the left of the next became exposed. As Barlow's men withdrew in disorder, Gibbon and Mott became vulnerable to the oncoming rebels. The second brigade of the Second Division quickly collapsed and four small regiments simply surrendered on Confederate demand. Mott lost four guns as his line gave way. On Barlow's front, Miles and his brigade held off the southerners until they exhausted their ammunition when they too were forced to join the rest of the division in retreating to their rifle pits. Once back in their works Barlow, Birney, and the other two division commanders were able to restore order, and Hill's attack was brought up short. Nevertheless, the rebels had gotten close enough to Birney's headquarters that artillery round shot flew around the officers' tents.[25]

Although they held their original positions and linked up with Wright the next day, the II Corps had been punched hard, and Barlow had been handed the kind of rough treatment he was accustomed to inflicting on his opponents. In the Battle of the Jerusalem Plank Road (also called the Battle of the Weldon Railroad) the II Corps losses were mostly in prisoners, 1700 in total. This was a larger number of prisoners than the corps had lost on the Peninsula, Antietam, Fredericksburg, and Chancellorsville combined.[26] Barlow also suffered heavily in his own personal staff. Since their commander frequently led from the front and undertook some of the army's most desperate assignments, Barlow's staff officers often found themselves going to the hottest places on the battlefield. Barlow once made a caustic comment about "using up his staff in a damn short time," a remark which some remembered bitterly after the battle.[27] Three of Barlow's staff officers, Derrickson, Brady, and Alexander were captured at the Jerusalem Plank Road, and Bird and Black were wounded.[28]

The main cause of the debacle was the gap between Wright and Birney, which Hill's Confederates had effectively exploited. Birney cited the gap as the decisive factor in the defeat, but also mentioned the large number of new, inexperienced troops in explaining the corps' poor performance in battle.[29] This opinion was supported by George Kelly of the 57th New York who later recalled "how, in my flight, I hopped over many fat haversacks which had been thrown away, probably by new recruits or conscripts, of whom there were many now in the army, and some of them sadly impaired the morale of the rest."[30] Barlow was more explicit in the report he wrote immediately after the battle. He too, identified the separation between the corps as the crucial element, but went on to state, "that the troops did not meet the attack with courage and determination. The brigades of my front line (Second and Third) are too unsteady from the loss of commanding and other officers and other causes, to be much depended on in circumstances requiring much nerve and determination."[31]

Few of the troops knew of Meade's orders sending Barlow forward with his flank in the air and at least some blamed him for the rebel breakthrough. Indeed, among the troops at least, the II Corps' rout became widely known as "Barlow's Skedaddle."[32] J. B. Hallinbeck wrote to Robert S. Robertson of Miles's staff, recuperating from his wound at Totopotomoy Creek, that "Barlow made a h-ll of a 'bull' the other day. He advanced his Division without any connection on his right or left and the consequence was we were flanked."[33] Hallinbeck gave Miles's brigade credit for changing position and holding the rebels back while "Barlow was endeavoring to rally the 2nd, 3rd, and 4th Brigs [sic] in which he partially succeeded." Nevertheless, Hallinbeck claimed that "Barlow's stock is below par and the most bitter feelings exist towards him by every officer and man throughout the Div. while Miles' stock is at a premium."[34] Hallinbeck also made it clear that he blamed Barlow for the severe losses among staff officers.

Hallinbeck's harsh assessment of Barlow's leadership stemmed from his ignorance of Meade's role in the affair, and Barlow's attempts to adjust his orders to prevent just such a debacle. But such a negative appraisal reveals resentments some officers and men held towards the young general. Barlow was hard and arrogant. He had his favorites, and he could act cold and aloof. The perceived failures of a commander as belligerent and harsh as Barlow may have provided the opening to vent accumulated grievances and animosities. There were those who judged Barlow overly rash in combat and some believed his reputation as a tough and aggressive fighter had been won at the expense of his men.[35]

Nor was Hallinbeck the only participant who laid the blame for the Corps' thrashing at Barlow's feet. John Haley of the 17th Maine wrote that Barlow took his men beyond his supports and then "went out in front of his line to a brook to bathe his feet," leaving his men unprepared for the rebel onslaught.[36] The charge lacks credibility. Had Barlow ridden forward and then dismounted to wash his feet, he would likely have been snatched up by the advancing rebels. If not, he would have had to ride for his life which would have been seen and reported. Regardless, the tale is valuable since it provides further evidence of how Barlow was perceived by some soldiers. It also suggests that Hancock's outburst on hearing that Barlow had stopped to attend his feet on arriving at Petersburg had become common knowledge—or, Barlow's fondness for the practice had passed into army lore. It seems likely many soldiers considered Barlow odd. His superior demeanor, hyperaggressiveness, obsessive protocol, youthful appearance and occasionally idiosyncratic behavior—climbing trees, washing his feet along the march, affecting a cavalry saber—may well have nurtured such a reputation. Even his friend Lyman considered some of his behavior as eccentric. Certainly Haley's explanation of what went wrong at the Jerusalem Plank Road supports the likelihood that Barlow was thought peculiar. "General Barlow is chiefly censurable for the entire transaction," Haley wrote, "It is an open secret that Barlow isn't just right in his head, and his performance lends strength to this insinuation."[37]

The Battle of the Jerusalem Plank Road proved, though the warning signs were there before, that the II Corps had become a ghost of its former self. Once the Army of the Potomac's strongest corps—its shock troops—the II Corps was now possibly the weakest. Condensing the May–June experience of the II Corps to a single jarring sentence, historian Bruce Catton wrote, "During the last two months almost all of the good men [in the II Corps] had been shot."[38] This was no exaggeration. Hancock's regiments suffered 20,000 casualties between 5 May and 23 June. More than twenty brigade commanders were killed or wounded with almost 100 regimental leaders suffering the same fate.[39] While the II Corps may have suffered most grievously in the fighting, Grant's campaigns had wreaked like devastation in the entire Army of the Potomac. Somewhat over 100,000 men left the Rapidan on 3 May. 60,000 of them had been shot. As a result, most of the 86,000 men on the Army's rolls in June were new men.[40] Even the best of them would require time to learn how to act effectively as soldiers and officers. Barlow himself was not immune from the strain resulting from the near incessant fighting, brutal heat, and the sight of so many of his men and officers being ground up in ineffective frontal assaults. In the end, even he found it impossible to keep maintain his verve and sangfroid indefinitely.

Francis did reap one benefit from the fight at the Jerusalem Plank Road. A Confederate colonel was captured riding what was described as a "superb" gray horse. Barlow bought it from the colonel, who would have no immediate need of it and was in no position to decline his offer. Troops noted how the "splendid animal became very fond of the General and would follow him around the camp begging for the lumps of sugar that the General would be pretty sure to have in his pocket with which to treat his equine friend."[41]

Barlow summed up the actions at Petersburg as "a whirl of marching and picket fighting . . . all of which has accomplished nothing."[42] Regarding the 22 June battle, Barlow wrote home vaguely that the "whole line had to fall back rapidly, by reason of the enemy appearing on our flank."[43] From his personal staff Barlow lost an aide, two staff officers, and an ordnance officer who he thought "were probably gobbled up by the rebs in confusion."[44] In the fighting before Petersburg from 13 June to 26 June Barlow's division suffered 2276 casualties, the highest number of losses suffered by any of the II Corps divisions.[45] Barlow seemed depressed by the inconclusive and bloody campaign, which had culminated in the semi-siege, and promised to drag on indefinitely. "Things do not look very bright," he confessed. As he had before when frustrated and annoyed by the inadequacies of the army, Barlow threatened to resign as soon as the campaign was over. He thought he could gain some position in the government service, but if not he was certain he could resume a successful career as a lawyer.[46]

Like most men in the Army, Barlow was keenly interested in the way the newspapers reported the war—especially when his name was mentioned. He was often either amused or disgusted by the papers' explanation and interpretations of events and had warned his family in the early days of the war not to trust all that they read. Newspaper accounts of his role in the first month's fighting before Petersburg he denounced as "nonsense."[47] His condemnation of newspaper reports grew more heated when he read newspaper accounts blaming the defeat at the Jerusalem Plank Road on his division. "It's an unmitigated lie," he wrote his brother Richard, going on to say he had written a letter to the papers to contradict it. Regarding his share of the blame in the near rout of the Second Division in the battle Barlow stated, "Gibbon was attacked on his own front independent of us and must bear his own burdens."[48]

At least to his brother, Barlow downplayed the setback. He totaled his losses as 240 prisoners and was satisfied he had lost no guns, colors, or suffered the destruction of regimental organization.[49] The version of events that he gave Richard was accurate as far as it went. Gibbon's men had broken and some units surrendered wholesale. But, Gibbon's retreat was at least partly caused by the rout of the First Division and Barlow's official report was more somber than his letter home. The difference between his official and personal remarks on the battle probably stems from his indignation over the newspaper report and, perhaps, a common soldier's habit of downplaying dangers and losses—and reverses.

Not everything Barlow read in the press was critical. On 9 July, *Harper's Weekly* ran a profile of the First Division's commander. Basically a puff-piece, possibly intended to buck up homefront morale which had not received much positive news from the Petersburg front, the article was accompanied by a line drawing of Barlow which overemphasized his youthful appearance. After explaining that General Francis Channing Barlow was "more familiarly known as General Frank Barlow" the article went on to declare that "throughout the campaign Barlow [was] conspicuous among the noble band of united heroes, officers and men, in the very active front of battle. He is just thirty years old, but he has made a name that the history of American liberty will forever honor."[50] The *Harper's* writer did not neglect Arabella in his praise. "The men of General Barlow's division," he continued, "would never forgive his biographer who should omit to record the unwearied service in the hospitals and among the wounded and dying Union soldiers from the beginning of the war to this day, of [Barlow's] faithful and devoted wife." Barlow no doubt dismissed the gushy article, at least as regards himself, as journalistic fluff. On the other hand, in a campaign in which nothing seemed to be going well, and where he had been subjected to unexpected criticism from within and without of the army, receiving public words of praise, even if overblown, may have been a pleasant change.

After the Battle of the Jerusalem Plank Road, the II Corps settled in for a continuous round of picket duty, skirmishing, and bombardment and counterbombardment. Barlow was well acquainted with the muggy Tidewater climate from the Peninsula Campaign, yet in the trenches in front of Petersburg the summer seemed exceptionally brutal. The situation was worsened by a near absence of rain since the torrents which drenched both armies at Spotsylvania. Lyman described the weather as sweltering. "The region is so beclouded with dust and smoke of burning forests . . . and so unrelieved by any green grass, or water, that the heat is doubled."[51] Barlow responded to the enervating heat by stripping down to his drawers and shirt whenever he was in his tent.[52] It was in just such garb that Lyman found him when he called for a visit in early July. Although his leisure-time dress was decidedly unmilitary, Barlow told Lyman his men were rested and he was ready for another go at the rebels. If the assault were of "real importance" he told Lyman, he'd lead it himself, as he wanted "no more trifling."[53] In light of the intensity of the combat in front of the railroad town, Lyman confessed he found Barlow's ideas of "trifling" as "peculiar." What the general probably meant was decisive.

Barlow was hardly the only officer to dispense with unnecessary clothing whenever possible. During lulls in the fighting, Hancock could sometimes be found wearing a simple white shirt and blue pantaloons. Barlow continued to affect the casual, careless dress that accentuated his youth and added to his aura of almost daredevil aggressiveness. When not lounging in his tent, he was usually seen in a checked shirt and old blue trousers when the situation allowed.[54] Whether he had more than one such shirt, or simply kept washing out a single such item, is not known. Yet, the combination, with the ubiquitous saber, had become his signature battle dress for the 1864 campaign.

Barlow derived some pleasure from another visit by his old friend Winslow Homer. Homer had frequently stayed with Barlow when he journeyed to the front lines and his sojourns with his distant cousin's commands had born fruit in numerous sketches, which often appeared in newspapers, or served as the basis of later paintings. Homer arrived at the Petersburg front shortly after the initial assaults and immediately began drawing what he saw. Some of his first sketches at Petersburg were of casualties from the II Corps opening attacks. *Wounded Soldier Being Given a Drink From a Canteen, 1864* may well depict Second Lieutenant Morton Havens of the 7th New York Heavy Artillery, who had suffered a head wound from a shell fragment during the 16 June attack.[55] Homer also made the preliminary drawings which were incorporated in one of the most famous of all Civil War paintings, *Prisoners from the Front,* that features an officer who looks like Barlow examining three Confederate prisoners. Homer's stay at Petersburg also led to the dramatic *Defiance: Inviting a Shot,* which presents a young Confederate soldier standing brazenly atop his earthworks defying Yankee snipers.

In addition to his own duties, Barlow kept abreast of the course of the war in other theaters and never felt constrained from offering his opinion on the conduct of other officers and men. In the middle of July, Barlow became enraged at the success General Jubal Early had enjoyed in driving Federal forces out of the Shenandoah Valley and raiding into Maryland as far as the defenses of Washington. Early's force comprised the bulk of Lee's Second Corps. Having successfully parried all of Grant's thrusts before Petersburg, the Confederate commander felt confident enough to detach Early and send him to the Valley to clear a Federal force operating there. Barlow was convinced Early faced no opposition until the VI Corps was dispatched to the scene. He denounced the Battle of Monocacy, generally considered a successful delaying action by the Union command in the area, as "disgraceful." Intemperate as always when he vented his indignation, Barlow was infuriated that a relatively small rebel force had penetrated so close to Washington before turning back. "I am only sorry that [Early's force] did not destroy every man and thing in Maryland and Pennsylvania," he wrote bitterly.[56] Barlow was especially infuriated by the behavior of Union citizens compared to their southern counterparts. He could not understand why no one had counted Early's troops, which he believed would have demonstrated how few in number the Confederates were. In contrast, Barlow stated that the northern soldiers "could not march a mile into the South without the Confederate government knowing what force we have." Barlow ended his tirade on Early's raid with the wish that the rebels had burned Baltimore and Washington.[57]

Though Barlow never showed much interest in controlling his temper, the heated language and tantrum-like outbursts in summer 1864 owed much to the accumulating stresses and frustrations of the campaign. He might have felt less angry had he known of new plans laid by Grant and Meade to breach the rebel lines by means of a mine. The tunnel, constructed by troops from the Pennsylvania coal country, was to be filled with enough explosives to blow a hole in the Confederate lines, allowing the Union troops to make the long desired breakthrough. Unaware of these preparations, Barlow was puzzled by the lack of any major action since the end of June and thought it strange that Grant would not try Lee's defenses while Early was away in the Shenandoah Valley. He expressed little confidence in the success of the siege operations before Petersburg. "I do not believe we shall starve out the rebel army by cutting the rail roads even if we could keep them cut. The inhabitants of Richmond and Petersburg may suffer but I believe they have enough rations to subsist their army all summer."[58] In terms of time, Barlow was prophetic. It would take all summer, winter, and the first few weeks of spring before the rebel lines before Petersburg were weakened enough to crack.

Nor were military operations the only cause of Barlow's ragged emotions and hair-trigger temper. As was so often the case, Arabella's work as a Sanitary Commission nurse brought her to the hospitals set up behind the battlefields where Frank was fighting. Despite her occasional proximity, their companionship during the Overland-Petersburg campaign was primarily a case of catch-as-catch-can. On 11 June, Arabella left the Tyler House near Cold Harbor and accompanied the wounded to the Union base at White House on the Pamunkey. From there she shipped out to City Point, destined to become the Union Army's major supply center and Grant's headquarters for the next nine months. She made her way to the First Division field hospital on 18 June just as the opening days' battles before Petersburg were coming to an end, and immediately began distributing food and drink to the wounded.[59] The hospital was located at the Henry Bryant house situated on a 264-acre farm three miles northwest of Prince George County courthouse.[60] In fact, it was she, along with some of her assistants, who gave the aforementioned Lieutenant Havens the first food or drink he received since being wounded.[61]

Whatever consolation Barlow may have received from his wife's presence turned to worry when she fell sick. Diseases were rife in military camps and hospitals, and Arabella apparently contracted an infection while ministering to the sick and wounded. Her condition deteriorated to the point where she had to relinquish her own duties and seek better treatment than was available in the hospitals at City Point. She took the steamer to Washington where she was cared for by friends, but soon decided to return to the front—and Frank. But her condition worsened and on 6 July, Arabella said goodbye to Frank at his headquarters near George W. Alley's farm on the Jerusalem Plank Road and prepared to return again to Washington. Frank walked her over to the First Division field hospital at "Bell Hill."[62] Unable to leave his command at the time, Barlow asked Dr. William W. Potter, one of the division surgeons, to escort her back to the transports at City Point. Potter and Arabella made the trip in an old family carriage which was found in a barn on the Smith estate. Although she made no complaint, the doctor thought she did not look well.[63]

Presumably, once back in Washington, Arabella could relax, recuperate, and receive more sophisticated medical treatment than was available in Virginia. Barlow was deeply concerned for his wife's health and described the high fever which accompanied her illness as dangerous. Nevertheless, she seemed to rally, and by 15 June, Barlow received word that the fever had broken.[64] He

anticipated a full recovery for her, but the burden of worry must
have weighed heavily on him. And his relief was premature.

During this period of inactivity and frustrations of war the
possibility of service with a black organization reappeared. On
12 June, Cornelia Hancock reported that Barlow was to be appointed chief of the Freedmen's Bureau. Whether she was repeating a rumor or was told something by Barlow is not clear. In her
estimation, he was just the man for the job. On a more practical
level, she hoped that her acquaintanceship with him would lead
to a job in the Bureau for her brother.[65] Whether or not a serious
opportunity for Barlow to join the Bureau still existed is unknown. What is certain is that he received no such appointment
and it was not mentioned again.

Although Barlow himself said nothing about a Freedmen's Bureau position at Petersburg, he continued to probe the feasibility
of joining what he now called the "darkey corps." Although the
Federal Army was segregated, and blacks confined to black regiments, the officers were white, and the government was especially interested in attracting proven, effective officers, to insure
that the experiment with raising black units would succeed.

In July, as he chaffed against the seeming futility of the Petersburg operations, Barlow toyed again with the prospect of leading
a black unit—certainly, a brigade if not a division. One of his
confidants was an officer named Forbes, but he also discussed
the possibility of getting an assignment with blacks with Charles
Dana, Brook Farm alumnus and Assistant Secretary of War, who
spent much time with the Army during the Overland Campaign
and the ensuing operations around Petersburg. Barlow's dislike
of slavery, and stated belief that anti-slavery men were the most
committed in the Army, did not make him particularly sensitive
to the position of the newly freed slaves as his use of the southern slang term attests. That he was capable of even more crass
language is illustrated by his remark, "If I go into the nigger business I ought to get a few days home."[66] In any event, Barlow's
somewhat desultory efforts to secure a black command bore no
fruit. He would finish the war where he began it—in the II Corps.

The involvement of Barlow's brothers in the war is not completely clear. At various times they spent time with him at camp,
apparently serving as volunteer aides. Edward Emerson Barlow,
Francis's older brother, put in a stint as an assistant adjutant
general with the rank of captain. Edward's official tour of duty
in this capacity ran from 27 October 1862, when Francis was out
of action due to the Antietam wound, to 30 July 1863, which en-

compassed the battles of Chancellorsville and Gettysburg where his brother was again wounded.[67] Edward seems to have spent some time with the Army of the Potomac's headquarters staff before joining his brother's staff in May 1863.[68] In June 1864, during breaks in the fighting on the Petersburg front, Barlow spoke of securing commissary positions for his brothers, though it is uncertain if they came through.[69] However, Richard was apparently employed at the Brooklyn Navy Yard during the previous year. Whether his brother helped arrange that post is unknown, but likely.[70] Richard never seems to have held an official position in the Army, and both he and Edward were generally visitors rather than participants.

Francis was never loath to secure advantage for family members and friends, and while at home Edward and Richard apparently watched over investments in which he was also a partner. At one point Frank asked for his portion in the *Enchantress,* a vessel in which the Barlows had invested. While fighting off flies and fatigue in his tent, Francis suggested that Edward find a position in the Quartermaster's depot in New York, which he thought should be easy to obtain. Barlow believed he could get the job for his brother if he could be sure it "was a good one"—by which he apparently meant lucrative.[71] Barlow was willing to use his influence to benefit family friends as well as relatives. He informed his brother Richard that he could secure a position for Richard's friend in the Commissary if the man would commit himself and come to Virginia.[72]

One last bit of domestic business to which Barlow attended in the respite after the June battles was the publication of the photographs Brady had taken after Cold Harbor. Copies reached the army and Barlow obtained some. He thought the photograph with all the staff officers was inferior, but he reported that the one with Hancock and the divisional commanders was considered good, "though I do not like mine. I presume no one likes their own."[73] Nevertheless, Barlow asked for four or five of each pose to be sent to him.

Continually seeking a soft spot in Lee's defenses, Grant began to pair his attacks at the Petersburg front with strikes north of the James. If Lee sent reinforcements to bolster his lines before Richmond, he would leave himself weaker at Petersburg. If one attack failed, the other would presumably have a better chance of success. In theory the one-two punch made sense, but, as usual, the execution proved difficult. This was especially true since Grant did not strike both wings of the rebel army simultaneously until autumn.[74] In late July, Grant initiated a two-prong offensive intended to find a weakness in the Confederate line and secure a major breakthrough. Using his superior numbers Grant prepared to launch an attack north of the James at Deep Bottom, divert Confederate strength from the Petersburg lines, and then spring another attack against the hopefully undermanned defenses at Petersburg. The II Corps was given the task of assaulting the Confederate works in the Deep Bottom sector. The mine, which the IX Corps had been digging, was almost completed, and the Federal general-in-chief intended the Deep Bottom operation to draw off troops which Lee might use to counter a breakthrough when the mine exploded. Grant had also grown unhappy with Meade's performance as commander of the Army of the Potomac and was considering replacing him. Hancock seemed an obvious choice. If the II Corps commander performed well at Deep Bottom a change in army commanders might be made.[75]

Meade and Grant both saw several potential advantages to the Deep Bottom operation. The most optimistic, if least likely, result was the possibility that Hancock would break the rebel line on the north side of the James and force the southerners back towards Chaffin's Bluff. If Hancock were successful in making such a penetration, Sheridan's cavalry, which was also involved in the offensive, would make a lunge for Richmond and take the capital. Should that appear impossible, Sheridan was to raid north of Richmond and sever the two railroad lines as far north as the Anna rivers. If nothing else, Hancock and Sheridan would hopefully convince Lee to send reinforcements across the James, leaving the Petersburg front more lightly defended when Burnside's mine went off.

On the afternoon of 26 July, Hancock's men were pulled out of their lines, and marched around the Federal positions. At 2:00 A. M. the next morning, the II Corps, led by Barlow's division, began to cross the James near Deep Bottom, where Butler's men had established a bridgehead on the northern bank. Originally, the II Corps was to cross on the upper, or west, bridge, but the Confederate defenses forced a change of plan. The rebels had set up strong entrenchments facing the bridge, and Meade authorized Hancock to use the lower bridge.[76] The shift in jump-off points from the upper to lower bridges meant that Bailey's Creek lay now between the II Corps and its primary objective, Chaffin's Bluff. To prevent the Confederate pickets from detecting the northern movements during the night crossing, straw was strewn on the pontoon bridge to muffle the sound of marching columns. The

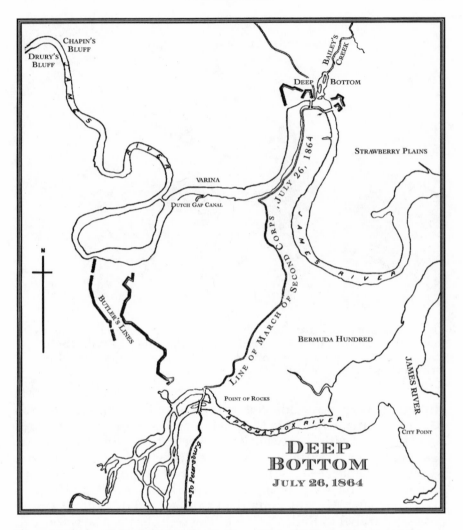

Deep Bottom, July 26, 1864. From Francis A. Walker, *History of the Second Army Corps*, **1887.**

march, as Barlow remembered it, was a "severe one" with bad roads and considerable straggling. By daybreak, Hancock confided to Humphries that the advantage of surprise was lost.[77] Nevertheless, the II Corps proceeded to test the Confederate lines with the First Division again in the van, the Third Division on its right, and Sheridan holding the right flank.

The first encounter with the rebels went smoothly. Coming up against Confederate positions along the New Market-Malvern

First Deep Bottom, July 27th, 1864. Nelson Miles' brigade captures four 20 lb. Parrott guns. The Confederate gunners flee with their sponge staffs to render the cannon at least temporarily unusable. Drawing by William Waud. *Library of Congress.*

Hill Road, Miles's brigade, led by the 28th Massachusetts, which had been transferred from the Irish Brigade, captured a series of rifle pits along with four twenty-pounder Parrott guns. Barlow was again in the forefront of the charge, right behind his skirmishers, wearing his checkered shirt, suspenders hanging over his hips, and his saber flashing in the sun.[78] The Confederates pulled back across the New Market-Long Bridge Road and dug into a strong position parallel to Bailey's Creek. The southern works were situated about 1000 yards behind the creek with a wide swatch of open land in front of them providing an excellent killing ground for the defenders.[79] Unsure where the Confederate line ended, Barlow sent the 26th Michigan, his only western regiment, forward to develop the southern flank. The regiment came under such intense fire that Barlow went personally forward and withdrew it to safety. While Barlow had gained some knowledge of the southern deployments on his front, he remained uncertain of the exact terminus of the rebel line.[80]

Other than Miles's capture of the four guns, little had been achieved by the Deep Bottom operation. On the night of 27 July, the Confederates reinforced their position along Bailey Creek. Grant, having become more cautious about frontal assaults, instructed Hancock not to attack but to see if he could turn the southern line. Before he could do so, the rebels began to probe the Federal lines and Hancock, sensing a counterattack, pulled his men back to a position near their original jumping-off lines. No assault was made. That evening Meade and Grant visited Hancock. Grant was convinced that the operation had at least succeeded in draining off men from Lee's lines at Petersburg and Mott's division was returned to Petersburg. Barlow and Gibbon remained to make demonstrations all day on 29 July to convince the southerners another attack was in the offing. Grant then ordered the First and Second Divisions back to their Petersburg position, and the entire Corps was again south of the James by 30 July—just in time for the men to watch the fiasco of the explosion of the mine and the ensuing Battle of the Crater.

Casualties suffered during the Deep Bottom operation of 27–29 July were light. Barlow's division, which had done the bulk of what fighting there was, suffered ninety-six casualties, only sixteen men being killed outright.[81] In light of the horrendous losses that had been incurred for small gain throughout May and June, the relatively light losses at Deep Bottom may have seemed a relief. Yet, low casualties could not assuage the knowledge that another attempt on Lee's lines—two if the fiasco at the Crater is included—had failed. Worse, the First Division was now regularly performing well short of its former effectiveness. And the deadlock at Petersburg showed no signs of ending.

8

Collapse and Resurgence

NELSON MILES COMMANDED THE FIRST DIVISION WHEN IT RE-
turned to its Petersburg encampment. On 28 July, Barlow received word that the redoubtable Arabella had died the previous
day of typhus in a military hospital in Washington. Throughout
the Overland and Petersburg campaigns, Frank and Belle had
managed to see each other as often as the whirlwind of fighting
allowed. They met several times at Cold Harbor, and Arabella's
service at the Petersburg front and nearby City Point hospitals
allowed the two to visit each other during lulls in the fighting.
But by early July, Arabella was exhibiting serious signs of illness
and fatigue. In a 2 July letter to his family, Francis described her
as dangerously sick and "all run down with a fever."[1] Four days
later, she left the Virginia front for Washington. Francis never
saw her alive again. Apparently she rallied for a while and on 15
July Barlow rejoiced that "her fever is broken and in time she
will be well again."[2] But such was not to be, and news of Arabella's
death was a bitter blow. Barlow, in the words of Theodore Lyman,
"was entirely incapacitated by this sudden grief,"[3] and stories
spread among the troops that Arabella's death "had driven Barlow insane."[4]

Hancock supplied a tug to carry Barlow from Deep Bottom,
and the stricken general turned his command over to his most
trusted lieutenant and friend, Nelson Miles, commander of his
first brigade. Barlow received a 15-day leave of absence to attend
to funeral arrangements and deal with his heartache.[5] Arabella
was buried in her hometown of Somerville, New Jersey. A stone
later erected over her grave, a white marble marker of the type
favored by mid-nineteenth-century Americans, bears her full
maiden name, Arabella Wharton Griffith. Beneath her name
carved in smaller italics runs the legend, "wife of Francis C. Barlow." In 1996, the local Somerville American Legion post placed

Gravestone and Memorial Plaque to Arabella Wharton Griffith Barlow, Somerville, New Jersey. *Author's Collection.*

a bronze plaque under the stone recounting her service as a military nurse and specifically including her importance in restoring Francis to health after his two woundings.

Barlow's letters to and from Arabella have not survived, and far less is known about their relationship than is desirable. Surely, her continual efforts to serve close to him, and his obvious enjoyment of her companionship, indicate that their union was strong, devoted, and affectionate. If Barlow wrote his family about his wife's death, those letters have not survived either. We can assume his family and hers, certainly his brothers, rallied around to provide sympathy and whatever aid they could. Those who knew Arabella and her tireless work in the military hospitals were stunned and saddened by her death. Belle and Frank's friend, the inveterate New York diarist and Sanitary Commission official, George Templeton Strong, read of Arabella's death in the *New York Post*. He recalled that on his previous visit to Washington, he had found her ill from disease she had contracted in the hospitals near Fredericksburg and Belle Plain. "She did great service there," Strong wrote. "She was a very noble woman."[6]

Those who had served with Arabella in the military hospitals during Grant's struggle with Lee lauded her work and deeply lamented her demise. Helen L. Gilson, who worked with Arabella among the wounded at Petersburg, was deeply moved by Arabella's passing. In a letter home to a friend two weeks after Belle died she wrote, "You say I am getting familiar with death. Yes; but death wears its most solemn aspect when it touches our individual lives. Sometimes it makes terrible voids in our hearts. I groaned aloud last night, so heavy was my heart, when I knew I should not again see Mrs. Barlow."[7] Dr. W. H. Reed ascribed Arabella's death to her labors in the "poisonous swamps of the Pamunkey" and the "malarial districts of City Point." Working ceaselessly in the scorching Virginia sun, Arabella, according to Reed, was

neither conscious that she was working beyond her strength, nor realiz[ed] the extreme exhaustion of her system, [so] she fainted at her work and found, only when it was too late, that the raging fever was wasting her life away. It was strength of will which sustained her in this intense activity, when her poor, tired body was trying to assert its own right to repose. Yet to the last, her sparkling wit, her brilliant intellect, her unfailing good humor, lightened up our moments of rest and recreation. So many memories of her beautiful constancy and self-sacrifice, of her bright and genial companionship, of her rich and glowing sympathies, of her warm and loving nature, come back to me, that I feel how inadequate any tribute I could pay her is worth.[8]

Nor were praiseful elegies confined to personal remarks or written remembrances. In an obituary titled "The Death of Mrs. General Barlow," *Harper's Weekly* extolled Arabella's service to the wounded as "amiable, accomplished, admired [and] beloved." The encomium concluded, "Mrs. Barlow from the first has been among the most eminent of the many heroines in this war whose names are not loudly mentioned, but whose memory will be forever fresh in the grateful hearts of their friends and country."[9] However deeply Barlow hurt for his lost wife, he was forced to cut his mourning period far short of the Victorian norm. On 13 August, Francis reported back from his leave of absence and resumed command of the First Division.

Barlow returned to command just in time to take part in another attempt by Grant to force Lee back towards the Confederate capital on the north side of the James. With troops from Lee's Second Corps detached to the Shenandoah Valley, Grant concluded that Lee's lines had been thinned out. Unbeknownst to Grant, however, Lee had dispatched only two of the Second Corps' three divisions to the Valley, and retained a stronger counterpunching capacity than the lieutenant general assumed. Grant opted for a replay of the Deep Bottom operation, using plans virtually identical to those of the previous July. Once again the attack called for Hancock to move his Corps across the James and assume operational control over the X Corps. The latter had already occupied a bridgehead position under the leadership of Hancock's former Third Division commander, David Birney. The X Corps was to attack almost directly west against the southern positions at New Market Heights, while the II Corps pushed inland and then turned west towards Richmond. Following the model of the previous operation, Gershom Mott would push his division up the New Market-Malvern Hill Road, and drive the rebels back to their old line on the west side of Bailey Creek. Barlow would move to Mott's right and attack near the Jenning's House. If he were successful in ripping a hole in the rebel line, Barlow was to shift left and "uncover" Mott who would be free to move up the New Market Road towards Richmond.

For the renewed Deep Bottom offensive, Hancock placed Barlow in command of both the First and Second Divisions. Francis Walker described Hancock's motives for giving Barlow this double responsibility in some detail. Hancock, he wrote, wanted to give Barlow a chance to get the

promotion which he coveted with the just ambition of a faithful soldier, and which he had abundantly merited for his services from the

Po to the Appomattox. General Hancock knew, moreover, that Barlow was an officer, not only of dauntless courage, but of great energy; and he desired the enterprise of this day to be prosecuted with the utmost vigor. Finally, he was influenced by the consideration that Barlow had held that part of the line from which the attack was to be made, at Deep Bottom in July.[10]

Unfortunately, Barlow was in no condition to shoulder the burdens of such an operation. Still shaken by the death of his wife, he was also suffering from dysentery, a debilitating disease which could result in death.[11] Although Barlow attempted to carry on as though nothing was wrong, both his energy and thinking were dulled by his deteriorating physical condition. Whatever hopes he and Hancock nurtured, the renewed attempt north of the James was to prove more frustrating and disappointing than the first.

The success of the Second Deep Bottom operation depended on speed. As far as possible, the men in the ranks were encouraged to think the corps was being pulled back to Washington to deal with Early. It was hoped any rebel ears gathering up soldier scuttlebutt for the Army of Northern Virginia would pass along this piece of disinformation. The plan called for the use of steamboats to ferry the Corps across the James in the belief that the appearance of large vessels increased the likelihood that the Confederates would fall for the ruse. The use of the boats, however, created problems for Hancock. In order to disembark the men quickly, it was expected that the transports would run up almost to shore and thrust their gangplanks out. However, the boats, sixteen in all, were oceangoing or large river craft, and they required deep water to maneuver. No one on Grant or Meade's staff seems to have realized the difficulty in taking them close enough to shore to land the troops.

The II Corps pulled out of its Petersburg position on 12 August and bivouacked at City Point. The heat was relentless—99 degrees—and took its own toll of both officers and men. Seven men from Miles's brigade and 15 from Broady's died of sunstroke on the march to City Point.[12] The troops were scheduled to begin loading on the transports at midnight on 13 August. In the meantime, Hancock grew increasingly concerned about the plan to sail the steamboats close enough to the shore to use the gangplanks. He made a personal visit to the landing site at Deep Bottom and quickly concluded that the nature of the shore and water would make the projected landing difficult. Returning to City Point, he ordered lumber sent

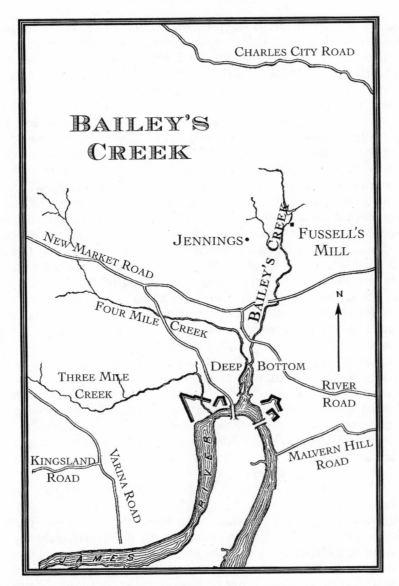

Bailey's Creek. From Francis A. Walker, *History of the Second Army Corps*, 1887.

to Deep Bottom with instructions to put the ruined wharves there in as sound a shape as possible, although such activity would clearly attract Confederate attention. Additionally, Hancock moved up embarkation time from midnight to 10 P. M.[12] It was not enough.

Any chance that the II Corps would achieve the goal of surprise was lost in crossing the James. Conveying the troops in the dark, the transports had to use lights and whistles to prevent ramming each other. In addition to their large draft, the steamers were not well suited as troop carriers, and some men had to cram the upper decks. The ruse of going to Washington initially deceived the soldiers if not the rebels. The men were so delighted to be escaping from the alternately tedious and frightening Petersburg front that some even broke out into song as they crammed on the transports. Their lightheartedness, however, quickly faded when tugs appeared to lead the transports across the River and the realization spread that the real destination was Deep Bottom.[14] The disembarkation, as Hancock had feared, was clumsy and slow. The men began to unload at 2:30 A. M., crowding each other in the dark and narrow passageways and decks. Those on the top decks could only descend in twos and threes. Worse, the vessel ferrying Barlow's fourth brigade became stuck on a sandbar in the James for several hours. Consequently, it was nine in the morning before most of the troops were ashore, and several more hours before the fourth brigade had finally unloaded and caught up with the rest of the First Division.

Hancock had intended for Barlow to keep his division intact and not "develop a battle" until he was properly positioned which ate up even more time. Due to the wooded and broken nature of the land, the II Corps commander himself found the overseeing of his divisions a difficult task. The heat beat down remorselessly— it reached 100 degrees on 14 August—and the advancing union troops passed men lying off to the sides dead from sunstroke. By the time Barlow reached Long Bridge Road 35 percent of his men had fallen from the ranks.[15] Mott reported 105 men overcome with heat from his division.[16]

Again and again, the losses in veteran troops and experienced officers, brutal heat, incessant marching, countermarching, and fighting combined to dull the fighting edge of what had been the Army of the Potomac's elite corps. Barlow experienced a tough time trying to coordinate his units and keep them moving in the concentrated mass necessary to break the rebel lines. The delays at the river prevented him from launching his attacks until noon which gave the Confederates time to begin shifting men from New Market Heights to the northern end of their defenses near Bailey's Creek and Fussell's Mill. Concerned about the rebels exploiting any gap in the Federal lines, Barlow left Smyth's Second Division to preserve his link with Mott leaving him with only his First Division to storm the rebel positions. Maintaining contact with the Third Division blocked any southern attempt to turn his flank and cut him off, but it further slowed the Union advance. Additionally Barlow's decision to keep contact with Mott left his regiments in a strung out formation making it difficult to concentrate them for an assault.[17]

After leaving one brigade to hold the New Market Road, Barlow moved up the Central Road until he came before Confederate entrenchments northwest of Darbytown Road. Feeling the pressure of the time lost in disembarkation, and believing, correctly, the position was only thinly held, Barlow decided to strike immediately before rebel reinforcements could arrive. Without waiting for his full division to come up, he sent Miles's men in against the southern works. Barlow ordered the 2nd New York Heavy Artillery under Major George Hogg to attack on the left while the remainder of the brigade advanced on the right. Barlow was astounded as he watched Hogg's men veer off in the opposite direction. The regiment finally halted in a wood where the remainder of Miles's brigade had stopped after capturing only the outer defenses of the Confederate line. The men became convinced the rebels were reinforcing their front with infantry and artillery and the officers found it impossible to get them to leave the safety of the woods and continue the attack.[18]

Nor were Barlow's other units to do much better. After Miles's attack had stalled, Barlow prepared another thrust with Colonel Levin Crandall's third (Consolidated) brigade. Keeping the balance of the brigade in reserve, he personally formed Major George Byron's third provisional regiment for the attack. Again, he chose to use only part of the force available to him, negating his numerical advantage. The regiment of 252 officers and men constituted the pitiful remains of the Irish Brigade. Barlow told the men that the rifle pits were held only by skirmishers and ordered them to take it with a bayonet charge. Byron's men succeeded in driving the Confederates out of their advanced works from which they fell back across Bailey's Creek and into their trenches below Fussell's Mill. Disregarding Barlow's orders to cross the creek, Byron halted his advance and eventually withdrew to the Federal lines citing lack of support on his flanks as well as raking artillery fire for his decision.[19] While Byron's explanations for withdrawing seem reasonable, Barlow saw it otherwise. The Irish Brigade, he wrote using their traditional name, "behaved disgracefully and failed to execute my orders. They crowded off to our right into the shelter of some woods, and there became shattered and broken to pieces."[20]

Barlow's men in skirmish order "12 miles from Richmond." Probably Deep Bottom, July 27-29 or August 13, 1864. Drawing by Alfred R. Waud. *Library of Congress.*

Barlow's first two attacks at Deep Bottom showed he was not thinking clearly. At this stage of the fighting, he was faced by less than a thousand rebels who were supported by two cannon. Rather than taking time to concentrate his units and create the mass necessary to breach the outmanned southern defenses, he fed his troops into action piecemeal. Although he had 10,000 troops under his command, only a fraction took part in any one assault.[21] Miles's men did not receive the support they needed to crack the Confederate front, and Byron's men charged alone without the rest of their brigade. A larger concentration might have given the men the morale boost they desperately needed as well as the momentum to carry out the task given them.

As Byron's regiment—the former Irish Brigade—fell back, Confederate reinforcements began arriving on the field, and Barlow concluded another assault in that direction was impossible. He then marched his third and fourth brigades a half mile north to a hill facing Fussell's Mill where he hoped to turn the Confederates' left flank. The Southerners had dug entrenchments behind the millpond which gave them a distinct advantage and were well prepared to meet an attack, but Barlow again believed the works were weakly defended. At 3:00 P. M. he organized Broady's fourth brigade into four lines and ordered them to take the position. The sun continued to take its toll on the attacking troops. Thirty-two percent of the fourth brigade had dropped out on the short march to Fussell's Mill leaving Broady with only 856 men for his attack.[22] When they moved forward, the Yankee units did no better than their Celtic counterparts. As Broady's brigade began their assault, Confederate artillery opened up on them and after being hit by a third salvo they broke and ran for the rear throwing their rifles and equipment away in the process. Barlow gave up hope of using them in another assault and was again harsh in his condemnation. "The troops exhibited such signs of timidity that I was convinced it was out of the question to employ them in this work," he wrote.[23]

Increasingly desperate to gain some success during the day, Barlow called up the Second Division and prepared for another attempt on the Confederate line. By this time, the odds were shifting as more southern regiments arrived from New Market Heights where Birney had failed to keep them occupied. Barlow arranged Smyth's brigades in the woods and cornfield from which Broady's men had attacked, and chose Colonel George N. Macy's first brigade to spearhead the assault. Macy's brigade had also been depleted by the sun and heat. 337 of his soldiers had been forced to quit during the march to Fussell's Mill, leaving about 1,000 available for the attack.[24] As Macy's brigade lined up, Barlow rode down the ranks trying to exhort and inspire the men. Upon reaching one regiment he asked for its name and was told it was the Minnesotans. The 1st Minnesota had been part of the famed "Iron Brigade" made up of regiments from the Great Lakes states. They had proved their mettle on many battlefields and were decimated at Gettysburg. Barlow was well aware of their impressive history. "If you fight like the Old First," he told them, "all hell won't stop you."[25] At 5:00 P.M., Barlow was ready and sent the Second Division men forward. The assault began badly when Macy had his horse shot from underneath him. Barlow quickly found him another and Macy returned to the attack. Before they even approached the main Confederate line, the oncoming northerners had to negotiate the gullies, ravines, and bogs formed by tributaries of Bailey's Creek. Macy's brigade came closest to gaining success, but after vicious hand-to-hand combat in the rebel trenches, it too was repulsed. Though the men fought hard and were forced to attack across broken terrain and cut through entanglements, Barlow pronounced their performance deficient, and asserted that the Confederate lines should have been captured by troops possessed of "reasonable vigor and courage."[26]

With Barlow's repulse, any possibility of meaningful success at Deep Bottom was lost. The Confederates were solidly ensconced behind their well-prepared positions, and quickly broke up the II Corps attacks. From the 16–18 August the II Corps, in the words of its commander, was "engaged daily in skirmishing with the enemy and on several occasions in considerable affairs, which at an earlier period of the war would have been dignified by the name of battles."[27] None of the fights had any significant result. The First Division suffered 434 casualties during the Deep Bottom operation, the first brigade receiving the heaviest losses since it was detached from the division after the first day and saw action away from the divisional lines.[28]

Regarding Deep Bottom, especially the first day's assault by Barlow, Hancock admitted being "considerably disappointed."[29] He accurately identified Barlow's failure to commit his men in massed formations as the fundamental reason for the operation's lack of success. "I must say," he admitted in his report on the battle "that had they [the troops] been kept more compact they ought to have broken through the line, then thinly held, by mere weight of numbers, and opened a hole for Mott."[30] Nevertheless, he did not blame Barlow whose "example to the troops was all that could be expected from his well-known gallantry and devotion to duty."[31]

Like Barlow, Hancock viewed the diminished quality of the II Corps troops as the key reason for the debacle at Deep Bottom. Indeed, there was much truth in the two generals' criticisms. Reinforcements from the North included increasing numbers of substitutes and bounty men whose reliability was suspect. Additionally, even those with a will to action often lacked experience. As was the case throughout the campaign, the losses in officers were felt in the performance of the companies, regiments, and brigades. "The troops are not behaving steadily to-day," Hancock reported back to Grant, as Barlow's first attack fell apart. Nor did the enervating heat and heavy marching aid the troops' spirits. "Many are straggling and sun struck," Hancock informed his commander.[32] Nevertheless, by placing full blame on the soldiers, Hancock and Barlow overlooked, or refused to admit, their own role in the unraveling of the Union offensive. Both Hancock's passive oversight of the operation and Barlow's feverishly ineffective field command played their role in the failure at Second Deep Bottom.[33]

If Hancock was disappointed, and probably embarrassed, by the performance of his troops at Second Deep Bottom, Barlow was beside himself with anger and frustration. He had pushed himself hard during the operation, perhaps too hard, and was enraged by what he deemed the incompetence of his officers and timidity— or worse—of his men. That he bore any responsibility for the failure at Second Deep Bottom did not appear to cross his mind. The failure of the 2nd New York Heavy Artillery to attack as ordered especially galled him. Barlow blamed the regiment's commander, Major Hogg, and asked for a written report of his conduct. Hogg's response, written in the field on 17 August, explained that the regiment's movements were caused by flanking fire which caused Hogg to change his line of assault and clear out some of the rebels. Following this, strong infantry and artillery fire prevented the 2nd New York Heavy Artillery from moving further as Barlow had ordered. Hogg concluded by saying he hoped his explanations were satisfactory to Miles, his brigade commander and "the general commanding division."[34] Whatever Miles thought, Barlow was unmoved. In his report on Second Deep Bottom, he described Hogg as "utterly unfit for command."[35] With the attack at Deep Bottom floundering, most of Barlow's casualties occurred in the first day. The small, for the campaign, losses of 434 men testify to Barlow's inability to organize a strong assault.[36]

Barlow was bitter about the conduct of his division on 13 August, and his assessments reflected his frustrations. Additionally, he was physically and emotionally stretched to the breaking point—a condition which likely colored his thinking. Hogg, for example, was cited for gallantry at Hatcher's Run the following December which does not seem to be the conduct of a man "utterly unfit for command."[37] Of course, there are several ways of looking at the situation. First, Hogg was correct. In the confused fighting, he had reacted to circumstances which Barlow could not see from his vantage point. It is equally possible that Hogg had made a mistake. If so, he had plenty of company at Deep Bottom. If this was the case, he clearly learned from his errors, and became the effective, brave officer who impressed his superiors at Hatcher's Run.

Perhaps the most intriguing aspect of Barlow's account of the Second Deep Bottom operation is his singling out of the Irish Brigade for scathing and detailed criticism. The brigade had long been considered one of the best in the Army of the Potomac, and had distinguished itself on many battlefields. Barlow had fought alongside it on the Peninsula and at Antietam. The Irish Brigade suffered heavy casualties at Gettysburg, but was recruited up during the winter of 1863–64. As was the case with all units in the Army of the Potomac, it had been used up during the Overland and Petersburg campaigns. The heavy losses had forced Barlow to reorganize his division. In June, he merged the second, "Irish" brigade with his third brigade, creating the consolidated brigade. Nevertheless, he was well aware that Byron's regiment contained the remnants of the Celtic warriors.

It would have been strange if Barlow's attitude towards the Irish Brigade had not been affected by his own background and experiences. Generally, the Boston elite looked upon the heavy

Irish immigration of the 1840s and 1850s with alarm. Their En-
glish-derived prejudices against a conquered people were but-
tressed by the visceral anti-Catholicism of their class and sec-
tarian heritage. The concern which many in the New England
elite felt for black slaves and freedmen seldom seemed to extend
to the poverty-ravaged Irish Catholics who had found refuge in
the larger cities of the northeast. Most likely, Barlow had absorbed
the prevalent anti-Irish, anti-Catholic prejudices of his time and
class.

Barlow's feelings about the Irish in his units, and the Federal
armies in general, are not as clear as those he held for the Germans. Like many, if not most, Federal officers, Barlow found
German troops inferior. The Irish, on the other hand, had a reputation as fighters. Theodore Lyman, for instance, who rated
Germans as "miserable" in soldierly attributes stated, "The Pad-
dies . . . will go in finely, and if well-officered, stand to it through
everything."[38] Barlow's references to the Irish Brigade are fleeting and reveal little about his attitudes towards them. While
convalescing from his Antietam wound, he praised the bravery
of the Irish Brigade during a visit from his friend and patron,
Judge Charles Daly. Shortly after the war, he told the Dalys that
he had grown "much attached" to his Irish soldiers and remarked,
"they would follow a brave leader anywhere."[39] Whether or not a
desire to please his influential Celtic host played any role in these
comments cannot be ascertained.

In official reports and private letters after previous battles,
Barlow found himself unable to fault the Irish, but he also said
very little about them. Tellingly, he never referred to his second
brigade by their famous name, until he made his negative report
after Second Deep Bottom. Throughout his tenure as commander
of the First Division, Barlow had demonstrated that he considered his first and fourth brigades, led by Miles and, until his
wounding at Cold Harbor, Brooke, his elite units. Certainly, the
lesson was not lost on the men of the Irish Brigade. According
to some accounts, Barlow had a "running feud" with the Irish
Brigade.[40] The zest, if not lust, for action, and disdain for danger,
which won Barlow many laurels and much admiration, was not
universally respected. William O'Meagher, in Conyngham's history of the Irish Brigade, gives a very different picture of Barlow
than the encomiums found in official reports:

The general, though commonly counted a brave, fearless soldier . . .
was exceedingly unpopular, not only with the Brigade, to which he

rarely omitted an opportunity of showing his dislike by the exhibition of many petty acts of tyranny and persecution, but with the whole division, by his reckless management of a splendid command. Even to his staff he was rude and overbearing, frequently and needlessly risking their lives in the execution of many useless commissions.[41]

O'Meagher's depiction of Barlow seems unduly harsh, and it is certainly exaggerated in certain respects. Clearly not all, if any, of Barlow's staff shared O'Meagher's opinion, as John Black's memoir of the storming of the salient demonstrates. However, the remark may allude to the heavy loss of Barlow's staff officers at Jerusalem Plank Road. But considered along with remarks made by troops in other brigades, O'Meagher's condemnation probably does convey how a not insignificant segment of Barlow's command viewed him. Barlow was a man of strong convictions and opinions, not all of them well-founded or examined. Barlow was not always a good "people" man. He played favorites and directed his caustic tongue towards anyone who did not measure up to his exacting personal standards. His successes depended partially on his own intelligence and unyielding will, and partially on the respect most men had for him. How many of his officers and men genuinely liked him is an open question. Lastly, O'Meagher's assessment suggests that the heated criticisms levied at Grant for the massive bloodletting which began in May 1864 extended to the officers who carried out the lieutenant general's orders.

Whether or not anyone in the Irish Brigade saw Barlow's report at the time, O'Meagher presented a very different picture of the Irish Brigade at Deep Bottom. According to this account the Irish Brigade assaulted an "almost impregnable" position and yet took the first line of rifle pits. At this point an "unusual stillness" occurred. Barlow, dismounting with his staff, assumed that the silence meant a repulse and "with a malignant satisfaction characteristic of a narrow intellect, he suddenly exclaimed 'that damned Irish brigade has broken at last.'"[42] According to O'Meagher, as soon as Barlow had voiced his bizarre indictment, the adjutant of the 69th New York rode up to him, told him the "Brigade" had taken the rifle pits, and awaited his further orders. Supposedly, Barlow was "so confounded at the sudden contradiction of his spiteful slander, that for a considerable period he did not regain his self-possession."[43]

Although this account is valuable as evidence of the poor relationship between the Irish Brigade and its divisional commander, it does not ring true. Barlow may have said something derogatory regarding the brigade's performance, but the truth was that Major Byron did not follow all of Barlow's orders and fell back from the ground he had taken. Additionally, stunned silence was not part of Frank Barlow's personality. Surprisingly, O'Meagher did not criticize Barlow for sending the remnant brigade—less than the size of a healthy regiment—to carry the Confederate lines without support. Though the entire truth of the incident cannot be determined, Barlow was correct that the brigade-regiment's performance lacked dash and determination. The Irishmen, like most of the Army of the Potomac, were simply not what they once had been.

Neither was Barlow. On 17 August, three days before Grant told Hancock to break off the operation and withdraw to Petersburg, Barlow handed over command of the division to Miles and reported to a military hospital at City Point. In his formal request to Hancock for permission to report to the hospital, Barlow stated,

> I have been suffering from diarrhea for the last seven weeks & have become much weakened thereby. I cannot have here the diet & [rest] emphatically prescribed by the surgeon as necessary for recovery. In my present condition I am unable to [function] & am becoming worse. By a few days of perfect quiet and proper food I shall probably become better & avoid the necessity of applying for a leave of absence.[44]

Barlow's outward ferocity at Deep Bottom was part of a vain attempt to mask increasing exhaustion. Along with his men, he had borne all the hardships of the campaign—the oppressive heat, hard marching, and near incessant combat. Additionally, he shouldered all the responsibilities of a division officer in seeing to the needs and performance of his command. If his men were stressed from the ardors of the campaign, Barlow was probably more so. Cornelia Hancock, who had come to know him well during the 1864 campaigns, wrote from her hospital that "General Barlow is here played out. Why are they not all played out?"[45] Grief at the loss of Arabella undoubtedly dealt him a heavy blow, and the poor performance of his division at Second Deep Bottom might simply have been more than he could handle. II Corps Assistant Adjutant Francis Walker described Barlow at this time as a classic case of burnout. Barlow, Walker wrote "had fought against disease and the effects of his ghastly wounds, received at Antietam and Gettysburg, no less bravely then he had fought against the public enemy. During the several days preceding [Deep Bottom] he had been more like a dead than a living man."[46]

Barlow's departure provided yet another opportunity for observers to comment on his leadership. St. Clair A. Mulholland of the 116th Pennsylvania, which served most of the war with the Irish Brigade but was transferred to the fourth brigade before Second Deep Bottom, remembered, "It was not without regret that the men of the Regiment saw General Barlow take final leave of the division. He was a fearless officer, perfectly reckless as regarded his own person and, in spite of wounds and disease, stuck to the work and remained with the command long after a man with less force of character would have given up the struggle."[47] Clearly, opinions regarding Barlow could vary greatly depending on the experience and outlook of the commentator.

While Barlow rested at the hospital, Grant and Meade began a southward thrust to rip up the Weldon Rail Road south of Petersburg. The II Corps was sent to support Warren in destroying the tracks southward towards Stony Creek Depot as far as Rowanty Creek. The troops, who had barely rested after returning from Deep Bottom, were more physically drained than ever, and Miles soon reported that the division was worn out from the continual marching. On 23 August, Barlow reported himself back for duty and resumed command of his division, which was operating near Reams Station. That night he sent a message to corps headquarters that he was in rifle pits about a mile and a half west of Reams Station on the road to Dinwiddie Court House. He informed Hancock of heavy cavalry action nearby, but stated he would continue destroying the railroad the following morning if things quieted down.[48] He never got the chance. If he could have functioned on willpower alone, Barlow might have been able to remain in command of his division. But, his return to the front was premature and he soon collapsed from exhaustion. On 24 August, he had to be taken to the rear on a stretcher, again handing over the reins to Miles.

Barlow's impatience to return to action was an error in judgment, but one that was true to his personality. We do not know his thoughts on being forced back to the Army hospitals, but in addition to his physical collapse, he was probably angry, disgusted, and frustrated as well. He was, however, spared the experience of the worst whipping the II Corps experienced in the war. On 25 August, a Confederate strike force sallied out of Petersburg and tore into Hancock near Reams Station. It was here that the downward spiral in the performance of the corps reached its critical mass. Many units of the First and Second Divisions broke, surrendered, or simply proved unwilling or incapable of responding to orders. Only the most energetic exertions of Hancock and Miles prevented a mauling from becoming a total rout. Reams' Station proved the nadir of the II Corps. Although Hancock suffered slightly less than the attacking Confederates in killed and wounded, the rebels took approximately 2000 of his men prisoners.

THE END OF THE GAME

Barlow was out on an initial 20 days' leave while Reams Station was fought and lost. What he thought about the disaster can only be surmised. It was while he was hospitalized that Hancock forwarded Barlow's name to Meade for a brevet commission as major general. Hancock's recommendation cited his "highly meritorious and distinguished conduct throughout the campaign," especially the attack on the salient at Spotsylvania. Hancock also recommended other First Division officers, Miles, Beaver, Brown, and Broady, for brevet promotions. Throughout Barlow's leave, Hancock continued to correspond with him, keeping him informed of the latest movements at the front. At first, Barlow was optimistic about the length of time it would take to restore his health and initially told Hancock he would soon return. For his part, Hancock regretted the delay in Barlow's rejoining the corps. The II Corps commander told Barlow that he expected a rigorous campaign throughout the fall and that new recruits and returning convalescents were coming in rapidly, though the corps' commander complained of a lack of good officers to lead them. Anticipating Gibbons's departure, Hancock presumed Miles would take the Second Division when his brevet came through, and went on to suggest that Barlow himself might be placed in command of the II Corps if Hancock left. The only competition Hancock saw for Barlow's rising to corps commander was Meade's Chief of Staff, Andrew A. Humphreys. But Hancock believed he would stay in command until the campaign ended.[49]

Such was not to be. Barlow's vigor did not return as rapidly as he or Hancock had hoped. Worse, Barlow's fragile health received an additional shock in the form of an unforeseen tragedy. Barlow had no contact with his father after David Hatch Barlow deserted the family when Francis was still a boy. The elder Barlow drifted southward into Pennsylvania and was living outside of Haddington in 1864. He was not in good shape, and had lost his sight in one eye, but he had managed to obtain some sort of position in a hospital there. Somehow, possibly through friends in Philadelphia, Barlow became aware of his father's whereabouts and took steps to reestablish some kind of contact with him. His duties at the front, subsequent breakdown, and possibly a sense of uncertainty regarding his father's reactions, led him to send his old friend and Harvard classmate, Phillips Brooks, to make the first approaches. Barlow had apparently heard of his father's reduced straits and uncertain health, and asked Brooks to offer him some sort of support, including living quarters and treatment. On 12 October 1864, Brooks informed Barlow that he had been to Haddington, but had not been able to locate David Hatch Barlow, although he was in the village.[50]

Brooks finally met the elder Barlow at the Haddington hospital on 29 November. He presented Barlow's proposal to offer him care, but the father declined, saying he would only agree if he lost sight in his other eye.[51] Hatch Barlow pressed Brooks for information about his son's life, about which he knew only what was publicly reported. Brooks was favorably impressed with Hatch Barlow's quarters and concluded that he was better off at the hospital than anyplace else. Before Brooks left, at about 5:00 P.M., Francis' father earnestly urged him to entreat his son to come for a visit so they could talk.[52]

The father-son reunion never took place. A shocked Phillips Brooks wrote his friend that after their meeting, David Hatch Barlow took a walk into Haddington, which was close by the hospital. On his way back he "received [a] blow which resulted in his immediate death."[53] Though Brooks' language suggests an assault, Hatch Barlow's death certificate states he died of "injuries received from a fall."[54] It is possible that Brooks used the word "blow" to indicate the elder Barlow had struck his head. It may also be that the cause of death was disguised in the official record to avoid any scandal—especially one involving the father of a prominent general. David Hatch Barlow's death, like much of his life, is shrouded in a cloud of uncertainty. Whatever the truth of his demise, his death gave another twist to the downward spiral of events which brought Francis Barlow low in the autumn of 1864. Barlow's immediate reaction is not recorded. But for a man already reeling from physical and emotional exhaustion, the death of his father on the eve of a possible reconciliation was likely devastating.

Even before he learned of his father's death, Barlow received an extended leave of absence running until 1 April 1865 which included permission to travel to Europe. Barlow's reasons for leaving the country are unknown. The most likely explanation is that he, and probably his doctors, believed a change of scene would provide the necessary restoratives for his health. Shortly before Barlow received his lengthy furlough on 5 November, Hancock wrote him again. He mentioned putting together the official reports of the summer's operations and asked Barlow to forward his on the Second Deep Bottom movement. Otherwise, Hancock sounded worn out and dejected. "I am tired of serving here," he wrote. "We do not get our share of the credit considering the fighting we do."[55] Referring to the Battle of Hatcher's Run (also called the Boydton Plank Road or Burgess's Mill), on 27 October, Hancock was positive, stating that the Rebels were "soon busted up." His spin on the operation was overly positive, as the Federals did not achieve any of their objectives, yet he may simply have been reacting to the behavior of the Corps which, if not functioning at the level it had in spring 1864, behaved far better than it had at the debacle at Reams' Station.

Hatcher's Run proved to be Hancock's last battle. In his 27 October letter to Barlow, he mentioned Grant talking to him about the Veterans Corps, an independent command made up solely of discharged veterans. In his letter, Hancock related that he told Grant such an assignment would suit him. He did not want command of the Army of the Potomac, and did "not want to serve ungenerous people always," although he did regret leaving the Corps he had commanded since Chancellorsville. As for Barlow, Hancock hoped for his speedy recovery and promised him "a magnificent division in the II Corps should you prefer to remain with it." Hancock counted somewhat over 7,000 men present for duty with the II Corps. As to its morale and capabilities, Hancock was a bit cautious. "Now our men as a mass are a *little* shaky for want of officers. But, by Spring the Second Corps will be a *power*."[56] On 27 November, Hancock left the II Corps and began recruiting for the Veteran's Corps. As he had predicted, with Barlow out of the picture, Andrew A. Humphreys assumed corps command.

Barlow left for Europe sometime in the winter of 1864–65. Unfortunately, this is another time period in which nothing about his activities are known. Where he went, what he did, whom he visited, or who, if anyone, accompanied him, remain undiscovered. In any event, he fulfilled the terms of his leave and was back in the United States no later than March when he reported himself available for duty. On his way back to the army, he stopped to visit his political patrons, the Dalys. Maria Daly noticed that he was wearing Arabella's ring on one of his fingers.[57] Maria, who had of-

Francis Channing Barlow. A written note on the photograph states "Rome. Jan. 1865" indicating that it was taken during Barlow's convalescent leave. *Massachusetts Commandery Military Order of the Loyal Legion and the U.S. Army Military History Institute.*

ten been catty about Arabella while she lived, lamented that some "young woman" would now share Barlow's "glory and property." "Poor Belle" she confided to her diary, "how little I ever thought so short a life for one so full of energy, so untiring."[57]

Initially, plans were put in motion to assign Frank to Hancock, who was in Cumberland, Maryland organizing the Veterans Corps. On 26 March, Grant wrote Halleck, informing him "General Barlow, an excellent officer, is for duty and can be assigned to General Hancock."[59] Two days later, acting on Grant's initial suggestion, the War Department ordered Barlow to report to Hancock for assignment to duty. Although Barlow likely felt a good deal of loyalty and affection for his old commander and friend with whom he had fought in so many desperate engagements, he had not returned to the war to join the Veterans Corps. Probably exploiting every political connection at his disposal, Barlow succeeded in getting back into the II Corps with a combat command. On 1 April, Assistant Adjutant General E. P. Townsend of the War Department inquired if Meade had any objections to Barlow's reassignment to the Army of the Potomac. Three days later, Meade replied that he had no objection, and the War Department contacted Barlow at the Eutaw House in Baltimore where he was staying. Here, he received the welcome news to report to the War Department in Washington, "as soon as practicable."[60] Two days later, the orders sending Barlow to Hancock were revoked and he was on his way to join Meade. Miles had led Barlow's old division since Reams' Station, and although Barlow could have pulled rank, Meade assigned him to the command of the Second Division, replacing Brigadier General Thomas Smyth. Barlow arrived on the field on 6 April as the Appomattox campaign was reaching its climax.

The situation on the ground had changed radically since the last time Barlow had been at the Petersburg front. Indeed, it had shifted drastically in the 10 days before he took over his new division. While many units in the Army of the Potomac might not have been at the level of combat proficiency previously seen, new recruits had beefed up the ranks and, as Hancock had foreseen, the battle worthiness of the Army had improved. Additionally, Lee's numerically inferior forces had seen similar losses of men and experienced officers. These losses were swollen by desertions stemming from lack of faith in the Confederacy's survival, and the fears on the part of troops from the lower south whose families and property lay in Sherman's path.

Using his superior numbers, Grant pressed his lines southwestward around Petersburg, hoping to cut all rail links into the city and maneuvering to prevent Lee from escaping south to join with what was left of Joseph J. Johnston's army in North Carolina. Having pulled so many rabbits out of his hat, and trouncing

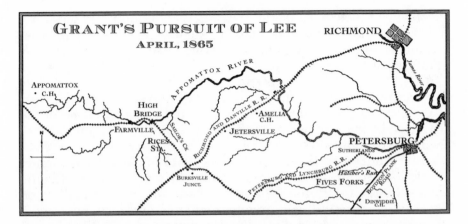

Grant's Pursuit of Lee, April 1865. From Francis A. Walker, *History of the Second Army Corps*, 1887.

the Federal forces more times than not, Lee, facing inevitable encirclement or the breaking of his lines, attempted once more to triumph through audacity. Building on a plan originally suggested by John Gordon, Barlow's alleged Gettysburg Samaritan, Lee put together a strike force aimed at cutting through the Union defenses at Fort Stedman on the northeast side of the city. If the breakthrough proved successful, Lee intended to split the Federal lines and drive towards City Point, forcing Grant on the defensive and staving off the inevitable. The assault temporarily ruptured the Federal lines, and for a brief period of time the rebels held Fort Stedman. Overwhelming Union reinforcement drove the Confederates out of the works they had captured and threw them back into their own lines. Northern troops followed them closely enough to capture the advanced Confederate rifle pits.

Grant, sensing the desperation in Lee's assault, and perceiving the significance of the insufficient force he had used to attempt a breakthrough, quickly launched a counterattack. On 1 April, Sheridan uncovered Lee's right flank by defeating George Pickett at Five Forks southwest of Petersburg. The next day Grant ordered assaults against several sections of the Confederate entrenchments. It was the VI Corps which achieved the final penetration of Lee's main line guarding the southwest approaches to the city. Ferocious resistance by the rebel defenders of Fort Gregg bought Lee some time, but their desperate stand could not save Petersburg. Lee began withdrawing his Army towards the west, searching for supplies and enough ground to allow him to wheel southward towards Johnston. With Lee abandoning Petersburg, the Confederate government fled Richmond. Grant, using his vast numbers, set off in rapid pursuit, determined to bring Lee to bay and end the war.

It was at this juncture, as the Federal forces swarmed over the fleeing Confederates, that Barlow arrived at Amelia Springs, west of Petersburg, to assume command of the Second Division of the II Corps. In fact, Barlow was the Division's third commander in twenty-four hours. On the morning of 6 April, II Corps commander Andrew A. Humphreys inspected his Second Division to check its preparations to move forward against Lee's fleeing troops. Instead of finding the units ready to march, the division lay in its camps with no arrangements to advance. Outraged, the corps commander rode to division commander William Hays's headquarters where he found everyone asleep. Humphreys immediately relieved Hays of command and sent him off to the artillery reserve. He then installed General Thomas Smyth as the new divisional commander.[61] Smyth was a seasoned officer who had commanded the Irish Brigade under Barlow at the Wilderness, but had transferred back to the Second Division after Spotsylvania. When Barlow caught up with the army later in the day he took command of the Division and Smyth resumed command of the third brigade. Barlow's presence was immediately felt, and the division pushed forward against the retreating rebels. In the late afternoon of 6 April, much of the Confederate rear guard and Richmond Reserve Corps under Ewell were caught at Sailor's Creek where they were driven from the field with heavy losses in prisoners and equipment. The II Corps was not directly engaged at Sailor's Creek, but were dueling with Gordon's men two miles north at Lockett's Farm.

Lee, hoping to shake off the northern pursuit and rest and feed his men, had ordered his units to cross to the north side of the Appomattox River. This maneuver handed Grant an enormous opportunity. The Federal forces south of the Appomattox River now had a shorter distance to cover in order to reach Appomattox Station, the last point where Lee could receive supplies from Danville and still make a turn southward toward Joseph Johnston. If one wing of the Federal army could block Lee at Appomattox, and another pin him down north of the river, the Confederate army was doomed.

Longstreet's Corps reached Farmville, and after crossing the river fired the railroad and wagon bridges to block Federal pursuit. Gordon's troops, along with those who had survived the rout at Sailor's Creek, were directed to cross the Appomattox at High Bridge. High Bridge was an engineering marvel of the age built by the South Side Rail Road in 1854. The entire span ran 2400 feet and rose 125 feet in the air. Twenty-one brick piers supported the tracks. A smaller wagon bridge ran parallel to the towering railroad structure with both bridges offering an escape route across the 75-foot Appomattox River.[62] The Confederates, mostly Gordon's men, made an unmolested passage at High Bridge, using both the wagon span and walkway along the railroad tracks to reach the north side of the river. The bridges were to have been destroyed, but the delay in the passage of some troops, and confusion and delay in issuing proper orders, meant that both bridges were intact when dawn broke on 7 April. Only then did the rebels attempt to destroy the bridges. It was too late.

Barlow, who had been racing north towards the Appomattox, reached High Bridge at 7:00 A. M., just as the last Confederates to cross the river blew up one of the two redoubts covering the bridges. The tall railroad structure, which gave the crossing its name, was already blazing, and Barlow sent Colonel Thomas L. Livermore of the II Corps staff and his engineers to save it. The men engaged in a high wire act 125 feet above the river as they endeavored to douse the fire. While part of the bridge was saved, their efforts were not successful, as three spans of the bridge were already gone and a fourth soon gave way. It was clear that seizing the smaller wagon bridge, which the southerners were also trying to ignite, was essential if Lee was to be brought to ground. If the II Corps failed to get across the river, Lee would have gained the crucial breathing space he needed to continue his resistance.

Eight months' rest and recuperation had not dulled Barlow's military skills. While Livermore and his detachment attempted to salvage the burning railroad bridge, Barlow ordered his first brigade, led by Colonel I. W. Starbird of the 19th Maine, to seize the wagon bridge and hold it. Starbird's men raced across the span and secured a bridgehead on the north side of the river. Other regiments from the first brigade came to Starbird's aid, and joined the struggle to expand the foothold on the north side. The Confederates counterattacked the isolated Yankees and had begun to gain ground, pushing the Federals back towards the crucial structure, when Miles's artillery opened up on them. Barlow's third brigade, under Smyth, then surged across the bridge and drove the rebel defenders away. Counting up the spoils from the engagement at High Bridge, Barlow found he had captured eighteen abandoned guns and 500 stands of Enfield rifles.[63] More importantly, the capture of the bridge meant Lee would have no respite from the relentless pressure of northern arms.

Once the entire Corps was across the river, Humphreys sent Barlow southwest along the railroad track towards Farmville while he led the bulk of the II Corps on a slightly northwest course, seeking to establish the position of the fast dwindling Army of Northern Virginia. Barlow came upon the Confederates entrenched at the intersection of High Bridge and Farmville Roads. The rebels were preparing to evacuate the position when Barlow struck their lines, cutting off a wagon train of 135 vehicles, which he promptly destroyed. At the beginning of the attack, however, Smyth, who had led his men to within fifty yards of Gordon's rear guard, was shot by a sharpshooter and fell from his horse, mortally wounded. He died two days later, unaware of Lee's impending surrender and earning the unfortunate distinction of being the last Federal general to die in the war. In the confusion following Smyth's wounding, an advance line of 103 men from the 7th Michigan and 59th New York were captured by North Carolina troops. Barlow soon redressed his formations and pushed after the retreating southerners. He followed the retreating rebels to the north side of the River facing Farmville when orders from Humphreys forced him to abandon his pursuit. In his absence the main body of the II Corps had run into stiffer resistance than expected and Barlow was called back for support. Though Barlow had no way of knowing it at the time, the fight near Farmville was the last of his military career. On the following day, the II Corps advanced without making serious contact with the retreating Confederates. As the corps drove relentlessly westward, rumors of a truce began to spread. On 9 April, Lee surrendered.

Barlow left no account of his feelings on hearing the news of the capitulation. It is hard not to believe that he felt a certain amount of jubilation that the object of four bitter and often frustrating years had borne fruit. Perhaps he felt a twinge of sympathy for the Confederates whose valor he had often praised as much as he despised their cause. He would have been thoroughly justified in looking back with pride over his military career—a four-year record of service, which had taken him across the many bloody roads and fields that led to Appomattox. He had seen more fighting than most enlisted men, let alone officers. His reputation as a combat commander was second to none. Whatever his shortcomings and flaws, he had carved a place in the annals of the Army of the Potomac that few general officers could equal and, arguably, none at his level of command could surpass.

He might have had other feelings as well. Neither Meade, Wright, Humphreys, nor any divisional commanders from the II and VI Corps were present when Lee surrendered to Grant. Although they were four miles from the surrender site facing Longstreet, their long years of service and participation in the heaviest fighting in the eastern theater might have led a more considerate commander to include them in the ceremony they had done so much to effect. Grant might simply have wanted the surrender over as quickly as possible and overlooked the desirability of inviting the veteran officers on the northern sector at Appomattox to the McLean House, where he met Lee. Even so, failure to include Meade, commander of the Army of the Potomac, while General Ord of the Army of the James was present, seems a slight. Nor did the men of the II and VI Corps get to attend the surrender of the Army of Northern Virginia—or what was left of it. Again, the V Corps and Ord's men oversaw that momentous, triumphant, and poignant occasion. While the remnants of Lee's army stacked arms and colors, the II and VI Corps were ordered to fall back east from Appomattox. Knowing Barlow's sense of honor and rectitude—not to mention his easily triggered sense of indignation—it is hard not to believe his feelings of triumph were not unalloyed with resentment at the Lieutenant General commanding.

Reflecting the effectiveness of Grant and Meade's quick pursuit of Lee, the Confederates had been unable to organize significant resistance and casualties in the Army of the Potomac were relatively light during the final campaign. Between 29 March and 9 April, the Second Division suffered 64 casualties—four killed, 59 wounded, and one captured or missing.[64] Following the formal surrender of the Army of Northern Virginia, the Army of the Potomac remained in Virginia facing the possibility that at least some of its Corps might be sent to help Sherman finish off Johnston. Johnston, however, surrendered to Sherman on the eighteenth and the scattered remains of Confederate forces across the South began laying down their arms, the last to do so surrendering on 26 May.

As the war flickered out, the Army of the Potomac began its final march. The II Corps retraced the route it had taken to Appomattox, marching first to New Store and then to Burkeville. On 30 April, the Army began its return to Washington by way of

Richmond. When Humphreys took a temporary leave of absence on 22 April, Barlow led the II Corps on the first leg of its last foray through southern territory. The corps marched from Burkeville to Manchester, just across the James River from the erstwhile Confederate capital. Then they crossed the James and finally entered the city they had striven to take for three years. Since the II Corps was fully engaged in pursuing Lee after Petersburg fell, this was the first time the men had seen the city whose capture eluded them for so long. During this last march through Virginia, the Army of the Potomac was concerned with maintaining the tightest discipline especially in regards to looting. On 1 May, Barlow issued an order calling upon the divisional commanders to observe the "strictest measures to prevent straggling. The necessity for foraging upon the country no longer existing, no mercy will be shown to any plunderers."[65] Barlow was clearly doing his part to begin reconstructing the hearts and minds of the recently avowed secessionists.

By 6 May, with Humphreys back in command, the II Corps troops filed out of Richmond and strode northward along Virginia's roads and turnpikes heading for the camps around Washington from which the Corps had begun its brief but glorious career in 1862. As the Army of the Potomac's corps traversed the barely 100 miles of the most contested ground in American history, it made a journey back in time, passing by, and sometimes through, the farms, villages and crossroads over which it had fought and bled during the previous four years.

No letters or other records exist to reveal what thoughts went through Barlow's mind as he traveled through scenes of hard-won victories and bloody, heartbreaking defeats. The sight, even the names of the southern rivers and streams—the James, the Pamunkey, the Chickahominy, the Rapidan, the Po, the Rappahannock—must have unleashed a torrent of memories of men and deeds, terror, and exhilaration. It is difficult to believe that he, like most of the other soldiers, was not consumed in a swirl of emotions—satisfaction, and triumph—mixed with a sense of loss for all who had fallen, including his wife.

On 10 May the corps reached Fredericksburg, where it had received a bloody repulse in the impossible attempt to clear Marye's Heights in December 1862. A few miles to the west lay the fields of Chancellorsville, the Wilderness, and Spotsylvania, where the bones of so many members of the Army of the Potomac lay mouldering. Did Barlow gaze westward as his mind returned to those recent desperate struggles? At any rate, there was little time to ruminate on the past as the Army of the Potomac neared its final bivouac. On 15 May, the men bivouacked in the now unnecessary defenses of Washington. From there, on 22 May, they crossed Long Bridge into Washington in preparation for the Grand Review of the Armies.

With the war over, Grant, back in Washington, considered sending the XXV Corps, comprised of black regiments, to Texas. Possibly, he hoped to ensure the surrender of isolated Confederate outposts, although he might have been sending a message to the French, who had been occupying Mexico. He knew the man he wanted to lead the Corps. On 22 May, Grant telegraphed Meade asking him to offer the job to Barlow. Meade tried to sweeten the pot by informing Barlow that the offer came with a "full commission as Major General."[66] But Barlow felt that an army career "would never suit me in peace."[67] Preparing for a return to civilian life he had activated his network of influential friends to scout out the best career prospects for his future. The only government position he thought worth considering was in the Revenue Service, though he personally favored returning to the law "if I can do really well."[68] Upon receiving the offer to command the XXV Corps, Barlow wrote immediately to Grant telling him that "very reluctantly and for imperative personal reasons I must decline a command which will take me so far as Texas at present."[69] The day after Barlow turned down the command of the XXV Corps, foregoing his last chance to lead a "Darky" unit, the Federal Armies held their grand review in Washington.

With a single exception, the days after the Grand Review were anticlimactic. On 25 May, despite having declined Grant's offer, he was promoted to major general of volunteers. Though Barlow was no doubt pleased by this hard-earned recognition of his service, he continued his preparations to leave the Army and busied himself in the process of demobilizing the once formidable II Corps. On 28 May he submitted a list of officers he recommended for promotion for distinguished performance during the Appomattox campaign. Apparently, he intended that those who had performed with conspicuous ability or courage should receive one last bit of recognition from the army before returning to private life. Previously, on 20 April, he had forwarded a promotions list which had been compiled by his brigade commanders. Since the promotions were for action which occurred mostly before he took command, Barlow sent it along to Corps headquarters without any comment since, as he stated, he lacked "sufficient knowledge" of the events involved.[70] Such was not the case in his recommendations of 28 May. This was his personal list, based on his own assessments, the last such he would make in the army. He urged promotions for the commanders of his first and second brigades as well as for Starbird, who had led the attack across the wagon bridge at High Bridge. Humphreys concurred with all Barlow's recommendations except those for staff, supply, or administrative services, which, he explained, he exempted from consideration for brevet.[71]

Two days after Barlow forwarded the names of those he recommended for brevet promotions, Meade asked for one last review of the II Corps before its remaining men left for home. The following day, the already diminished Corps turned out for their army commander. Immediately thereafter, the discharge process resumed, and the northern hosts melted away. Barlow's last known official act with the II Corps took place on 6 June, when he consolidated his brigades into regiments as entire companies were released from the service.

Barlow's own time in the Army was drawing to a close. On 27 June, the II Corps was reduced to one division. Humphreys nominated Gershom Mott for the job of corps commander. Apparently, many expected Barlow would receive the assignment and, in his recommendation of Mott, Humphreys specifically stated that Barlow did not want the command, which had apparently been offered to him.[72] Two days later, the entire Army of the Potomac was reduced to one provisional corps under the command of Horatio Wright. The orders reorganizing the former Potomac Army listed a number of "supernumery" officers, who were directed to "repair to their respective residences." Among these was Francis Channing Barlow, whose Civil War was finally over.[73]

9
Peaceful Pursuits

THE POLITICO

HAVING DECLINED COMMAND OF THE XXV CORPS, THERE WAS little reason for Barlow to retain his commission, and on 16 November 1865, he resigned the major generalcy he had so recently attained. As he had predicted during the siege of Petersburg, he quickly resumed his legal practice, returning to New York and renewing his partnership with Bliss. On 25 November, at a dinner with the Dalys, he candidly spoke of the usefulness which his military record could bring to his legal career.[1] Barlow's ambitious talk led Maria Daly to fear that he might become "a very hard, money making, selfish man" as he grew older.[2] Those fears were not born out. Barlow made money enough, but was too bound by his sense of duty and honor to descend into crass selfishness.

Like many veterans of the Civil War, Barlow hoped to parlay his reputation and record into politics. He accepted the Republican candidacy for secretary of state for New York running against another former general, Henry W. Slocum.[3] The Democrats were on the defensive in the 1865 elections. Many New York Democrats, most notably former governor Horatio Seymour, were identified with the "peace" wing of the Democratic Party which had advocated a negotiated peace with the Confederacy. The northern victory, coupled with the assassination of Lincoln, made it difficult for Democratic supporters of the war to avoid some of the taint connected with their less committed brethren. While Barlow respected and was quite willing to work with Democrats who supported the Union military effort, he viewed the party in general with distrust. From his perspective, its strength in the south, and the presence of so many former secessionists in its ranks, made the Democratic Party suspect. In his mind, while not all Democrats were rebels, all rebels were Democrats.[4]

Though totally sincere in his beliefs about the opposition, Barlow certainly understood the Democrats' vulnerability and he played the loyalty card in his contest with Slocum. Slocum himself possessed a superb war record, fighting first with the Army of the Potomac and ending the war in command of the XX Corps in Sherman's army, and Barlow was careful not to attack his steadfastness to the Union. In a speech he made before the election, Barlow conceded that Slocum had rendered excellent service when he was "marching against the enemy." But, he explained to his audience, as a Democrat candidate he was "now marching against their friends [Unionist Republicans]."[5] He appealed to his audience not to betray the memory of the struggle and the sacrifices of the Union soldiers by voting for a member of a political party which was dominated by traitors and waverers. "I have seen your sons die for their country," he told his listeners, emphasizing his role in the war. "They struggled, they fought, they died and they were conquerors. Their glory, the trophies and the treasures they have won, they have left to your care. Those trophies will not let you sleep. You, too, I have firm faith, will watch, and struggle and fight. And I believe you, too will be conquerors."[6]

Barlow defeated Slocum and won his first political office. His first foray into the political arena was brief. He failed to be reelected at the expiration of his term, and between 1866–69 Barlow busied himself with his law firm and family life. The partnership with Bliss, which had been kept open throughout the war, had been disbanded by 1868 and Francis became a principal in Barlow & Hyatt which maintained offices at 5 Beekman Street. In the mid-1870s, he changed his law associates again and formed Barlow and Wetmore, which operated from quarters at 208 Broadway. This partnership was supplanted by Barlow and Olney which operated a few doors away at 206 Broadway in 1877.

The death of Arabella stung Barlow deeply, contributing to the breakdown of his health during the Petersburg campaign. Nevertheless, her untimely death left him a highly eligible young bachelor. Once back in civilian life, with a legal practice going and a career in government in the offing, Barlow felt ready to marry again. His second wife was Ellen Shaw, whom he wed 24 October 1867. She was the sister of Robert Shaw, Barlow's former pupil and hero of the assault on Battery Wagner by the 54th Massachusetts. The Shaws were old friends of the Barlow family, and had, like the Barlows, moved to New York before the outbreak of the war. At the time of their marriage, Ellen was living with her family on Staten Island, only a ferry ride away from Frank. Barlow's second marriage seems to have been a happy one, and was not plagued by the chronic separation which had characterized his

Ellen Shaw about the time of the Civil War. She married Francis Channing Barlow in 1867. *Staten Island Museum of Art and Science.*

first. Francis and Ellen had three children: Robert Shaw Barlow, who was born on 4 July 1869 on Staten Island; Charles Lowell Barlow, born 10 October 1871; and Louisa Shaw Barlow, born 27 July 1873. Robert followed his father into Harvard and the law, although he practiced in Boston. He died on 3 September 1943.

Charles also returned to the ancestral city of Barlows and Shaws and was living in Boston at the time of his brother's death. Louisa married Pierre Jay, a member of a long-prominent New York family, on 23 November 1897, and it was she who donated her father's letters to the Massachusetts Historical Society in 1942. Louisa and Pierre had two daughters, Frances Barlow Jay and Louisa Jay.[7]

Barlow's political prospects brightened after the election of U. S. Grant in 1868. Although Grant had been unable to get him to accept an Army corps appointment, Barlow was amenable to a commission as United States marshal for the southern district of New York. In the nineteenth century, governmental appointments were largely seen as an opportunity to make money through favoritism, bribery, or what Tammany leader George Washington Plunkitt later termed "honest graft," that is, using inside knowledge to secure property, which could then be sold to a government agency for a profit. Additionally, Barlow was appointed at a point when the egregiously corrupt Tammany Hall Democratic organization, led by William Marcy Tweed, controlled the City and sometimes the state as well. Barlow adamantly refused to play by the political rules of the time or engage in graft, honest or otherwise. Thoroughly honest, and totally contemptuous of those who were not, Barlow swept the office of timeservers, incompetents, political appointees, and filled the positions under his control with those he deemed competent and honorable.[8]

Barlow's actions provoked a storm of outrage from the New York City Union Republican Club which charged the new marshal with rejecting their advice "in relation to the distribution of patronage of his office." Worse, according to members of the Club, his refusal had been couched "in the most offensive and autocratic manner."[9] Consequently, on 2 July 1869, the Club voted to petition Grant for Barlow's removal. The marshal was not without his supporters, however, and the same day the New York City Republicans were denouncing Barlow the *Albany Journal* ran an article supporting him. According to the Albany paper, the delegation from the New York City Republicans "impudently demanded the appointment of a list of placemen and hangers-on" which they had compiled. Barlow, according to the *Journal,* "politely" told them he did not need their assistance in making his appointments, and also declined to limit his choice for subordinate positions to New York City residents, which the committee had demanded.[10] The *Albany Journal* writer claimed that the New York City Republican Club's general committee was not representative of the City's Republicans and was under control of "bosses and degenerated into a mere factious machine."[11] The version of events as reported in Albany is probably close to what actually occurred when the "subcommittee" called on Barlow. Whether he was "polite" as opposed to proper is an open question and the Republican Club's charge that he was autocratic and offensive has a familiar ring.

Typical of the time, and not unheard of today, Barlow was assessed a contribution to his party which was based on the supposed amount he could amass through the standard practices of charging special fees, taking bribes, or engaging in favoritism in return for some sort of remuneration.[12] Barlow refused to pay his assigned "contribution," declaring that while he would make a donation to the Republicans, it would be based exclusively on his legal salary. Moreover, he imposed his standards of government ethics on his subordinates and prevented them from receiving any fees other than those prescribed by law.[13] Needless to say, none of this endeared him to his party's leaders.

Perhaps Barlow's most dramatic action as United States marshal was suppressing a filibustering expedition to Cuba. American interest in Cuba predated the Civil War and would ultimately lead the United States into the Spanish-American War. At this juncture, however, Grant wanted to prevent Americans from providing material support to the Cuban rebels. Under an 1818 statute, Barlow was given command of the combined United States military forces in the New England States, New York, and New Jersey and assigned the task of preventing arms shipments and other supplies from leaving the United States to Cuba. In accordance with Grant's policy, Barlow seized a shipload of Cubans carrying arms and munitions and blocked other attempts to provide assistance to Cuban revolutionaries.[14]

The suppression of military assistance to Cuban revolutionaries had international ramifications. The United States was pressing Britain for payment of damages inflicted on United States' shipping interests by the operations of Confederate commerce raiders, especially the *Alabama*. Despite the British government's failure to recognize the Confederacy, and international prohibitions against third parties providing war materials to belligerents, Confederate agents succeeded in having the *Alabama* built and outfitted in Britain from whence it sailed to wreak havoc on the northern merchant marine. Barlow's effective action in blocking outside support to the Cuban revolutionaries demonstrated the United States' adherence to the recognized principles of international law which, in turn, strengthened the

American case against Britain.[15] Nevertheless, the case of the *Alabama* claims dragged on until the Treaty of Washington in 1871, whereby both nations agreed to submit the dispute to an international tribunal in Geneva. The American case prevailed and the United States was awarded fifteen million dollars in damages. Perhaps more importantly, basic principles of international law were reaffirmed and the United States and Britain entered a period of rapprochement which would ultimately affect the balance of power in Europe and throughout the world.

Barlow resigned as United States marshal in 1869. According to the *New York Times* the duties of the office "were not congenial to him."[16] Always quick to anger or indignation, Barlow may have found the continual pressure to accept bribes or show favoritism to the politically connected increasingly distasteful. Additionally, he considered his marshal's salary inadequate to his needs, and the job prevented him from undertaking any outside legal work, which would have augmented his income.[17] Barlow had also gotten involved in a dispute with John T. Hoffman, the Democratic governor of the state. Hoffman was elected in 1868 in what some historians have called "probably the most corrupt election in the history of New York."[18] To ensure Hoffman's election, Tweed arranged for the illegal naturalization of large numbers of immigrants, who were then herded to the polls and instructed to vote for the Democratic ticket. This device built up Hoffman's downstate margin to offset the upstate Republican vote—which was often as fraudulently inflated as the Democratic tally.

Barlow, whose tongue was as sharp as ever, denounced Hoffman as a scoundrel and despite Barlow's federal appointment the governor apparently threatened to have him arrested.[19] The dispute arose at a sensitive time, as Ellen was about to give birth to their first child. Under the circumstances, Barlow decided he could not afford to dismiss Hoffman's utterances as mere bluster. The Barlows were then living at Ellen's father's house on Staten Island, and Francis, still holding Grant's commission as head of the state's military forces, ordered a battery of artillery to camp on the lawn of the estate to dissuade any of Hoffman's supporters from attempting to carry out the gubernatorial threat. When wife and child were ready to travel, the troops formed a protective square around Francis, Ellen, and Robert, and escorted them to a revenue cutter, which took them to Bridgeport, Connecticut from where they left for Lenox, Massachusetts.[20] The removal to Massachusetts was designed to protect Ellen and his newborn son from danger. Any attempt by state officials to arrest or otherwise interfere with a United States marshal who was also a friend of the president, not to mention famously pugnacious, would have placed those making the attempt in serious legal—if not physical—difficulties. Nothing came of Hoffman's threat and, having seen Ellen and his newborn son to safety, Barlow was soon back in New York, where he quickly resumed his legal and political careers.

One other factor probably influenced Barlow's decision to let go the Unites States marshal's position—the possibility of advancing to a more prestigious position. He was again returned as New York Secretary of State in 1869, a post he held for one year. On 7 November 1871, he was elected to the more influential position of Attorney General of New York State.

Shortly before he was elevated to the state's highest prosecutorial office, Barlow took an active role in the efforts to found the New York Bar Association. His official duties and concern for the ethics and reputation of his profession led him into a confrontation with David Dudley Field, lead attorney for James Fisk and Jay Gould. Fisk and Gould, financial operators whose machinations helped set the stereotype of "robber barons," attempted to build a transportation empire based on their control of the Erie Rail Road, hence their popular nickname, the "Erie Gang." They also had the Fall River Steamship line in their hands, and in 1871 attempted to gain possession of the Albany and Susquehanna Rail Road. In order to ensure political protection, they allied themselves with Tweed who was cut in for a piece of the action.[21] In a series of letters which ran in the *New York Tribune* in February and March 1871, Barlow charged Field with using unprofessional, illegal, and corrupt means to keep the railroad in the hands of Fisk and Gould. In the process he claimed, with considerable evidence, that New York judge George G. Barnard was in Field's pocket, (which was true since he had been appointed to the State Supreme Court by Governor Hoffman which meant he was ultimately Tweed's man) and the two had colluded to rig a stockholder's convention to place the railroad in the "Erie Gang's" hands.[22]

After two of Barlow's broadsides, Field responded with a letter to the *Tribune* charging that Barlow had "been busy the last few weeks going from office to office to gather scandal, and abuse me. I am glad that he has, at last, made an open attack, though if I were to have a controversy, I should have preferred an opponent of some standing and experience at the bar. His long and confused misrepresentations, downright falsehoods and garbled quotations can be readily refuted."[23] The *Tribune* printed Field's defense, with the added comment that Field was "unwise" in "provoking comparisons" between himself and Barlow. Field's name, the paper continued, was

> most intimately associated with Judge Barnard's court, with Jim Fisk's finances, with legal proceedings which respectable judges [Justice Darwin E. Smith of the New York State Supreme Court] have from the bench denounced as fraudulent and flagitious. General Barlow's name is most intimately associated with Fair Oaks, with Antietam, with Gettysburg, with the Wilderness, with a career in the service of his country that began in the ranks and ended with a major general's commission, universal honor and many wounds. If he has been fewer years at the bar than Mr. Field, he has at least won the confidence of the profession, escaped the rebukes of an upright bench, and stood in no fear of expulsion from the bar association. The comparison which Mr. Field invites is not one which General Barlow need shrink.[24]

Barlow himself replied on 20 March with a detailed presentation of the Albany and Susquehanna case. His letters on the case were subsequently reprinted in a 32-page pamphlet. In his 20 March reply, Barlow explained that he was responding to Field's printed challenge that none of his critics presented any facts to support their contentions. He also stated that Field was the first to resort to the papers rather than answer the private letters Barlow sent him. As a result, Barlow had no choice but to go public with the dispute. At the end of his exhaustive analysis of the misdeeds of Fisk, Gould, Field and their judicial allies, Barlow concluded, "As concerns Mr. Field I shall take care that his conduct is investigated before a body of men who can not be deceived by small tricks and petty evasions"—in other words, an inquiry before the newly formed New York Bar Association.[25] Field countered that Barlow could have the investigation "with all my heart" and castigated him for not going through the Bar in the first place. In Barlow's last letter on the topic, he explained that the Bar had met at least once since the letter war began, and that Field said nothing about the controversy at the meeting. The former general and rising lawyer-politician ended his rebuttal by declaring, "By becoming a member of the Bar Association, I did not surrender my right to denounce iniquity wherever I see it, and in any form I choose."[26]

Barlow's campaign against the activities of the "Erie Gang" led the New York City Bar Association's Committee of Grievances to draw up a report condemning Field's activities. But the document was never voted on, and Field remained an active lawyer going on to defend another Barlow target, William Marcy Tweed.[27] Indeed, as agitation rose against the corruption of the Tweed Ring, the "Committee of Seventy" comprised of civic and business leaders, was formed to press the case against the Tammany machine. Barlow was a founding member of the Committee and soon became their paid counsel.[28]

While he was unable to have Field expelled from the legal profession, Barlow had better success with Judges George G. Barnard and Albert Cardozo. Governor Hoffman had put both men in their positions and both were part of Tweed's network of corrupt governmental officials. Barnard had incurred Barlow's special wrath for his part in protecting Fisk and Gould's control of the railroad. As attorney general Barlow played a key role in the campaign to remove the judges, and devised a two-pronged attack against them. He first convinced the New York Bar Association to condemn Barnard and Cardozo, and then used the Bar to lobby political/governmental leaders for the judges' removal. He also enlisted the aid of Samuel J. Tilden to unseat the corrupt justices.[29] Tilden, a prominent New York City attorney, was the reform-minded state Democratic chairman, and a somewhat tardy opponent of Tammany Hall and its many subsidiaries, satellites, and collaborators.[30] Tilden, ultimately, went on to embrace many of the causes and policies first staked out by Barlow during his term as attorney general. In order to coordinate the assault on the judges, Barlow organized a meeting between a delegation of the New York Bar and influential legislators at his office on 23 April 1872. Barlow's campaign finally bore fruit and on 20 August 1872, Barnard was removed from his judgeship by a unanimous vote of the state senate. Shortly after, Cardozo resigned, rather than suffer the humiliation of a similar fate. Barlow's role in the impeachment was praised by the *New York Times* which editorialized that "General Barlow, although making no boasts, has always struck at the right moment, and has done more to bring to pass the removal of the corrupt judges than half the papers which crow about the victory."[31]

Barlow's elevation to the state Attorney General's office was itself an indication that the winds of change were finally blowing against the Tweed-Erie forces. The *New York Times,* which had been an early opponent of Tammany, was effusive in its praise of Barlow's candidacy. "Francis C. Barlow" their endorsement began,

is well known to the people of this City as one of the most earnest
and indefatigable laborers in the cause of Municipal Reform and as
an uncompromising enemy of the entire gang of thieves who have
grown rich in the plunder of our taxpayers. His services as counsel
in the procedures that have already been taken, and that are about
to be taken, to expose their villainy and bring them to justice have
been of great value to the people, and, if elected to the position of
Attorney-General, he will use the whole power of his office to rid the
community of their presence and, to restore to the people their stolen
plunder.[32]

By the time of Barlow's election, the Tammany sachem was
already on the defensive and the blatantly corrupt management
of the Erie Rail Road had aroused opposition in New York's busi-
ness-financial community which belatedly recognized that the
activities of Fisk, Gould, and Drew jeopardized not only the
American stock market but the ability to sell American shares
abroad.[33] Measures to reform the situation went forward on two
levels. On the first, official level, the state legislature began to
consider the repeal of the Classification Act. This Act, passed on
Erie's behest in the late 1860s, gave managers, not stockholders,
the ultimate control of corporations. Repeal would once again allow shareholders to determine their board of directors and restore the will of the stockholder to corporate life.

Barlow supported both the repeal of the Classification Act as
well as a measure which became known as the "Attorney General's
Bill." While this legislation was directed at Erie, it would give
Barlow broad power to investigate all corporations, including the
right to interrogate members of boards of directors even before
trial.[34] Not everyone was happy with this attempt to extend the
attorney general's power, and even some who had no love of the
Erie Gang thought Barlow was overreaching. The *New York Tribune* accused Barlow of wanting to be the "King of the State," and
charged that he wanted the state senate's judiciary committee,
where the bill was introduced to "sanction his outrageously ambitious idea of obtaining power by process of law to place him above
the Supreme Court of the State and make him grand 'Inquisitor
General' against any corporation whose private business he may
desire to question."[35] Barlow did not get his "Attorney General's
Bill," but the Classification Act was repealed on 20 March 1872.
But, even before that, Gould and his supporters had lost control
of Erie through nongovernmental maneuvers.

This second, unofficial, method of shaking out the Erie Gang
entailed a private suit in which Barlow soon became involved. In

the late nineteenth century, the United States was a major re-
cipient of foreign, especially British, investment capital. Among
those with business interests in the country was James McHenry,
an Englishman who owned the small Atlantic and Great Western
Rail Road which ran between western New York and Ohio. Mc-
Henry found himself totally dependent on the Erie Rail Road's
connectors, and decided Gould had to be removed from Erie's board
and men favorable to himself installed in the management. Consequently, joined by other Londoners who had invested in Erie
Rail Road stock, McHenry engaged Daniel Sickles, controversial
New York politician and Civil War general, to bring a lawsuit,
independent of the Classification Act's repeal, against the Erie
managers. Sickles contacted Barlow, who was by then in the New
York State Attorney General's office in Albany, and asked if he
would undertake to bring the case to court. Barlow replied that
though his opinion about the "outrages" of the Erie managers was
well known, the case remained a private matter. Nevertheless,
he undertook to organize the legal team which would pursue the
matter against the "Erie Gang" and used the $10,000 Sickles sent
to retain legal counsel for the task.[36] Sickles had initially asked
Barlow to lead the case himself, but the new Attorney General
thought this might detract from his official duties. He had no objection, however, to orchestrating the campaign from behind the
scenes. "Of course," he assured Sickles, "I shall control and direct
the conduct of the proceedings and the counsel will take their
direction from me."[37] Barlow would subsequently find that his
quasi-official leadership in the case left him open to accusations
which would cause him some uncomfortable moments in the
future.

Sickles was too impatient, and perhaps too wily, to wait for the
case to work its way through the imperfect state courts. Instead,
he bribed enough members of the Erie Board of Directors—who
also saw which way the wind was blowing—so they would resign
their seats and allow the selection of a new board which would remove Gould as president of the railroad. On 11 March 1872, nine
days before Governor Hoffman signed the repeal of the Classification Act, Gould was turned out during a riotous meeting which
included shareholders, a rebellious board of directors, Gould's
goon squad, New York City police, and United States marshals.[38]
In the aftermath of what Barlow later termed a "coup d'etat," the
private case which Barlow had been nursing collapsed. He was
forced to abandon legal proceedings against the "Erie Gang" when
the British and German investors whom Sickles represented

asked for discontinuance while the election of a new Board of Directors was arranged.[39] Although Barlow was no doubt glad to see Gould and his followers out of power, he was disappointed and disgusted that Gould had escaped without penalty and, indeed, seemed poised to increase his influence and wealth on Wall Street. However, he saw no reason to continue with the suit if the stockholders no longer desired it. He wrote bitterly that if the Erie stockholders wanted Gould and his fellows to "plunder them" it was their business and not something worth public expense.[40]

But if Barlow was through with the Erie case, it was not quite through with him. On 12 October 1872, the *New York Tribune* printed charges accusing Barlow of taking Sickles' $10,000 to do his official duty in conducting state business. The attorney general, so the allegations ran, had received the money in an " illegitimate, unprofessional and possibly corrupt manner."[41] Of all the accusations to hurl at Barlow, corruption was the most grievous, striking at the core of Barlow's self-image. Not surprisingly the charged provoked outraged indignation. Barlow rebutted the allegations in letters to the *Times,* then a Republican organ, whose editors also took up his defense. Charging the *Tribune,* which was generally pro-Democrat, with a "mean, malicious attack," Barlow described his role in the Erie case as a perfectly honest and desirable undertaking. The Erie stockholders wished to bring a suit against the Erie directors in the name of the state, but the state treasury would not pay the fees. Barlow explained that it was necessary for the attorney general to control the case and he used the $10,000 from Sickles to assemble a legal team. $8,692.81 was spent in prosecuting the suit before it was dropped. The remainder was returned to the Erie stockholders.[42] The *Times* also ran letters from others involved in the case who supported Barlow's explanation of how the money was raised and disbursed. The attorney general emphasized that he had received no compensation for his work on the case.

Despite Barlow's explanations, enough attention was focused on the unusual nature of the Erie suit that a state legislative committee opened hearings on the allegations. Testimony was taken at the Fifth Avenue Hotel in New York City with the major players in the case attending. Barlow himself appeared twice, on 18 March and 9 April 1873. Barlow reiterated the statements he made in his letters of the previous fall but went into more detail about the legalities. He explained that under state law, any action for removing corporate directors had to be undertaken by the attorney general. He also pointed out that while he was legally entitled to compensation for his work in the suit he never accepted any. "[B]esides my action as Attorney General," he frankly admitted, "I was personally interested in getting rid of these people."[43] But, all his efforts went for naught when Sickles and his party dropped out of the case. "I discontinued the suit reluctantly and with annoyance," Barlow told the legislators. In fact, he was so indignant with Sickles "that I have since ceased to treat with him."[44] Barlow's defense was accurate, authoritative, and supported by both documents and witnesses. For Barlow, however, the experience was galling and may have led him to question the desirability of pursuing a career in public service. After all, if a man with his proven standards of rectitude and abilities could be forced to defend himself against spurious charges in the popular press, perhaps governmental office was not worth the price.

One way or another most of the cases involving political corruption and judicial malfeasance originated with Tweed. Even as the case against Erie was collapsing, Barlow stepped up the legal assault on the Tammany Hall Democratic machine and Tweed himself. The charges and cases were complex, and often overlapping, and the undertaking would require several years to complete, extending beyond Barlow's tenure in office. Nevertheless, Barlow's initiatives laid the basis of whatever success the legal campaign against Tweed accomplished.[45] The attorney general was well along with civil and criminal proceedings against Tweed and his henchmen when a report surfaced claiming that the "Ring's" leaders were buying their way out of prosecution. Barlow quickly took up pen and wrote a lengthy rebuttal which ran in his favorite journal the *New York Times*. Barlow stated categorically that the suits against Tweed, Peter Sweeny and the other Tammany leaders was proceeding "as fast as the machinery of the Courts will allow." He revealed that the previous January he had been approached by persons purporting to speak for the Tweed party who sought a "compromise" in return for a cash payment.[46]

Barlow rejected the offer out of hand. He went on to state that the civil cases were moving forward as fast as possible in light of the appeals process, but he had held back from lodging criminal complaints as long as they would come under the venue of Barnard and Cardozo, who were still on the bench in New York City. "The cases will be tried as soon as there is a judge on the bench in whom the public have confidence," he continued.[47] Barlow concluded his report with the comment that he had explained the situation to a *Tribune* reporter the previous week, but that the

paper had ignored his statement and gone on to write that the
case had been shelved as the result of a political bargain. The following February, Barlow worked out an agreement with the New
York City Corporation Counsel, Delafield Smith, to coordinate
the various state and city suits against Tweed. Barlow expected
to press the state suits first since "they are further advanced and
we have bail therein."[48] Indeed, while both city and state attorneys conducted the case against Tweed and his men, it was the
state's special counsels, Lyman Tremain and Wheeler H. Peck-
ham, acting on Barlow's behalf, who "really had full charge of the
prosecution."[49]

Barlow did not remain in office long enough to witness the conviction of Tweed, several of his lieutenants, and the temporary
eclipse of Tammany Hall, the New York City Democratic organization. But, the legal war against the Democratic chieftain began
when Francis Barlow initiated the prosecution against him. Nor
was Tammany the only group of grafters in Barlow's sights. He
also began the campaign against the "Canal Ring," a bipartisan
group of politicians and politically connected citizens who had
grown rich and powerful through their control of the enormous
sums expended in repairing and extending the state's canal
system.[50] Canal contractors would lowball potential contracts,
agreeing to do them inexpensively, and, once the contracts were
awarded, receive increases from the state's Canal Board, which
was in on the operation. The contractors also petitioned the state
legislature for "relief bills" which also granted fee increases to
the canal contractors.

As attorney general Barlow challenged the constitutionality of
the relief bills in court, setting in motion the legal maneuvers
which would put an end to such practices. As was the case with
Tweed, the defeat of the "Canal Ring" occurred after he had left office. Samuel J. Tilden took up Barlow's investigation of the "Canal
Ring" when he became governor in 1874 and succeeded in breaking their hold on the state's canals. The governor's growing fame
as a political reformer pushed him into the front ranks of prominent Democrats which led to his winning the Party's nomination
for president in 1876. Nevertheless, those who followed the course
of events knew who deserved the greatest credit. As *Harper's
Weekly* put it in an 1875 editorial, Barlow "did not shrink from the
duty of grappling single handed with the ["Canal Ring"] . . . and
when the obituary of the Canal Ring shall at last be written, the
chivalrous attack which that honest public officer directed upon
the peculators will be remembered to his everlasting honor."[51]

In addition to launching high-profile cases against Tweed and the canal bosses, Barlow's duties as attorney general led to his involvement in a wide variety of civil and criminal actions, including the sensational "Kelsey Outrage." Charles G. Kelsey, a love-smitten young man living in Huntington, Long Island, had been tarred and feathered by his erstwhile love's other suitor. Shortly after this event, Kelsey disappeared. The trunk of his body, which showed evidence of castration, was subsequently found floating in Oyster Bay and was identified by a watch chain. Although several people witnessed the tarring and feathering, and more than one person was required to transport Kelsey's body to the Bay, both state and local authorities had been unable to break the wall of silence surrounding the crime. As Barlow put it, "they [the perpetrators] hang together with considerable persistency."[52] While preparing to leave office in December 1873, Barlow prepared a lengthy document for his successor, Daniel Pratt, explaining the various cases still pending. Concerning the Kelsey case, Barlow suggested that the suspects, especially Rudolph and Royal Sammis, be subjected to "a severer cross-examination than they have yet undergone, in hopes of bringing down some of them."[53] Such was not to be. None of those under investigation cracked, and Royal Sammis left Huntington for New York City where he married the young woman who had fatally attracted Kelsey.

Barlow originally refused to seek renomination as attorney general. The New York Times commented on his decision by stating that Barlow had done his duty faithfully "but such an office requires a man to devote nearly his whole time to it, and it is not surprising that Gen. Barlow should not be prepared to make so great a sacrifice on a second occasion."[54] Efforts were made to change the attorney general's mind and on 29 August the Times ran an article reporting that "reformers" in New York City were greatly disappointed that Barlow chose not to run again. Barlow was again lauded for his energy in pursuing the "municipal plunderers of New York," and fears were expressed as to whether the pending cases "would be safe in other hands." The article concluded that another term would "involve considerable personal sacrifice on the part of Gen. Barlow; it is equally obvious that it would be a decided public gain."[55] A group of prominent citizens sent a letter to Barlow, which was later reprinted in the Times. The writers praised Barlow's efforts against Tweed and his machine, and maintained that it was clear Tilden, who was now governor, wished to retain him. They argued that the "great partisan and mercenary pirates" hoped to escape justice without Barlow in the attorney general's chair and they closed their letter with an appeal to Barlow to make "the pecuniary and other personal sacrifices" and run again.[56]

Faced with these entreaties, Barlow reluctantly agreed to serve again. But the Republicans did not renominate him. Barlow's initial refusal to seek another term no doubt affected the party's decision. His prickly, acerbic personality probably played a role in their thinking as well. Additionally, as a prominent member of the reform faction of the Republican Party, Barlow was sometimes at odds with the party's regular organization, which he later (and perhaps at the time) referred to as a "machine."[57] Perhaps the decisive element in the Republicans' calculations may be found in *Harper's Weekly's* observation that Barlow had taken action "against the corrupt agents in State politics, and he is cordially hated by them of *all* parties"[58] (emphasis added). Uncorruptible himself, he would root out bribery, graft, kickbacks, and favoritism wherever he found it, whenever he could. As a result, as would be the case of Theodore Roosevelt a generation later, there were many Republicans who were as fearful of Barlow as their Democratic counterparts. By the time the Republican nominating convention met in Utica in September 1873, Barlow had already been passed over for consideration as the party's candidate for attorney general. While he did not attend the convention, he made his presence felt. A letter from Barlow was circulated among the delegates describing William B. Taylor, the incumbent State Engineer whom the Republicans had just renominated, as "an officer for which no honest man ought to vote."[59]

Barlow's letter was precisely the kind of action which made even his natural political allies nervous, and explains why they were more comfortable with a more predictable personality. Indeed, in the course of nominating Benjamin D. Stillman as the party's candidate for attorney general at the state Republican Convention, Delafield Smith remarked that the attorney generalship should "not be made a school to educate young lawyers in," which was taken as a slap at Barlow. The assertion, according to reporters from the *New York Herald*, "was greeted with great laughter by the delegates who were unfriendly to Barlow." Stewart L. Woodford, permanent chairman of the convention, sought to spike any intraparty dissension and since Barlow "did not hav[e] a friend visible anywhere" he made some favorable comments about Barlow while supporting Stillman's nomination.[60]

Although snubbed by his party, Barlow was likely relieved at not continuing in office. His initial insistence that he did not want the position was sincere, and his agreement to consider running again was unenthusiastic. His reluctance to continue may have stemmed partly from his unhappiness with the amount of time he had to spend in Albany away from his family. As was true with the federal marshal's position, he might also have calculated how much more he could earn in private practice, and decided that he was hurting his family's prospects by remaining in government. It is also likely that he had had enough of public service. Assured of his own rectitude, confident of the righteousness of his course of action, he was likely infuriated at finding himself under attack from partisan newspapers, political hacks, and their corrupt lawyers. Although he easily disposed of the allegations raised against him during the Erie case, he might well have found it demeaning to be forced to explain himself before a state committee. He may also have been frustrated that his best efforts had not yielded greater results. Gould was ousted from Erie, but thriving on Wall Street. The Tweed prosecutions seemed to drag on, and few of the miscreants were behind bars. Field, whom he considered as corrupt as Barnard and Tweed, was still practicing law. True, Barnard and Cardozo were gone from the judiciary, and the Bar Association was taking steps to reform legal ethics and behavior, but with all the targets surrounding him, the removal of two judges might have seemed small consolation to an ambitious, energetic—not to mention self-righteous—attorney general.

At its core, Barlow found his experience in holding an elected office in the rough-and-tumble democratic politics of the late nineteenth century simply beneath him. He had done his best and rendered diligent service to the state. All the major cases were well under way. Now, they could find someone else to finish them.

Barlow returned to private practice in 1874, though he remained active in New York's Republican Reform Club, but was drawn back into public life by the heated controversy over the presidential election of 1876. In the electoral contest of that year Samuel Tilden, Governor of New York, received a majority of the popular vote, and seemed to have defeated his Republican rival, Rutherford B. Hayes. However, Republican-controlled Reconstruction governments, propped up by Federal troops, remained in three states: Louisiana, Florida, and South Carolina. The returns from these states were initially fragmentary, and Republican

Francis Channing Barlow, probably in the mid-1870s. *In Memoriam. Francis Channing Barlow.* **1923.**

supporters and political leaders quickly realized that if the vote in these states were reversed, Hayes would take the presidency by a single electoral vote.[61] Charging voter fraud, Republicans declared that the three states had actually gone for Hayes, which threw the election into doubt. With tempers running high and each party accusing the other of attempting to steal the election, a recount was ordered.

In order to determine the validity of the votes cast, state canvassing boards were directed to review the returns in all the disputed states and turn their finding over to a returning board which would determine the validity of the votes and then certify the winner of the election. Both parties sent semi-official delegations of "visiting statesmen" to monitor the proceedings, and hear the evidence presented before the canvassing boards, which would be forwarded to the returning board and, as it turned out later, the courts and Congressional investigating committees. Accepting the role as Grant's personal representative, Barlow accompanied the team of "visiting statesmen" which monitored the Florida canvass. The high-powered group also included E. F. Noyes, Senator John A. Kasson, General Lew Wallace, Senator John Sherman, and Congressman James Garfield. Sherman and Garfield, the future president, were close friends of Hayes as was Noyes, the ex-governor of Ohio. Another major player in Florida was William E. Chandler. Chandler, a member of the Republican National Committee, was primarily responsible for devising the party's recount strategy. Grant was so confident of his abilities that he personally requested that he remain in Florida until the canvass was completed. Together, Chandler and Noyes were the key figures in the Republican efforts in Florida.

The canvassing boards, which determined the validity of the votes, were controlled by Republicans and "consistently and ruthlessly used [their] discretionary power in favor of the Republicans."[62] Names of Republican voters were placed on the polling lists to give Hayes a majority in some counties, while Democratic votes were invalidated on transparently partisan technicalities.[63] The returning board which had the responsibility of deciding the legality of the county canvasses was equally partisan. Its members consisted of a "carpetbagger" Republican, a former deserter from the Confederate army who had become a "scalawag" Republican, and one Democrat.[64]

While a Republican sent by a Republican administration, Barlow had never allowed purely partisan considerations to interfere with his judgment and direct his course of action. Indeed, Barlow had formed many warm friendships with those Democrats he deemed honorable, beginning with Judge Daly before and during the Civil War. He had also shown a readiness to work with reform-minded Democrats in his campaigns against Fisk, Gould, and Tweed. In fact, his reputation as a man of unsullied integrity and political courage probably loomed large in Grant's decision to appoint him as the president's personal representative. Barlow's attitude towards Tilden was somewhat complex. Tilden, who had led the reform wing of the New York Democrats, had pursued many of the suits Barlow had initiated, particularly the prosecution of the canal and Tweed rings. It was known that

Barlow heartily approved of Tilden's policies—unsurprising since
they were also his—but he nevertheless held deep reservations
about the Democratic Party in general. Shortly before election
day, Barlow was asked if he had been campaigning for Tilden.
His reply, contained in a letter written 6 November 1876, reveals
his political thinking at the time. "I have been on the stump for
Hayes," he responded,

> doing what I can, and I have the strongest confidence that we are go-
> ing to elect him, and that is because I believe there is too much good
> sense in the American people to turn this Gov't and its credit to those
> who 10 or 12 years ago were trying to destroy it. Neither Mr. Tilden
> nor anyone else can stem the rebel influence if he is elected. I have
> always said that I thought that Tilden if elected by the Republican
> Party would make an admirable president, but with the rebels and
> copperheads of the democratic party, with all its villainies behind him,
> he will ruin us.[65]

Clearly, Barlow shared the fears of many Republicans that the
end of military occupation and Federally controlled Reconstruction in the south would result in a resurgence of power by southern Democrats which might set back, or even negate, the fruits
of Union victory in the Civil War. Barlow had invested far too much
of his life in the conflict to see its outcome undone by politics.

Barlow arrived in Tallahassee, the Florida state capital, on 17
November intending to do his part to prove that Hayes had actually won in Florida. Unfortunately, he was proceeding on the
assumption that Grant was in earnest when he instructed the
Republican dignitaries and canvassers to "make a fair count of
the votes actually cast." Although he had dealt with corruption,
bribery, and chicanery in New York, most of it had come from the
opposition party, and he was initially unprepared for the campaign of deception and deceit the Republicans were waging in the
southern state. In this instance, his own sense of ethics and assumptions about politics temporarily misled him.

Assuming that his fellow Republicans were on the same track,
he failed to see that Chandler, Noyes, and the Republican canvassers were enthusiastically aiding and abetting fraud to deliver the state to Hayes. Upon meeting Chandler in Tallahassee,
he told the Republican leader that he was there at Grant's request
"to see that there was a fair count and that nothing wrong was
done on either side."[66] He also shared his atypically naïve belief
that Hayes "would not take the presidency if there was any fraud
in connection with the count. That if [Hayes] thought there was

a danger of his being counted in by fraudulent methods some
elector chosen as a Republican would vote for Tilden at Hayes'
request."[67] Chandler immediately realized that Barlow had no
idea of what was actually going on in Florida and might pose a
problem for the Republican effort. The Republican strategist also
understood that it would serve no purpose to alienate or irritate
the former general. Barlow, as Chandler later stated, was a man
of "many idiosyncrasies"—among which he seems to have counted
honesty—and, he proceeded to treat the well-connected "visiting
statesman" with all due courtesy and propriety while keeping
him under close observation and ignorant of the true nature of
the Republican mission.[68]

Barlow was originally selected to present the Republican case
for the count in Alachua County before the state returning board.
The county was under control of L. G. Dennis, who had falsified
the election returns by adding 219 Republican votes to the tally.[69]
Dennis had heard a rumor that Barlow was negotiating a deal
with the Democrats which would give the state to Hayes while
the Democrats took the governor's chair.[70] The story is impossible on its face as everything in Barlow's being and career
demonstrated his loathing of political corruption. Additionally, he
showed total uninterest in the gubernatorial contest during his
stay in Florida and afterwards, and even his most bitter critics
never lodged the charge against him. The rumor may have had
its roots in the Republicans' increasing concern about Barlow's
insistence on evenhanded scrutiny of both Democratic and Republican testimony and returns. In particular, Dennis and his men
worried that Barlow would find out the truth about the county
returns and expose them. They took their fears directly to Noyes,
who was Hayes's de facto personal representative in the state.
The agitated local Republicans told Noyes that the state's returns could not be split, that Florida could not give its electoral
votes to Hayes and install a Democrat in the governor's mansion
in Tallahassee. Barlow, they demanded, had to be removed from
managing the Republican efforts in the county.[71] Noyes sent his
visitors away with his assurances that all would be arranged. The
result, as Dennis put it dryly, was that "Mr. Barlow did not present the case as first intended."[72]

While personally and politically opposed to a Democratic victory, Barlow could not dismiss the dishonesty and trickery per-
petrated by Republican canvassers in Florida. While he arrived
in Florida innocent of Republican plans, the odor of fraud and
corruption grew unmistakable, and he would not ignore it. He

became increasingly convinced that Tilden had legally won the state by a slim margin, and began to argue his views openly. At a personal meeting in his rooms with Dr. F. A. Cowgill, one state Republican canvasser whom he thought was honest, Barlow pressed his case. Cowgill finally concurred, saying, "I agree with you. I can not conscientiously vote the other way; I can not conscientiously vote to give the state to the Hayes electors."[73] Unfortunately, Chandler was informed that Cowgill had gone to Barlow's rooms, and he sent one of his men to find out what they were up to. Honestly, but perhaps foolishly, Barlow told Chandler's man that he had been explaining the dishonest nature of the Republican canvass to Cowgill. Chandler's investigator made no reply but managed to get Cowgill to leave with him. The Republican canvasser soon fell back into line and Barlow never saw him again.[74]

The recount process reached its fraudulent conclusion when the returning board threw out enough Democratic votes, and accepted the Republican returns for Alachua County, so that a Tilden margin of 93 was reversed to a Hayes majority of 924. On 5 December, the returning board certified Hayes's electors, and the next day they cast their electoral votes for the Republican candidate.

Barlow, however, was not done. Fulfilling the assignment Grant had handed him, he submitted his report of the Florida vote, which the *New York Times* printed on December 15. Barlow described the Florida situation as complex and confusing and confessed, "I do not feel sure to-day whether the vote as actually cast gave Hayes or Tilden a majority."[75] But if the "actuality" were unknowable, the evidence on which the constitutional and legal issues were decided was not. And it was on this ground that Barlow took his stand. He stated that he came to his conclusions with "great hesitation, and I am conscious that in my desire to do exact justice, I may have borne too severely against my own party. But, if so, my errors of judgment will readily be detected, the evidence upon which I base my opinions being fully set forth. I have simply tried to put myself in the position which an impartial court would occupy in the matter."[76] The bulk of Barlow's report was a county-by-county analysis of the recount and the conflicting testimony of Democratic and Republican witnesses and canvassers. While he was critical of both Democratic and Republican teams and methods, he unequivocally presented his contention that many Democratic votes were unjustifiably rejected. Those who read the entire report with pen or pencil in hand could see that Barlow gave Florida to Tilden by a paper-thin margin.

Barlow's report was so detailed, however, that many apparently had difficulty negotiating its thick legalese and were uncertain as to its conclusions. Having been informed that some remained unsure of his meaning, Barlow wrote a letter, published in the *New York Herald,* in which he condensed and abstracted his brief, and boldly stated his conclusions. "I was not willing to give my own views without at the same time giving the evidence," he explained, "and hence my report was 'so long'."[77] Concerned that some readers might have erroneously assumed that he had deliberately buried his finding in a wordy, bureaucratic report, Barlow continued that he was "not unwilling to express my opinions, nor do I object to having any one to whom they are of consequence know them."[78] This time Barlow did the math himself and gave Florida to Tilden by a minuscule 55 votes.[79] Not surprisingly, Barlow's report and his more readily digestible letter were not well received by fellow Republicans. On 19 December, the *New York Herald* described Congressional Republicans as depressed by Barlow's letter "virtually conceding the state to Mr. Tilden. The letter produced a decidedly blue sensation among the republican [sic] senators."[80]

Grant neither commended Barlow's labors nor sent his report to the Senate.[81] Despite his evidence, a special electoral commission, tilted towards the Republicans, accepted the Republican returns in all three contested states and declared Hayes the winner of the election with 185 electoral votes to Tilden's 184. Most politicians, if not the entire public, knew the truth of the election of 1876. Hayes himself had personally supported the illegalities used to ensure his election and soon rewarded several members of the southern canvassing boards with government positions.[82] Although Grant's role was more ambiguous, he was fully aware of the measures taken to ensure Republican control of the White House.[83] The political price paid by the Republicans for reconciling the Democrats to the loss of the presidency was the removal of Federal troops from the south and the abandonment of the Reconstruction governments. Once Hayes ordered the end of Federal occupation, the disputed states quickly overturned the Republican governments, and elected conservative Democrats in their place. The South would remain "solid" for the Democrats until the 1960s.

The 1876 election investigations proved Barlow's last public service. As his first memorialist, Edward H. Abbot, put it, Barlow was never forgiven for telling the truth about the situation in Florida. Retribution followed quickly and Barlow was ostracized from Republican councils and became the subject of harsh criticism. Three years after the election, irate Republicans got their chance to publicly punish Barlow for betraying the party line. On 1 June 1878, the House of Representatives authorized a committee to investigate allegations of fraud which had emerged during the 1876 election and the southern recount. The Potter Committee, as it was popularly known, took its name from New York Democratic Congressman Clarkson N. Potter who had called for its creation and served as its chairman. At first, the Committee concentrated on charges of fraud in Louisiana, but in February 1879, it began to hear testimony about the Florida recount.[84] Called before the committee, Barlow found himself excoriated by Republican questioners as well as his Florida colleague and nemesis, William E. Chandler, who also appeared as a witness. The basis of the attacks was that, in addition to his role as "visiting statesman," Barlow was also a lawyer and therefore a "counsel" to the Republicans. As a "counsel," the Republican argument ran, he had a duty to support and maintain his client, Hayes, and his denunciations of Republican fraud and ultimate support for Tilden were "treacherous" and "dishonorable."[85] Barlow countered that he was never a counsel in the sense that he was a legal representative of the Republicans. In his role as "visiting statesman," his primary objective was to ensure an honest recount, though he was willing to lend his party the benefits of his knowledge.

Republican papers picked up Chandler's contention that Barlow was duplicitous for agreeing to serve as a Republican counsel and then presenting arguments that supported the Tilden cause. Trumpeting the party line, New York Times took a swipe at Barlow stating that he "has views regarding the privileges of a non-partisan and independent observer, and the obligations of a trusted legal counsel, which are not as his previous reputation would have led the public to expect of him."[86] Specifically, the Times denounced Barlow for helping the Republicans with their concluding arguments before the Returning Board and then trying to persuade Cowgill to give the state to Tilden. "A more judicious distribution of his zeal," the Times editorialist continued in cool but bitter language,"would have saved Mr. Barlow's character, which once stood very high, from harsh judgments, which however they may be regretted, appear inevitable."[87]

Barlow immediately reached for his pen and responded to the

Times' denunciation of his actions in Florida. In his lengthy letter, which the *Times* printed in its entirety on page two, Barlow
refuted all the allegations brought against him by Chandler and
the paper. "Your criticism in *The Times* of yesterday," he began,
"upon my course in Florida would be just if the facts were as you
understood them. But it is not true that I ever assumed the position or responsibilities of counsel or that I ever did say or entered into any agreement at all inconsistent with what I finally
did."[88] Barlow reiterated that he went to Florida to "see a fair
count . . . I understood this to mean that I was to do what I could
to see that both sides had fair play, and to announce my opinions
whatever they might be."[89] He then quoted Chandler's own testimony in which the Republican operative testified that after
informing Barlow that he wanted him to be the lead Republican
counsel, Barlow explained that he was there at Grant's request
to ensure an honest recount. Barlow vehemently disputed Chandler's contention that he was in Florida under the obligations of
counsel.[90] Nor did Barlow see any contradiction in serving on the
Republican team and working towards an honest recount. "Is it
an inconsistent and untenable position," he asked the *Times,* and
through its pages the public, "for a man to say I will gladly serve
for the Republican Party as to those . . . questions in which I think
it is right, but I will not press points which I do not believe in,
and if I think the party is wrong I will say so, and try to prevent
the injustice from being done?"[91]

Barlow admitted that his position was "curious and anomalous."
"But," he hurried to say,

> the whole situation was anomalous and curious—the going down into
> a state to see that the proceedings were justly conducted, which is
> what "seeing a fair count" seems to me to mean, if it means anything.
> On the one hand was my wish to have the Republicans succeed, im-
> pelling me to do for them all I honestly could, and, on the other, my
> desire to have exact justice done, and a fair and true account given of
> the proceedings as each man understood them. But however anom-
> alous the position, I cannot see that it was a dishonest one as long as
> it was freely avowed and fully understood which I say it was.[92]

Grant's former personal representative denied he had delivered
the Republican summation before the Returning Board, which
his critics offered as proof that he had indeed been their legal
counsel. When he was asked to make the concluding statements
Barlow explained that he had rejected the task ". . . on the express ground (among others) that this would involve my taking

the Republican grounds on all points which I would not do unless I believed in them."[93] Barlow did agree to present the Republican position in those areas where he concurred and to "present some remarks on the general principles which I thought should guide the [returning] board." In no case, Barlow emphasized, was the document which Barlow prepared for presentation to the Returning Board a summation of the Republican case.[94] Regarding the accusation that he had attempted to convince Cowgill to accept findings favorable to Tilden, Barlow stated that his discussions with Cowgill, and later public announcements of his findings, were made after all the evidence and arguments had been placed before the board and after he had informed the other members of the Republican team of his conclusions.[95] As far as Barlow was concerned, everything he had done was above board and honorable.

The *Times* did not agree. To its credit it ran Barlow's defense brief in a conspicuous spot, but it commented critically on it in the same issue. "Of course [Barlow's] disclaimer must be accepted as final as far as his position is concerned," the *Times* conceded. "[But] one can not but regret, however, that it was not made more clear to those intimately concerned in understanding him correctly at the time."[96] The *Times* charged that Barlow had made public arguments for the Republicans and reserved his reasons for supporting Democratic positions for "private meetings" with canvassers. This alleged practice, the *Times* went on, "may not have been inconsistent with his own standard of political and professional honor but which stands no chance of being approved by the general public."[97] The *Times* editorialist concluded his hostile analysis with the remark "To the casual observer, uninitiated in [Barlow's] peculiar mental processes his conduct seems very much like that of an advocate of one side who went over to the other."[98]

Nor was the *Times* finished with Barlow. On 24 February, they ran a short piece on page one under the heading "Gen Barlow's 'Neutrality'. A Letter Which Shows That He Did Assume to Act As Republican Counsel."[99] The letter in question had been entered before the Potter Committee by W. E. Chandler and a copy was forwarded to the *Times* for quick publication. The letter, written early in the canvass by Barlow to Judge James Bell of Monticello, Florida, was a recommendation for a post office employee on the grounds that he understood the Republican position and would help in the party's recount campaign. The *Times* crowed that the letter proved that Barlow was acting as a counsel and that "he was fully trusted as such by the Republican managers."[100]

Actually, the letter did not contradict Barlow's assertion that he aided his party where he could, but would not do so in instances where he believed them wrong. But the *Times* and the other Republican papers were determined to maintain the validity of Hayes' election. Barlow's flouting of party solidarity had threatened a Hayes victory in 1876 and helped cast a cloud of doubt over the legitimacy of his presidency. As far as most Republicans were concerned Barlow had betrayed his cause and must suffer the consequences. It was also true that Barlow's position was complex and that his actions in Florida seemed to shift. He came to the state expecting that his role as a Republican "visiting statesman" was perfectly compatible with his legal position. Mounting evidence of Republican chicanery probably came as an unwelcome surprise, and Barlow soon found himself torn between his desire to help his party and his commitment to honest politics. He tried to straddle the gulf between the competing objectives by aiding the Republicans where he could and lending his support to the Democratic argument when he felt he had to. In the end he had to come down on one side or the other. He stuck with his convictions. Most of his fellow Republicans would not or could not accept this. When the opportunity came to smear and defame him, they took it.

While many partisan Republican papers took their cue from Barlow's critics on the Potter Committee and piled on, the beleaguered war hero and former politician had his defenders. The reform-minded *Harper's Weekly,* which had long been a Barlow admirer,[101] charged that the committee's "cross-examination of General Barlow seems intended not to throw any light upon the question of fraud, but to be an attempted act of discipline of the witness for not insisting through thick and thin that the Republicans did carry Florida. The only result of such a course is to raise the question of whether the Republicans really did carry it."[102] *Harper's* heartily endorsed Barlow's position that his only legal obligation to the Republicans was to give him the benefit of his knowledge and expertise. "Just that," the *Harper's* editorialist wrote, "and that subordinated to . . . the supreme duty of seeing a fair count, not a Republican count."[103]

Barlow's galling experience before the Potter Committee and its aftermath no doubt confirmed his negative opinion of politics and politicians in general. It certainly reinforced his own resolve to avoid overt political participation—in the unlikely event that the Republicans were ever inclined to nominate him or appoint him to a position again. But Barlow's political problems ran deeper than his actions in the south. If further proof were needed, his work in the Florida recount demonstrated that he was simply not cut out for democratic politics. In addition to his unwilling-ness to indulge in, or at least tolerate, the political corruption of time, his unfiltered frankness would win him few friends among political timeservers or the public at large. As Abbot observed, "There is an unhappy significance in the fact that almost all of the high public functions which Barlow administered and which gave him the opportunity to do great deeds, came to him rather by appointment than election."[104] Barlow would have concurred. In a letter written in 1888, he identified the basic source of his inability to maintain a political career:

> The one thing which impresses and influences me most, after many years of experience is the unwillingness of most men ever to take any position hostile to themselves or their friends. Of course public offi-cers *must do this,* but most men have never been public officers and they regard only the obligations of a friend to a friend.[105]

Unfortunately, many public officials did *not* believe they had an obligation to place honesty, justice, and the public trust above self-interest or the advancement of friends and political allies. In peace, as in war, Barlow followed his conscience and went his own way. Unsurprisingly, this sometimes led to conflict and hard feel-ings. It did not lend itself to successful politicking.

Barlow did perform one last—minor—bit of public service in a presidential election. When the votes from New York City were counted in the presidential election of 1884, both Republicans and Democrats selected teams of counsels to monitor the proceedings in order to avoid charges of fraud or other irregularities. The Re-publicans sent five attorneys to monitor the proceedings, while the Democrats fielded 10 counsels to represent their interests. Francis Channing Barlow was one of them.[106]

FADE AWAY

Barlow no doubt realized that he had committed political suicide by his stand in the Florida matter. Ignoring the storm of abuse many Republicans tossed at him, he returned to New York and picked up his private practice which continued to prosper, un-affected by his flouting of the party line. Shortly after his re-turn from Florida, however, Barlow became embroiled in a bizarre dispute with fellow lawyer Elihu Root, who later became Theodore Roosevelt's Secretary of War. Root and Barlow were opposing lawyers in a case involving the Bank of North America. The suit was tried before a referee, William Stanley, and when it began to drag on, Stanley asked both counsels to conclude their arguments by means of written briefs. The two lawyers exchanged their summations before Christmas, and Barlow returned Root's, asking for his back. Root, assuming that each lawyer was to keep the other's written argument, had made notes on Barlow's statement and declined to return it, as this would reveal his defense. Barlow seemed to take Root's refusal as a breach of ethics, and he sent a formal notice to Root threatening a lawsuit if his brief were not returned. Taken aback by Barlow's heavy-handed reaction, Root fired off a note reading, "Dear Sir: Don't be a damned fool."[107]

Whether or not Barlow had acted in an overly officious and uncollegial manner, Root's decision to call Barlow a "fool" was ill-advised. It is unlikely Barlow would ever have turned the other cheek in the face of such a comment, and occurring as it did shortly after the Florida recount he might have been more short-tempered than ever. Additionally, Root had been one of Tweed's attorneys in 1873, a role guaranteed to incur Barlow's disdain. On 27 December 1877 he sent Root a lengthy reply, which was certainly meant—at least partly—facetiously, though Root did not see it that way. He began by stating that he had hoped their dispute could have been conducted in court without involving them personally. Then affecting an inability to decipher Root's handwriting, he asked Root to clarify whether he had written "damned" or "darned." Barlow, clearly enjoying himself, conceded that the latter expression was possibly less offensive and requested that Root explain which word he had chosen. Whichever one it was, however, he demanded that Root withdraw "the entire expression" of his offensive reply. Should Root decline to do so, Barlow asked whether he would meet him the following week at a designated spot in Canada "that we may settle this matter of difference in a dignified way"—in other words, a duel.[108] If Root refused the challenge, Barlow warned him "to be prepared to defend yourself (of course I mean by use of a firearm) whenever and wherever I may meet you."[109] In the event Barlow had not received satisfaction for his injury before the two lawyers were to meet with the referee on 6 January, Barlow mischievously suggested that Root "notify Mr. Stanley of our intentions, that he may absent himself from the room until the result of our meeting is determined."[110]

Root was shaken by Barlow's reaction and returned a note

stating that since it contained "a threat of assassination," he
could consider nothing else in Barlow's letter. Root then sought
the counsel of friends, who on looking over the letter advised him
that Barlow was in earnest and urged him to go to the district attorney, Anthony Phelps, for protection. The frightened lawyer
and his friends assured the district attorney that Barlow "was a
very excitable man and would just as soon kill Mr. Root as eat
his dinner."[111] After reading the letters, the district attorney
pronounced Barlow's missive a joke—which it certainly was. But
since the dispute involved men of stature and prominence he
consulted with Judge Noah Davis, who then called on Barlow to
get to the bottom of the matter. Barlow professed to be "aston-
ished" at the purpose of the judge's call and described his letter
as a jest, a declaration he later put into an explanatory letter to
Root's friends—although not to Root himself.[112]

The incident soon blew over though it caused a certain amount
of entertainment for the reading public and created a minor up-
roar in the legal circles. The *Times,* perhaps less pleased with
Barlow after his Florida declaration, commented that Barlow did
"not like to be called a fool, so he set about to make a fool of himself by sending the challenge to Mr. Root."[113] The judgment seems
overly harsh though it may reflect the temper of the times. But,
if Barlow suffered any embarrassment from the incident, and
there is no evidence either way, it was largely his own fault. However he meant it, the challenge to Root was likely to strike most
people as odd. Distinguished war heroes, and former attorneys
general, did not ordinarily demand satisfaction on the field of
honor. On the other hand Barlow had a lifelong reputation for eccentricity, and his decision to needle Root may be simply another
instance of his quirkiness. Barlow, who was aware of his reputation, might have consciously played upon it, not seriously intending to fight a duel, but to amuse himself by throwing a scare
into Root. He might also have seen it as a method of teaching the
young lawyer a little respect for someone of Barlow's experience
and position. One wonders if his actions amounted to a little psychological displacement. The course of action he facetiously suggested to Root might have been one he fantasized about handing out to those who had first sandbagged him, and then
condemned and abandoned him in Florida.

Although he had eased back into private practice after completing his work on the Florida inquiry, Barlow still kept abreast
of political events. In June 1877, he sent a letter to the *New York
Times,* arguing that civil service reform, a movement that was

then picking up speed, would not be practicable unless it was based on non-partisan appointment and tenure of office.[114] Having begun the prosecution, Barlow keenly followed the developments in the Tweed case as they unfolded. He developed a friendship with Charles S. Fairchild, who became deputy attorney general of New York State in 1874, the year after Barlow left the attorney general's office. Fairchild rose to attorney general in 1876, and ended his government service as Secretary of the Treasury under Grover Cleveland. A reform Democrat, Fairchild completed the prosecution against the Tweed Ring winning Barlow's respect and good will in the process. Barlow sent him written support when Fairchild came under fire in the press for not accepting a written confession made by Tweed. Barlow's distrust of newspapers and newspaper accounts stemmed from his experiences with the press during his military and political careers and the attack on Fairchild reawakened old grievances. "Newspaper editors are incapable of forming just conclusions," he wrote, "in some cases, even if the facts are before them." He went on to denounce the injustice of the criticism leveled at Fairchild as "disgusting and it makes me *sick*."[115]

In this instance, Barlow's condemnation of newspaper criticism directed at a friend may have been more than a knee-jerk reaction. Fairchild had rejected a written confession from Tweed, which went into detail about the nature and scope of the Ring's activities. The fallen boss also promised to supply more information which, together with his confession, would have provided a sweeping account of the Ring's operations including names, dates, and numbers. Tweed's documents could have provided the evidence necessary for the city to defend itself from nine million dollars in fraudulent claims, which were then being pressed by companies which had done business with Tweed.[116] Tweed had offered his confession in return for release from jail, an agreement to which Fairchild had originally assented, but then retracted after he had seen Tweed's letter. Fairchild's refusal to accept Tweed's admissions, and the cancelled checks and other papers Tweed promised to submit, effectively ended the prosecution of the Ring.

It is most likely that Fairchild, possibly directed by Tilden, suppressed Tweed's written confession and the other existing evidence, since it would implicate a wide variety of highly placed, highly respectable men in the city and state.[117] Or as the *Times* mused, "Could even Mr. Tilden afford to have Tweed's story told?"[118] Many highly respectable people of both political parties had found it useful and profitable to deal with Tweed when he was in power. It would prove embarrassing—perhaps, legally actionable—if their involvement or cooperation with the Ring came out in the aftermath of Tweed's fall. Good society had to be protected and Fairchild acted as their shield. With his legal knowledge and attorney general's experience to guide him, Barlow could not have failed to see the significance of Fairchild's maneuver. As willing as he was to flout public and political opinion and follow his own conscience, Barlow probably accepted that allowing the whole truth about the Tweed years to become public knowledge would amount to what the late twentieth century would call "mutually assured destruction." Like most of the other reformers he seemed satisfied to see the Ring broken and Tweed in jail. He would live to see Tammany Hall revive under bosses who had inherited Tweed's machine and improved on it.

Barlow's friendship with Fairchild continued until the general's death. In 1886, Fairchild was involved in a case designed to improve health and sanitation services in New York City. Barlow congratulated his friend on his actions in the matter and told him that he expected "to see the New York local health authorities driven to honest action by your decision."[119] In the same letter, Barlow demonstrated that he was not totally opposed to using his personal connections to the advantage of his law firm. He informed Fairchild that he had spoken "affectionately" of him at a social event, but, he went on to state chidingly, "*I* should have talked still more affectionately if you had gotten me into the Bell Telephone litigation."[120]

Fairchild returned Barlow's warm friendship. He later recalled that he had come to know Barlow when the latter was attorney general engaged in bringing suits against Tweed and the corrupt canal contractors. Watching him in action, Fairchild had been impressed by Barlow's sense of duty and disregard of the consequences of doing the right thing. " I see, as I recall it now," Fairchild mused, "Barlow set me a standard of public duty that has influenced all my life since."[121] Fairchild credited Barlow for paving the way for Tilden's politically profitable drive against corruption in the state. But it was Barlow who launched the assault on chicanery and malfeasance in New York State and Fairchild remembered that he had begun it "under circumstances of great difficulty and great danger to himself, for he was all alone. Not another state officer dared stand with him at the beginning of the fight."[122] Summing up Barlow's tenure as attorney general Fairchild concluded "that the State owes General Barlow more than it does any other single man for results without which the life of an honest man would have been intolerable in this state."[123]

Barlow's military career had been the central event of his life, and he looked back on his wartime experiences with pride and satisfaction. While he never wrote his memoirs or recollections, he presented his account of the storming of the Mule Shoe Salient before a meeting of the Massachusetts Commandery of the Military Order of the Loyal Legion of the United States which published it in 1879. He also kept up with the literature on the war, including campaigns in the west with which he was not involved. Unsurprisingly, he also participated in various veterans' events, such as meetings of the 61st New York veterans group and was elected president of the "2nd Corps Club" in July 1888. In late June of that year, he traveled back to Gettysburg with a few friends including a dozen whom he described as "mugwumps."[124] The latter reference was to the "reform" members within the national Republican Party, who had bolted the party to support Democrat Grover Cleveland during the 1884 election. Barlow, who had thought and acted like a "mugwump" before the word was coined, probably counted himself among their numbers. Whether Barlow went as far as supporting the Democratic candidate is uncertain, but Cleveland's Republican opponent, James G. Blaine, was widely regarded as corrupt, and Barlow's experience in Florida and its aftermath may have led him to embrace the total "mugwump" line.

Barlow's closest friend from the army was Nelson Miles. Miles had stayed in the army after the war and had gone on to carve out a distinguished record in the campaigns against the western Indians. The two men had maintained their friendship, and Barlow had followed Miles's military career in the west. In 1886, the position of major general in the regular army, one of the highest ranks in the small, nineteenth-century peacetime army, had opened. Barlow launched a lobbying campaign to help his old friend and comrade win the position. Among those he hoped to enlist in the cause was Samuel Tilden, now one of the Democrats' "elder statesmen." With Grover Cleveland, the first Democrat to win the presidency since 1856 in the White House, Barlow reckoned Tilden's support of Miles would carry considerable weight. He probably expected that a request for aid from a personal friend and former colleague—particularly one who had sacrificed his own political career on Tilden's behalf in the 1876 election—would induce the ex-presidential candidate to come out on Miles's behalf.

On 7 January 1886, Barlow sent Tilden a detailed letter, almost a legal brief, recommending Miles for the position and asking for Tilden's support in winning it. Three other officers, Terry, Crooke and Howard, had seniority over Miles, but Barlow pointed out that the President was not bound by that consideration alone. He dismissed Terry as a one-hit wonder, having gained only one isolated success in the war, the capture of Fort Fisher. Crooke, Barlow explained, was made a brigadier general by Grant in 1873, but "since then he does not appear to have done anything to warrant this new promotion."[125] Barlow personally admired Howard but did not think he was really in the running. The contest as he saw it was between Miles and Crooke. Barlow reviewed Miles's distinguished war record and emphasized the number of New York regiments in the First Division, II Corps in which Miles served under Barlow and later commanded. More to the point, Barlow argued that Miles was "superior in military ability to the others and has, certainly since the war, rendered more valuable and conspicuous service."[126]

The latter remark referred to Miles's record in the Indian Wars. According to Barlow, the factor that should convince Cleveland to waive seniority in the appointment was "the great skill and success of Miles in dealing with the Indians in *peace* as well as war."[127] Barlow went on to spell out Miles's expertise in Indian matters and the advantages it gave the nation and administration:

> I think it can not be questioned that he has the confidence and respect of the various tribes in a far greater degree than any of the other officers named has. He has thoroughly studied the question of the management and civilization of the Savages, and has long entertained the views on the subject which are expressed by the President in his late messages.[128]

To add a little more heft to his brief, Barlow drew Tilden's attention to the governor's own previously stated interest in Indian affairs. Additionally, he invited Tilden to make his own inquiries to test the accuracy of Barlow's presentation of the facts. "If you feel at liberty, and are willing, to aid General Miles, both he and I shall feel very grateful," he wrote in conclusion.[129] Despite the cogency of his appeal, Barlow was fated to be disappointed in his solicitation of Tilden's support. The former governor replied that he lacked sufficient knowledge to interfere in the appointment of a major general, especially since he had made it a rule not to make recommendations for appointments to federal positions.[130] Knowing Barlow's warm affection for Miles, and his proven practice of tapping political connections whenever he thought it useful, it seems unlikely that Tilden was the only influential politician contacted by Barlow. Any other efforts he might have made on Miles's behalf are not known, but whatever they were they did not result in instant success. Miles had to wait four years until 5 April 1890, before receiving his promotion to major generalship. Five years later he reached the pinnacle of his career when he was appointed as commanding general of the army.[131]

In 1893, Miles invited Barlow, his son Robert, and several other old friends on a trip to the west. During the trip the two old friends reminisced and swapped many stories about their wartime experiences. Barlow recounted one which not only got a rise out of Miles, but also sheds some light on the history and composition of Homer's *Prisoners from the Front*. In 1938, Robert Gould Shaw Barlow sent a letter to the Metropolitan Museum of Art, which owns the painting, explaining how Homer created one of its central figures:

> During the war Winslow Homer had been at the front and painted pictures of soldiers there. . . . One of Homer's pictures represented some confederate prisoners being inspected by a Union officer. Miles was a very fine figure of a man, and my father was nothing special in this respect. So Homer got Miles to pose for the officer's figure. Then when the figure was finished, Homer put my father's head on top of Miles' body, apparently merely because my father held higher rank than Miles. At any rate Miles was seriously annoyed.[132]

In the late 1880s, the Grand Army of the Republic (GAR), the major Union veterans organization—not without considerable internal dissension—pressed the government to provide a pension, for any veteran of 90 days service and more who had any sort of disability, war related or not.[133] The measure became law when President Benjamin Harrison refused to veto it as had his predecessor, Grover Cleveland. Barlow was adamantly opposed to such a program. After discussing the issue with E. L. Godkin, editor of *The Nation* and fellow Mugwump, Barlow wrote out his thoughts on the matter and sent them to Godkin who arranged for them to be published by the *New York Evening Post*. The letter, intended for publication, appeared in the August 9 edition taking up the better part of a page. In the course of his argument, during which he referred to his own wartime experiences, Barlow charged that the pension bill was "not only a great wrong to the taxpayers of this country, but is fatal to its military spirit, and to the manhood of the solders who served during the late war, and to that of the future soldiers of this country."[134] Barlow made it clear he had no problem with earlier pensions that went to those who had been wounded or disabled or to the wives and children of those who had been killed, but that otherwise soldiers should be satisfied with the knowledge that they have done their duty out of patriotism. "A soldier of our army always has and always will have especial honor from his fellow citizens," he wrote:

> Other things being equal, he will always stand higher in public estimation than his neighbors who did not share in the dangers and toils of war, and in almost all states he is preferred to others in the civil service statutes in public employment. This and his own approving conscience is a soldier's surplus reward over and above that the government agree to pay him.[135]

Barlow's bitter hostility to the pension plan drew fuel from his knowledge that "many men who served in the army (who however large in numbers, were of course small as compared to the whole number of soldiers) did not render any such service as entitles them to any consideration. Mortifying as it is, and disagreeable as it is, the truth requires it to be stated that there were cowards, stragglers and shirkers in the army."[136] Barlow cited some of his own frustrations in attempting to rid the army of such men. "More than once," he explained, "I secured the dismissal of an officer of inferior rank from the service because of cowardice or misconduct and some months afterward I found him riding about as a colonel."[137] That such men should be eligible for any sort of pension infuriated Barlow. Perhaps thinking of Arabella, he also voiced his opinion that many soldiers, particularly those on short-term garrison duty, had it easier than civilians who were involved in the war effort.[138] Barlow contrasted the hordes of often undeserving northern veterans seeking a handout (whom he satirized as acting as the mythical "Daughters of the Horse Leech") with Confederate veterans who "never complained," and relied for such assistance as they needed upon "the people of their own localities as should be done in the case of northern veterans who were not disabled in the service."[139]

In Barlow's estimation, the end result of such a poorly conceived pension plan was the demoralization of America's future soldiers. "If we ever become involved in another war," he asserted,

> every man who personally remembers this pension legislation, or who derives knowledge of it from tradition or from history, may justly

feel that valor and duty are the last things which he need consider. He will feel that when the war is over, an organization of those who have served in it can, without any necessary reference to their merits, so influence the legislation of the country, that whether he has been brave, faithful, and steadfast, or whether he has fallen out at the approach of the enemy, or has run away in battle, or whether when he was captured, he has enlisted in the army of the enemy and fought against his comrades, or whether, without ever having approached the enemy, he has been incapacitated by disgraceful diseases, he will still be a hero to his countrymen, and be entitled to all the honors and benefits which should only be bestowed upon brave and faithful soldiers.[140]

As usual when storming an enemy position, Barlow held nothing back and he blamed the GAR for the offensively generous pension. The now aging "Boy General" asserted that many GAR posts were dominated by those "who do not know what the army and war really were."[141] Nevertheless, Barlow recognized the potency of such a large and well-organized lobby in dealing with Congress. The only recourse Barlow saw was a revolt of the taxpayers, ousting Congressmen who voted for the plan. An experienced politician, Barlow probably held little real hope for such a turn of events. However logical his arguments, his campaign against the pension plan was one he was destined to lose, and it was likely that he knew it from the start.

Possibly because of the wounds he bore from his non-military service in Florida, Barlow increasingly refrained from public ceremonies and commemorations of the war. Moreover, he found military displays and memorial ceremonies increasingly overblown and self-aggrandizing. "Since the war there has been too much tendency to show," he complained. "We can not have the slightest military or quasi-military display without an exhibition of absurd inflation."[142] Worse, some of those prominently involved in such celebrations did not deserve the honor. "Within the last few years," Barlow observed bitterly, "I read an account of some imposing ceremonial upon the dedication of a monument to the memory of brave men upon a conspicuous battlefield. The orator on this occasion (so far as I can know from the newspaper reports) was a general officer who had been dismissed from the service for cowardice in action."[143]

The war, its memories, and those he had fought with and against, were never far from Barlow's mind. Occasionally the past would intrude into the present in the most unpredictable ways. In the spring of 1895, Barlow and his son, Charles Lowell Barlow, made

Francis Channing Barlow's final resting place, the Penniman family tomb, Walnut Street Cemetery, Brookline, Massachusetts. Barlow's maternal grandparents, mother, and brothers are interred with him. The bronze plaque, installed by the Lafayette Post 140, Department of New York, Grand Army of the Republic, is inscribed "Francis Channing Barlow. Born Oct. 19, 1834. Died Jan. 11, 1896. Enrolled as a private soldier, Apr. 19, 1861. Appointed Major General of Volunteers May 26, 1865." *Author's Collection.*

a visit to Thomasville, Georgia. One night a knock came on the door and the two Barlows admitted a man who explained, "General Barlow I am the night watchman and was the Confederate soldier who picked you up at Gettysburg."[144]

Barlow continued at his law practice until his death. He never again sought public office, and showed an "unwillingness to exhibit himself on public occasions."[145] The daring, aggressive, and courageous general, who had figured prominently in official reports and papers during the Civil War, began to slip into public obscurity, years before his death. While many Civil War officers retained their celebrity until the time of their deaths, and some basked in the status of national legends and heroes, Barlow's withdrawal into conventional law practice and family life made him unfamiliar to those who had not lived through the war. Abbott observed that he spent the last years of his life so quietly that "the generation now at the front scarcely appreciates how large a figure he was during the War of the Rebellion and the next ten years while he continued his public life."[146]

In December 1895, Barlow fell ill, and it was clear his situation was serious. Among those who came to visit him at this time was James A. Scrymser, an old friend who, after the Civil War, had gone on to a distinguished and lucrative career organizing telegraphic cable communications with Latin America and Cuba. Not surprisingly, the conversation between the two men often drifted back to the war which they had fought in their youth. Scrymser found that Barlow's mind kept returning to Arabella.[147] Frank predicted that the time would come for "the finest monument in this country" to be built to the memory of the "loyal women of the Civil War." Although in failing health, Barlow grew empathic about the monument and said that someone should take the lead "in reminding the country of the immense debt of gratitude which it owed the heroic women of the war."[148] Barlow's deathbed enthusiasm about the subject indicates that Arabella's memory remained vivid to him, and he was anxious to ensure some recognition of her importance in his life while he still could. Scrymser promised his old friend that he would do all he could to carry out his wishes and see to the erection of such a monument. Though Scrymser kept his pledge and did all in his power to fulfill Barlow's request, he was thwarted in the end by politics.[149]

Barlow died at his home at 39 East 31st Street on 11 January 1896. The *New York Herald* reported that he had died of Bright's disease.[150] According to The *New York Times,* Barlow had been ill for several weeks before his death. The *Times* account stated that he had been struck with a severe attack of the "grip" a year previously, and had never fully recovered. The small headline over the *Times* story proclaimed "The Gallant Soldier a Victim of the Effects of Grip."[151] Whether it was Bright's disease or the grip, Barlow was dead. He was 61 years old at the time. The funeral service was held two days after his death at the Church of the Incarnation on Madison Avenue and 35th Street. Though Barlow had spent all his professional, military, and political life in New York, the pull of his native state apparently never left him. His body was returned to Brookline, Massachusetts where he was interred in a tomb with his mother and brothers.[152]

10
Afterlife

As Barlow slipped into public obscurity during the last 20 years of his life, his exploits still found themselves into print. Excluding veterans and those absorbed by military history, Barlow's fame among the general public rested on the widespread dissemination of his supposed encounter with General John Gordon, after he fell on the first day at Gettysburg (see chapter 4). The first appearance of the incident is not precisely known. Nevertheless, the *Boston Transcript* ran a lengthy account of the meeting between Barlow and Gordon in early 1879. This version, picked up by other papers throughout the country, including the south, includes detailed conversation between the two as Gordon supposedly came to a fallen foe's aid and Barlow, fulfilling the expectations of mid-Victorian sentimentality, asked Gordon to read his last letter to his wife, and tell her of his whereabouts before he died. The alleged meeting of the two men at a dinner party in Washington after the war also appears in the *Transcript* story.[1]

The Barlow-Gordon encounter soon took on a life of its own and became one of the most enduring legends of the war. A slightly more elaborate rendition of the meeting appeared in *McClure's Magazine* in the 1880s. This version was reprinted in *Campfire and Battlefield,* a popular illustrated history of the war published in 1894.[2] Gordon, who had been using the incident in speeches for many years, included it in his published memoirs, *Reminiscences of the Civil War,* in 1904. The touching story continued to be accepted and repeated, apparently without contradiction or challenge, into the 1960s. Montgomery's *The Shaping of a Battle. Gettysburg* (Philadelphia & New York: Chilton Company—Book Division Publishers, 1959) recounted the battlefield meeting including most of the courtly dialog. Ezra Warner's *Generals in Blue* (Baton Rouge: Louisiana State University Press, 1964) contains a mention of the story, albeit briefly. However, in 1985 the accepted truth about Barlow's fate at Gettysburg was challenged

248

in print.[3] This belated debunking of the Gordon-Barlow encounter resulted from scholars researching his wartime letters—especially his 7 July 1863 missive—which became publicly available in 1942. In the letter describing his experiences at Gettysburg, Barlow mentions visits from several Confederate officers, but Gordon was not among them.[4] Since that time, it has become common among Civil War historians to dismiss the Gettysburg meeting as a well-intended fabrication.

But consigning the Barlow-Gordon exchange to the status of apocrypha leaves many questions unanswered. To begin with, the 7 July letter is incomplete. Although the letter breaks off after the point where Barlow describes the Confederates he met while in their hands, it is simply impossible to know what else he wrote. Moreover, the Barlow-Gordon meeting had achieved wide currency by 1880, 16 years before Barlow's death. He must have been aware of it, and asked about it as well. No evidence exists which indicates that he ever denounced the story as a fabrication. On the other hand, no evidence survives showing that he affirmed it either. His silence, however, allowed the story to gain widespread currency as an authentic wartime incident which he could have demolished with a single statement if he so chose. Everyone who ever had any contact with Barlow, those who liked him and those who did not, agree that he was bluntly honest, even when it worked against his personal interests. If the Gordon story was entirely false, his silence on the subject is entirely out of character. Additionally, Barlow did meet Gordon on several occasions after the war and at least once at a conspicuous public ceremony.

In July 1888, the 25th anniversary of the Battle of Gettysburg was commemorated with a reunion of both Federal and Confederate veterans, the unveiling of memorials, and events featuring major participants in the battle. James Longstreet and John Gordon were the most distinguished ex-Confederate leaders present. While former Union Corps commanders Daniel Sickles and Henry Slocum received most of the attention on the northern side, Barlow also attended.[5]

On the morning of 3 July, Barlow and Gordon met on the site of the first day's battle. According to the *New York Times* "The two men met for the second time in 25 years and the meeting was rather affecting. Gen. Barlow was left upon the field on the first day's fight. He was found by Gen. Gordon, who not only saw that he was taken care of, but allowed Mrs. Barlow to come through the lines to nurse her husband."[6] The *Times* account of the generals' personal reunion at Gettysburg lends credence to Gordon's descriptions of their wartime meeting. Furthermore, its appearance in a major New York daily gave Barlow another opportunity to dismiss it as a myth. He did not.

In the absence of any definitive statement by Barlow, it is likely there will always be an element of uncertainty regarding the events at Blocher's Knoll on the first day at Gettysburg. The most likely scenario is that Gordon did pause and speak to him on the battlefield and possibly later when he was held prisoner. After all, Barlow was a celebrity captive, and it is likely Confederate officers wished to see him and possibly interrogate him. On the other hand, the story certainly became embellished over time. It is most unlikely that in the swirl of battle, with one man down and badly wounded and the other trying to press his attack, that the two men engaged in the type of drawing room conversation that appeared in later accounts. Barlow may have accepted the exaggerations as insignificant annoyances to be borne to aid in the larger goal of national reconciliation. It is hard to see him remaining silent in the face of a complete falsehood involving his name.

Shortly after his death, Barlow's public exploits were commemorated by his alma mater. At the time, the Class of 1855—Barlow's graduating class—held the right to nominate two candidates to fill the last vacant windows in Harvard's Memorial Hall. Though Harvard maintained a rule that only those who had been dead 100 years were eligible for this honor, the Class of 1855 requested that two men from its own graduating year be depicted on the windows. A groundswell of support arose pressuring the University to waive its usual practice and permit the class to honor their own. Shortly after Barlow's death, Edward H. Abbot argued that the two vacancies honor Phillips Brooks and Francis Channing Barlow. Brooks, who had acted as Barlow's go-between in his attempt to re-establish contact with his long-estranged father in 1864, went on to become a popular preacher and the Episcopal bishop of Massachusetts. Barlow, of course, had a distinguished military and political career. In the end, Harvard's regulations were circumvented by installing stained-glass windows which ostensibly depicted Bernard of Clairvaux, a 12th-century reforming monk, and Godefroy of Bouillon, a leader of the First Crusade, who was described as "the perfect type of Christian knight." In selecting models for the subjects' faces, however, the artist, Edward Sperry, chose individuals much closer to him in time. It is certainly no accident that the knight bears Barlow's face, while the abbot has Brooks' visage. Tacitly, Harvard had bowed to its alumni's demands, and permitted the figures of "two graduates of unique history" to appear on the Memorial Hall windows.[7]

The most conspicuous memorial to Barlow's services was the eight and one-half foot statue of the "Boy General," which the New York State Monuments Commission erected at Gettysburg. Even before the Civil War was over, veterans of battles erected monuments commemorating fallen friends and marking their participation. As the United States government began creating the National Battlefield Parks system in the early twentieth century, both state governments and veterans organizations became involved in placing monuments, markers, and memorials, some extremely elaborate, on various parts of the old battlefields. Gettysburg, widely considered the decisive battle of the conflict, became studded with all types of memorials from markers denoting regimental positions, to large and ornate state monuments, as well as statues of leading personalities. Eight New York generals are memorialized by statues at Gettysburg.

In summer 1920, as part of the preparations for the 60th anniversary of the battle, The New York Monuments Commission chose Francis Channing Barlow as the subject of a statuary memorial. In 1921, the state legislature appropriated the necessary funds for the project.[8] The model for the statue, which depicts Barlow on foot, bareheaded and facing the direction of the onrushing Confederates, was designed by J. Massey Rhind. The actual eight and one-half foot statue was placed atop a 10 foot, one inch pedestal of New Hampshire granite. The entire monument, statue and base, cost $9,899.30 somewhat under the $12,000 the state had appropriated.[9]

Most fitting, the statue was situated on "Barlow's Knoll," where he had vainly tried to hold off Early's division before going down with an abdominal wound.[10] On 6 June 1922, the official ceremonies dedicating the monument were held. New York State had allocated an additional $8,000 for the event and a special charter train provided by the Pennsylvania Rail Road transported the most prominent of the 140 participants to the ceremony.[11] Barlow's immediate family, his widow, Ellen, sons Robert Shaw Barlow and Charles Lowell Barlow, as well as daughter Louisa Barlow Jay, were present on the field. The next generation was represented by his granddaughters, Frances Barlow Jay, who unveiled the statue, and Louisa Barlow Jay. Colonel Lewis R. Stegman, Chairman of the New York Monuments Commission and Civil War veteran, made a lengthy address. Nelson Miles, who knew Barlow's military career more fully and intimately than anyone else

Participants at the Dedication of Barlow's Monument at Gettysburg, June 6, 1922. Barlow's son, Charles Lowell Barlow stands second left in hat. The bespectacled girl in the middle is Barlow's granddaughter, Louisa Jay. *In Memoriam. Francis Channing Barlow, 1923.*

present, delivered only a few words. The obligatory state officials put in their appearances and the ceremony was filled out with musketry and a commemorative poem which was about as good as could be expected.[12] The following day, the dedication party visited Antietam, where they no doubt gave special attention to the sunken road.

Unfortunately, Barlow's last-minute hopes for a monument to

celebrate the service of Arabella and the other loyal women of the war never reached fruition. James A. Scrymser, who had promised Barlow he would take the lead in arranging such memorial, proposed it to the New York Commandery of the Loyal Legion in 1911. Scrymser proposed raising $500,000 for such a monument to be erected in Washington and pledged $50,000 of his own money.[13] Despite his efforts, Scrymser was unable to raise the required amount and shifted gears by offering to use the funds raised by the New York Commandery of the Loyal Legion to build a Red Cross headquarters which would be dedicated to the memory of the "Loyal Women of the War." All that was left to do was for Congress to appropriate the necessary funds to acquire the site for the building. But southern Congressmen choked on the word "Loyal" and the appropriations bill failed to pass.[14] Scrymser and the New York Commandery withdrew their organization's support, but Scrymser personally contributed $100,000[15] to a new proposed a Red Cross headquarters which was to be dedicated to "the heroic women of the Civil War both north and south." On December 6, 1914, the *New York Times* ran an article describing the memorial building and explaining Scrymser's efforts in its inception. Almost half the article was devoted to the story of Frank and Arabella's marriage, Barlow's deathbed request that a memorial be erected to his wife and the other loyal women of the war, and the change of dedication to encompass both Union and Confederate womanhood.[16] While not what Scrymser had in mind when he undertook the project, he took some comfort in "partially" carrying out Barlow's wishes.[17]

Scrymser's book itself is partly a memorial to Barlow. While a memoir of his activities, especially his work in establishing telegraphic communication with Latin America, Scrymser includes some detailed information about Barlow during the 1860–62 period, and again during his final days. There is no reason to doubt his friendship with Francis—his attempts to gain the Arabella/loyal women monument attest to that—but unfortunately some of the fascinating anecdotes he tells are at odds with the official records. The most glaring discrepancy concerns his account of how he and Barlow signed up with the 12th New York infantry on the night of 19 April 1861. The official rosters published in *New York in the War of the Rebellion, 1861–1865* do not list Scrymser as a member of the regiment.[18] Nor is there any record of his service in that regiment in the National Archives. He is, however, found in the returns for the 43d New York Infantry, in which he served from 2 October 1861 to 16 February 1863. It is, of course, possible that his name was inadvertently omitted from the rosters of the 12th New York, but this does not seem likely. Scrymser also states that Frank decided to join the 12th New York after running across Captain Alfred Jones, the regiment's chaplain, whom Scrymser described as a friend. Jones described the 12th as a "damned good regiment" and Barlow, amused by the alleged chaplain's profanity, decided he and Scrysmer should join up. Unfortunately, like Scrymser himself, Jones was not listed in the ranks of the 12th New York, nor on the roster of any other New York regiment for that matter. Scrymser's falsification (if it was) of his service record casts doubt on the rest of his reminiscences regarding Barlow. Consequently, it is difficult to determine when he was accurately presenting his experiences and when he was inventing or embellishing for effect. At the very least his account cannot be taken at face value.

While Barlow's political career faded quickly from public memory, and later historians largely overlooked it, his military experiences figured prominently in many of the works penned by veterans in the latter nineteenth century. Francis A. Walker's *History of the Second Army Corps* (1887) contains numerous references to Barlow, especially during the 1864 campaign. Walker depicts Barlow as a tough disciplinarian—a characteristic which was emphasized by everyone who wrote about him—an excellent officer, and brave, aggressive fighter. Unit histories and personal memoirs also tended to paint a positive picture of the general. Charles Fuller's *Recollections of the War of 1861,* which appeared ten years after Barlow's death, is almost idolatrous in its praise of Barlow. While Fuller agrees with all other sources that Frank Barlow was a strict, unbending taskmaster, he is credited with getting his men ready for combat, and leading them successfully in battle. John Black's memoir of the Mule Shoe Assault, which was published in 1898, presents an intelligent, conscientious commander, carefully preparing his men for the dangerous and risky assault which had been assigned to them. Like most regimental histories of the time, Frederick Gilbert's record of the 57th New York, which served in Barlow's third brigade, is primarily devoted to regimental officers. Yet, Barlow's disciplinary procedures are mentioned favorably—they increased combat survivability—and Barlow is described as strict but "tender hearted," a phrase seldom found in recollections of Frank Barlow.[19]

Negative descriptions of Barlow were rare in memoirs and unit histories. While soldiers and officers wrote critically about him, such passages were primarily found in letters and unpublished memoirs. The major exception to this pattern is Conyngham's *History of the Irish Brigade and Its Campaigns* (1867). Strong criticism of Barlow is found in the section on the 1864 campaigns which was written by William O' Meagher, who describes Barlow's poor relationship with the Irish Brigade as coming to a head during the Second Deep Bottom Campaign. (See chapter 7.) In O'Meagher's account, Barlow, though personally brave, was a harsh, unpleasant, callous martinet given to disparaging his troops and wasting their lives. While parts of O'Meagher's tale of the Irish Brigade at Second Deep Bottom sound exaggerated, they reveal genuine friction between Barlow and this renowned unit. It is likely that many who served in the heavily German regiments in the XI Corps would have seconded this assessment. Certainly, private letters and accounts, while citing Barlow's courage, show that many thought him unduly harsh and unjust.

The only other negative recollection of Barlow which was published in the nineteenth century was Captain Robert S. Robertson's memoir of the relatively small-scale actions along the Totopotomoy line on 30–31 May 1864.[20] While refraining from commenting on Barlow's behavior, he uses his remembrance of Barlow's own words and demeanor to convey the image of an inflexible, unimaginative commander who persisted in trying to throw green troops against an impregnable defensive position. Although one of the more unflattering presentations of Barlow in action, Robertson's memoir was not widely circulated and does not seem to have been used by later historians.[21]

One of the more important firsthand accounts of the 1864–65 campaigns which contains many references to Barlow was Theodore Lyman's *With Grant & Meade from the Wilderness to Appomattox*. Based on a collection of Lyman's letters to his wife, the volume was not published until 1922. Lyman, who had been a classmate of Barlow's at Harvard, includes personal anecdotes as well as accounts of his abilities as a divisional commander and combat leader. Though Lyman describes Barlow as a unique, somewhat idiosyncratic personality, as a soldier Barlow emerges from Lyman's pages as an organizer and fighter of the first rank.

The era of major firsthand accounts receded with the aging of the Civil War generation and a decline in public interest as two world wars raged across the world. After World War II, a new generation of historians returned to the Civil War, inaugurating an outburst of scholarly activity which has dipped and peaked, but never entirely faded ever since. Of course, any discussion of the Virginia campaigns required at least some consideration of Barlow.

Perhaps the most influential Civil War historian of the 1950s and 1960s was Bruce Catton. Catton was an experienced journalist, who combined solid research, sober judgments, and sharp, lucid, and gripping prose. He was among the first of the modern generation of historians to mine the memoirs, diaries, and narratives of the common soldiers which had been turned out in considerable numbers in the late nineteenth century but that had largely gathered dust after 1918. In addition to editing *American Heritage,* Catton turned out two studies of Grant's generalship; a special three-volume centennial history of the war; a single-volume history of the conflict, *This Hallowed Ground;* and a three-volume study of the Army of the Potomac. The last volume of this series, *A Stillness at Appomattox* (Garden City: Doubleday, 1953), a study of the 1864–65 campaigns in Virginia, won a Pulitzer Prize for its author.

A Stillness at Appomattox includes a detailed description of Barlow on the eve of what might have been his most dramatic assignment of the war—the attack on the Salient. With his perceptive eye and gift for language, Catton created an accurate and memorable verbal picture of the "Boy General":

> he was a slight, frail looking man with no color in his cheeks, a loose-jointed unsoldierly air about him when he walked, with deadly emotion-less eyes looking out of a clean-shaven face, and when he spoke his voice seemed thin and lackluster. To all appearances he was no soldier at all, but the man who went by Barlow's appearance was badly deceived. He was hard and cold and very much in earnest, a driving disciplinarian who began by making his men hate him and ended by winning their respect because he always seemed to know what he was doing and because the spirit of fear was not in him . . . . underneath everything there was a ferocious fighting man who drove himself and his men as if the doorway to Hell were opening close behind them.[22]

Catton's capsule assessment of Barlow's character was based mostly on written sources, but it seems also influenced by the photograph taken of him with Hancock, Gibbon, and Birney at Cold Harbor. Most of the photographs of Barlow taken during the war were profile, as was Homer's perspective in *Prisoners from the Front.* Brady took three photographs of Hancock and his divisional leaders at Cold Harbor. In the close-up, head-on shot, the most frequently published of the group, Barlow struck a casual pose with his saber, staring straight at the camera, possibly even leaning against the tree behind him. His gaze, as Catton described it, does seem both deadly and emotionless, yet it suggests the fire and drive mentioned in virtually all written descriptions. Of course, reading too much into a single picture can be dangerous. It took about 20 seconds to make a photograph using the technology available to Brady, and this might have affected Barlow's expression. On the other hand, his attitude stands apart from the others in the photograph, and the man in the photograph certainly fits the image of the Barlow who comes across in written accounts.

As the number of new works and reprints increased in volume during the Civil War Centennial and after, Barlow's role in the conflict and his battlefield performance received increasing mention. The most up-to-date study of the Battle of Antietam, Stephen Sears' *Landscape Turned Red* (New York: Ticknor & Fields, 1983), credits Barlow for breaking the Confederate position at the Sunken Road. Sears describes Barlow as possessing a "ruthless, driving energy" and approvingly describes him rushing to the hot spots on his front where he was most needed and could do the most good.[23]

The most extensive previously published study of Barlow is found in Thomas Buell's *The Warrior Generals. Combat Leadership in the Civil War.* (New York: Crown Publishers, Inc., 1997). Buell approached the Civil War by selecting several generals, Union and Confederate, whom he believed personified the different approaches and experiences in the conflict. Some of his choices are obvious: Lee, Grant, Sherman, and George Thomas whom he rates most highly as an Army commander. More originally, Buell examines the war through the careers of Barlow and John Bell Gordon, two men who rose through the chain of command on the strength of their performance in battle. Somewhat subjectively, Buell assigns each of his subjects a descriptive title intended to summarize the military personality of his subjects. Lee, for example, is "The Aristocrat," Grant "The Yeoman" and Gordon is designated "The Cavalier" which is neatly balanced by dubbing Barlow "The Puritan."[24] Buell is quick to point out that he does not mean "Puritan" in a theological sense, but rather as a system of values. One sees what Buell has in mind, though a Puritan in a non-theological sense is akin to a Marxist in a non-economic sense. Yet, in many ways, the term is appropriately applied to Barlow. Barlow's own family roots were certainly Puritan in all meanings of the term, though the theological system was effectively dead in New England by the time he was born, being replaced by either Presbyterianism or, in his case, Unitarianism. As a way of describing Frank's unswerving, and unquestioning, belief in his own values, opinions, and actions, the term "Puritan" is not entirely off base. On the other hand, a major component of New England Calvinism was an emphasis on community cohesion and conformity of thought which were totally alien to Barlow's nature. In many ways Barlow might have been better dubbed "The Maverick" or "The Egoist."

Whatever the plusses and minuses of Buell's descriptive names, he was the first author to present Barlow's entire wartime history in any detail. Additionally, he unearthed some previously unpublished information about Barlow's fractured family background. His narrative is accurate and readable, although the nature of the book precludes a fully developed study of Barlow's military and political careers.

Francis Channing Barlow was a man of consummate self-confidence. He believed in himself and his abilities—and duties—in a way that few men did. Intelligent, thorough, fearless, Barlow brought to both his military and political careers a burning sense of commitment and lust for success. In the war, he made himself into a first-rate field commander who seldom failed in his assignments. He was not flawless. His self-confidence easily slid into arrogance, and he sometimes alienated men unnecessarily. At times, primarily during the increasingly stressful and debilitating Overland-Petersburg campaign, he made errors.[24] Among these were insisting on a charge at Totopotomoy, blundering on the road to Petersburg and refusing to admit it for what it was, feeding his men in piecemeal at Second Deep Bottom, and letting personal biases color his relations with German and Irish troops. All these actions and attitudes demonstrated questionable judgment or outright mistakes. Against that must be balanced his continual success in transforming his commands into some of the sharpest, most reliable, combat effective units in the army. Additionally, he drove himself at least as hard as his men, typically led from or near the front, and developed a keen sense for storming into the critical point on the battlefield. Commensurate with the size of the units he led—regiment, brigade, and division—Barlow earned a place on a select list of the most effective fighters in the Army of the Potomac.

His bravery, refusal to compromise principle, and an almost contempt for possible negative consequences of doing his duty, carried over from his military to his civilian career. Here these attributes were less effective. While he provided good—sometimes excellent—service to his state and nation in the various posts he held 1865-76, his bare-knuckled frankness was simply unsuited for a democratic politics—especially as practiced at the time. Yet, if his influence and circle of political friends and acquaintances declined, and the public forgot or never knew him, he could take pride in a life spent in the performance of duty to himself and his country. He had kept faith with himself, his principles, his family and his country. A man cannot do more.

Notes

CHAPTER 1. THE APPRENTICE WARRIOR

1. Susan Barlow Holmes, "Barlow Clearinghouse." Barlow Webpage. Ancestry.com.

2. Anna Barlow Nielsen, "History of General Francis Channing Barlow's Family," 1998. Unpublished mss. Author's collection.

3. Robert N. Hudspeth, *The Letters of Margaret Fuller,* Vol. I (Ithaca: Cornell University Press, 1983), 212.

4. Louisa Barlow Jay, "Data on the Barlows. Compiled by Louisa Barlow Jay, for Ham and Ellen Shaw and Leake Barlow Keen. March 1951." By permission of the Houghton Library, Harvard University. bMS Am 1910, 175.

5. George William Curtis, *Early Letters of George William Curtis to John S. Dwight. Brook Farm and Concord,* ed. George Willis Cooke (New York: Harper & Brothers Publishers, 1898), 74, 94.

6. Ibid., 74.

7. Edward Bliss Emerson was the brother of Ralph Waldo Emerson. When Edward Emerson died in Puerto Rico in October 1834, Hatch Barlow wrote a poem in his memory which greatly pleased Ralph Waldo Emerson. Letter, Ralph Waldo Emerson to David Hatch Barlow, 24 October 1834. By permission of the Houghton Library, Harvard University. bMS Am 1280.226. (1709)

8. The church, located at 50 Monroe Place, later took the name Church of the Savior.

9. Edith Roelker Curtis, "A Season in Utopia," *American Heritage,* April 1959, 58.

10. Ibid., 60.

11. The exact causes and nature of David Hatch Barlow's psychological problems are not known, but he apparently suffered from hallucinations. Writing to James Russell Lowell from Dedham in 1844, Barlow described a "vision" which "I saw with my own eyes in a state of high nervous excitement, though otherwise in complete possession of my faculties." In his vision, a large building appeared in open country, and from it emerged a long procession of men and women in long, dark robes which passed by his window. Among the figures were his dead mother, an old family nurse, Almira, and "my beautiful infant boy," probably Richard, who was the youngest. At the end of the column came a man with a rifle who pointed it at Barlow's head exclaiming, "I'll kill him." As a result of such visitations, Barlow concluded, "the air about us is filled with good & bad spirits acting on men. I suppose that I was near death & that the wall of flesh separating the material from the spiritual world had /so to speak/become so thin that I saw & heard what was going on in the latter." Letter, David Hatch Barlow to James Russell Lowell, 30 December 1844. By permission of the Houghton Library, Harvard University. bMS Am 765, 162.

12. Louisa Barlow Jay, "Data on the Barlows."

13. Cooke, 74.

14. John van der Zee Sears, *My Friends at Brook Farm* (New York: Desmond Fitz Gerald, 1912), 54.

15. Lindsay Swift, *Brook Farm. Its Members, Scholars and Visitors* (New York: 1900; reprint, New York: Corinth Books, 1961), 27.

16. Grenville Hicks, "A Conversation in Boston," *Sewanee Review,* vol. XXXIX, no. 2 (April–June 1921): 134.

17. Letter, Margaret Fuller to Almira Penniman Barlow. Groton, 9 March 1834 in Hudspeth, 198–200.

18. Sears, 39.

19. Ibid., 40.

20. Ibid.

21. John Thomas Codman, *Brook Farm. Historical and Personal Memoirs,* (Boston: Arena Publishing Company, 1894), 57.

22. Swift, 127.

23. Ibid., 127–28.

24. According to Swift, "The impression, if a wrong one, is hard to escape, that Hawthorne had this lady's personal fascinations in mind when he formed certain characteristics of his Zenobia." (128). On the other hand, he later states that Zenobia might have been a blend of Almira and Margaret Fuller as "there is certainly an intimation of both" (173). Cooke was of the latter opinion believing Zenobia was partly based on Fuller and Mrs. Ripley but resembling Almira in "her luxurious tastes" (94).

25. Cited in Katherine Burton, *Paradise Planters. The Story of Brook Farm* (London and New York: Longmans, Green & Co., 1939), 48. Although Burton claimed to have derived all her direct citations from primary sources and that she used no "interpolation of fancy" (ix), some of her conversational material flows remarkably smoothly, and suggests at least some reconstruction or authorial tweaking. Nevertheless, her depictions and use of quotations seems straightforward and fit the known characteristics of the thoughts and words of her subjects.

26. "Oh Mr. Hawthorne, you have a wonderfully poetic way of talking," Almira reportedly gushed at one point (Burton, 62), "I feel it steal into my memory where it will always remain. Please don't ever give over saying such wonderful things." Even the narrator of the dark side of New England could not withstand such an entreaty and he replied, "After such inestimable praise I could not" (cited in Burton, 62–64).

27. Burton, 92.

28. Ibid., 154.

29. Ibid.

30. Ibid.

31. Cooke, 74.

32. Louisa Barlow Jay, " Data on the Barlows."

33. Interestingly, in September 1843, she arranged for her son, Edward, possibly because he was the oldest, to continue at the Brook Farm. Almira paid $2.50 a week in tuition, and the Farm had the use of Edward's part-time labor. Louisa Barlow Jay, "Data on the Barlows."

34. Cooke, 74.

35. Cooke claimed that Barlow's sojourn at Brook Farm was responsible for his "love of justice, his unflinching courage in opposing self-seekers and par-

tisan patriots, and his trust in the ultimate worth of what is right and true" (103).

36. Nielsen.

37. Edward H. Abbot, "Francis Channing Barlow," *Harvard Graduates Magazine* (June 1896): 11.

38. Ibid., 12.

39. Sears, 39.

40. Letter, Edward Barry Dalton to Charles Henry Dalton, 3 June 1861, "Charles Henry Dalton Papers," in *Proceedings of the Massachusetts Historical Society, October 1922–June 1923,* vol. LVI (Boston: Massachusetts Historical Society, 1923), 366.

41. Emerson, Ralph Waldo. Letter to Francis Channing Barlow, (FCB) 27 August 1855. By permission of the Houghton Library, Harvard University. bMS Am 1910 (4–6).

42. New York Monuments Commission, *In Memoriam. Francis Channing Barlow,* 1834–1896 (Albany, NY: J. B. Lyon Co., 1923), 136.

43. Letter, Francis Channing Barlow (hereafter FCB) to E. L. Godkin, *New York Evening Post,* 9 August 1890, 7.

44. Ibid.

45. According to James A. Scrymser, Barlow predicted a war over the slavery issue in 1860. Unfortunately, Scrymser's account is suspect. See footnote 60. Barlow's father, David Hatch Barlow, kept up his anti-slavery activities even while suffering from psychological afflictions. Letter David Hatch Barlow to James Russell Lowell, 30 December 1844. By permission of the Houghton Library, Harvard University. BMS Am 765 (162).

46. Letter, D. R. Lauter to author. 26 November 2000.

47. E. F. Conklin, *Women of Gettysburg, 1863* (Gettysburg, PA: Thomas Publications, 1993), 18.

48. Don Richard Lauter, "Once Upon a Time in the East. Arabella Wharton Griffith Barlow," in Eileen Conklin (ed.) *The Journal of Women's Civil War History,* vol. I, ed. Eileen Conklin (Gettysburg, PA: Thomas Publications), 8

49. Letter, D. R. Lauter to author, 26 November 2000.

50. Letter, FCB to Almira Penniman Barlow, 24 December 1861. Francis Channing Barlow Letters (hereafter FCBL). Massachusetts Historical Society (hereafter MHS).

51. Lauter, "Arabella Wharton Griffith Barlow," 9.

52. D. R. Lauter, *Winslow Homer and Friends in Prince George County, Virginia, June, 1864* (Disputanta, Virginia: Lauter, 1999), 5.

53. George Templeton Strong, *The Diary of George Templeton Strong, Vol. II, The Turbulent Fifties, 1850–1859* ed. Alan Nevis and Milton Halsey Thomas (New York: Macmillan Co., 1852), 217.

54. Ibid., 22.

55. Homer was also a distant cousin of Barlow's.

56. Strong, vol. III, 132.

57. Maria Lydig Daly, *Diary of a Union Lady,* ed. Harold Earl Hammond (New York: Funk & Wagnalls, 1962), 80.

58. Daly, 80. An ironic statement, as Barlow was sometimes charged with the same failing.

59. Ibid.

60. James A. Scrymser provides an elaborate description of Barlow's enlistment and departure for Washington with his regiment. See James A. Scrymser,

Personal Memoirs In Times of Peace and War (New York: 1915) Unfortunately, Scrymser includes material which is at odds with official records. He stated, for example, that he and Barlow enlisted in the 12th New York at the same time. However, Scrymser does not appear in the roster of the 12th New York contained in Frederick Phisterer (compiler) *New York in the War of the Rebellion, 1861–1865* (Albany, NY: D. B. Lyon and Co.). Scrymser is recorded as having joined the 43d New York on 2 October 1862 and was discharged from that unit on 16 February 1863. It seems reasonably clear that Scrymser knew Barlow and had some knowledge of his activities, but it can not be ascertained when he was recording what he saw and knew, what he heard, or even what he might have imagined.

61. New York Monuments Commission, 13.

62. Daly, 46.

63. Letter, FCB to APB, 2 May 1861. FCBL. (MHS).

64. Letter, FCB to Edward Barlow, 18 June 1861. FCBL. (MHS).

65. Ibid.

66. Letter, FCB to APB, 9 July 1861. FCBL. (MHS).

67. Letter, FCB to EB, 18 July 1861. FCBL. (MHS).

68. Ibid.

69. Ibid.

70. Ibid.

71. Ibid.

72. Ibid.

73. Ibid.

74. During this hiatus from his military career, Barlow spent much of his time at Somerville, possibly to save money, commuting to the city by rail to work at Bliss's office. Letter, FCB to APB, 25 October 1861. FCBL. (MHS).

75. Ibid.

76. Charles A. Fuller, *Personal Recollections of the War of 1861* (Sherburne, NY: New Job Printing House, 1906; reprint, Hamilton, NY: Edmonston Publishing, Inc., 1990), 9.

77. Abbot, 6. Unfortunately, Miles does not say what Barlow read. Most likely he read Jomini (*Summary of the Art of War,* 1838), which was in vogue at West Point and among American professional military circles, and possibly Hardee's tactics as well. The works of Dennis Hart Mahan, the most influential instructor at West Point, were widely read as well. His *Complete Treatise on Field Fortification* (1836) and *Out-Post* (1847) which was concerned with tactical offensives, were readily available. See Perry D. Jamieson, "Background to Bloodshed. The Tactics of the U. S.–Mexican War and the 1850s," *North & South,* vol. 4, no.6, 24–31.

78. Letter, FCB to APB, 12 December 1861. FCBL. (MHS).

79. Fuller, 10.

80. Letter, Samuel S. Parmalee, 9 April 1864. Samuel Spencer Parmalee and Uriah N. Parmalee Papers. Duke University.

81. Robert Gould Shaw, *Blue-Eyed Child of Fortune. The Civil War Letters of Robert Gould Shaw,* ed. Russell Duncan (Athens, GA: University of Georgia Press, 1992), 191.

82. Hammond, 173.

83. Letter, FCB to APB, 14 December 1861. FCBL. (MHS).

84. Ibid.

85. Letter, FCB to EB, 28 December 1861. FCBL. (MHS).

86. Fuller, 12.

87. Ibid.

88. Letter, FCB to APB, 18 January 1862. FCBL. (MHS).

89. Ibid.

90. Letter, FCB to APB, 23 January 1862. FCBL. (MHS)

91. Letter, FCB to APB, 18 January 1862. FCBL. (MHS).

92. Letter, FCB to EB, 28 December 1861. FCBL. (MHS)

93. Letter, FCB to APB, 14 December 1861. FCBL. (MHS). See also Fuller, 9–10.

94. Letter, FCB to APB, 30 January 1862. FCBL. (MHS).

95. Ibid.

96. Francis A. Walker, *History of the Second Army Corps in the Army of the Potomac* (New York: Charles Scribner's Sons, 1887; reprint, Gaithersburg, MD. Butternut Press. 1985), 48.

97. Letter, FCB to APB, 13 March 1862 FCBL. (MHS).

Chapter 2. Initiation in Blood

1. Stephen W. Sears, *George B. McClellan. The Young Napoleon* (New York: Ticknor & Fields, 1988), 125.

2. Ibid., 163.

3. Quarstein, John V., "The Siege of Yorktown and the Engagements Along the Warwick River" *Civil War,* 51 (June 1995): 29.

4. Barlow, Francis Channing. Letter to Almira Penniman Barlow, 17 March 1862. FCBL. (MHS).

5. Quarstein, 29.

6. Ibid.

7. Letter, FCB to APB, 11 April 1862. FCBL. (MHS).

8. Ibid., 18 April 1862. FCBL. (MHS).

9. Ibid., 23 April 1862. FCBL. (MHS).

10. Ibid.

11. Charles A. Fuller, *Personal Recollections of the War of 1861* (Sherburne, NY: New Job Printing House, 1905; reprint Hamiliton, NY: Edmundston Publishing, Inc., 1990), 14.

12. Letter, FCB to Gov. Edwin D. Morgan, 13 May 1862. By permission of the Houghton Library, Harvard University. bMS Am 1649.25 (29–30).

13. Ibid.

14. Letter, FCB to APB, May 15, 1862. FCBL. (MHS).

15. Ibid., May 17, 1862. FCBL. (MHS).

16. Sears, 193–94.

17. Craig L. Symonds, *Joseph Johnston* (New York: W. W. Norton, 1992), 163–65.

18. Letter, FCB to APB, 2 June 1862. FCBL. (MHS).

19. From Nelson Miles's report on the Battle of Fair Oaks,2 June 1862,quoted in Edward H. Abbot, "Francis Channing Barlow," *Harvard Graduates Magazine,* June 1896, 7.

20. United States Department of War, *The War of the Rebellion: A Compilation of the Official Records of the Union and Confederate Armies,* series I, vol. II, part one (Washington, DC: Government Printing Office, 1880–1901), 772 (hereafter cited as *OR*).

21. Letter, FCB to APB, 2 June 1862. FCBL. (MHS).

22. Report of Major General Oliver O. Howard, "The Battle of Fair Oaks," *OR,* I, II, 1, 769.

23. Ibid.

24. Fuller, 19.

25. Letter, FCB to APB, 2 June 1862. FCBL. (MHS).

26. Report of Colonel Francis Channing Barlow, "The Battle of Fair Oaks," *OR,* I, II, 1, 773.

27. Letter, FCB to APB, 2 June 1862. FCBL. (MHS).

28. Letter, FCB to APB and Edward Barlow, 10 June 1862. FCBL. (MHS).

29. Ibid.

30. Fuller, 40.

31. Maria Lydig Daly, *The Diary of a Union Lady,* ed. Harold Earl Hammond (New York: Funk & Wagnalls, 1962), 228.

32. Letter, FCB to APB, 5 June 1862. FCBL. (MHS).

33. Fuller, 20.

34. Ibid., 47.

35. Barlow, "Battle of Fair Oaks," *OR,* I, II, 1, 757.

36. Letter, FCB to APB, 3 June 1862. FCBL. (MHS).

CHAPTER 3. VALOR AND FRUSTRATION: THE SEVEN DAYS

1. Steven H. Newton, "The Battle of Seven Pines (Fair Oaks)," *Civil War* 51 (June 1995): 49.

2. Stephen W. Sears, *George B. McClellan. The Young Napoleon* (New York: Ticknor & Fields, 1988), 207.

3. Letter, FCB. Letter to Almira Penniman Barlow, 3 June 1862. FCBL. (MHS).

4. Letter, FCB to Richard Barlow, 18 June 1862. FCBL. (MHS).

5. Letter, FCB to APB, 12 June 1862. FCBL. (MHS).

6. Letter, FCB to APB, 10 June 1862. FCBL. (MHS).

7. E.F. Conklin, *Women of Gettysburg, 1863* (Gettysburg, PA: Thomas Publications, 1993), 19.

8. Ibid., 12 June 1862. FCBL. (MHS).

9. Emory M. Thomas, *Robert E. Lee. A Biography* (New York: W. W. Norton, 1995), 243.

10. Michael J. Andrus, "The Battle of Beaver Dam Creek (Mechanicsville)," *Civil War* 51 (June 1995): 60.

11. Sears, 213.

12. Charles A. Fuller, *Personal Recollections of the War of 1861* (Sherburne, NY: New Job Printing House, 1906; reprint, Hamilton, NY: Edmonston Publishing, Inc., 1990), 24.

13. Letter, FCB to Edward Barlow, 4 July 1862. FCBL. (MHS).

14. Peter S. Carmichael, "The Battle of Savage's Station," *Civil War* 51 (June 1995): 69.

15. Fuller, 25.

16. Fuller, 26. Fuller thought the general to whom Barlow was speaking might have been Kearney, but in his 4 July letter, Barlow makes clear it was Robinson.

17. Ibid., 26.

18. Fuller, 36.

19. Fuller, 35.

20. Cited in New York Monuments Commission, *In Memoriam. Francis Channing Barlow, 1834–1896,* (Albany, NY: J. B. Lyon, 1923), 78.

21. Ibid., 79.

22. Sears, 220–22.

23. Fuller, 40.

24. Ibid.

25. Letter, FCB to EB, 4 July 1862. FCBL. (MHS).

26. Francis A. Walker, *History of the Second Corps in the Army of the Potomac* (New York: Charles Scribner's Sons, 1887; reprint Gaithersburg, MD: Butternut Press 1985), 82.

27. Fuller, 44.

28. Letter, FCB to EB, 4 July 1862. FCBL. (MHS).

29. Ibid.

30. Ibid.

31. Ibid.

32. Ibid.

33. FCB, Service Record, Record and Pension Office, Washington, DC, 25 February 1896, 7. FCBL. (MHS).

34. Letter, FCB to EB and Richard Barlow, 12 July 1862 and FCB to APB, 9 August 1862. FCBL. (MHS).

35. Letter, FCB to Gov. Edwin D. Morgan, Harrison's Bar, 2 July 1862. By permission of the Houghton Library, Harvard University. bMS Am 1649.25 (29–30).

36. Ibid., 13 July 1862. Private Collection.

37. Ibid.

38. Sears, 229.

39. Letter, FCB to RB, 8 July 1862. FCBL. (MHS).

40. Letter, FCB to E B and RB, 12 July 1862. FCBL. (MHS).

41. Letter, FCB to APB, 28 August 1862. FCBL. (MHS).

42. Letter, FCB to APB, 6 September 1862. FCBL. (MHS).

Chapter 4. From Antietam to Gettysburg

1. Russell F. Weigley, *A Great Civil War: A Military and Political History, 1861–1865* (Bloomington, Indiana University Press, 2000), 144. See also Steven E. Woodworth, *Davis & Lee At War* (Lawrence: University of Kansas Press, 1995), 184.

2. Woodworth, 191.

3. Stephen W. Sears, *Landscape Turned Red. The Battle of Antietam* (New York: Popular Library, 1983), 97–98.

4. Letter, FCB to Edward Barlow, 6 September 1862. FCBL. (MHS).

5. Sears, 123–25.

6. Charles A. Fuller, *Personal Recollections of the War of 1861* (Sherburne, NY: New Job Printing House, 1906,) 58; reprint Hamilton, NY: Edmonston Publishing, Inc., 1990.

7. Fuller, 58.

8. Michael A. Vasile, ed., *"The Diary of Martin Sigman, 1861–1864"* (Little Falls, NY: Cattaraugus County Museum, n.d.), 12.

9. Letter, Ezra Ripley, 21 September 1862, in James B. Thayer "Ezra Ripley"

in Thomas Wentworth Higginson, *Harvard Memorial Biographies,* Vol. I (Cambridge: Sever & Francis, 1867), 103. Ripley, who believed Barlow had been killed when he wrote his letter, concluded his account of Barlow's performance at Antietam stating "He chased the enemy from the ground and drove them almost a mile—he and two other regiments following him—and then died as a soldier should. His loss affected me more than anything else that has happened here. I admired him, and enjoyed his society." Ibid.

10. Fuller, 59.

11. Miles A. Nelson, "Report on Battle of Antietam" 18 September 1862. *OR,* 1, 19, 1, 291.

12. Fuller, 59.

13. Letter, FCB to Almira Penniman Barlow, 18 September 1862. FCBL. (MHS).

14. Miles, 291.

15. Sigman, 13.

16. Or in Barlow's own words, "I was wounded in the groin by a piece of spherical case shot and know nothing of what subsequently occurred." FCB, "Report on the Battle of Antietam," 22 September, 1862. *OR,* 1, 19, 1, 290.

17. Not all of the soldiers were sorry that the attack was stopped. Martin Sigman of the 61st New York stated that Barlow's wounding "saved us from another hard charge." Vasile (ed.), Sigman, 13.

18. Fuller, 63.

19. Letter, FCB to APB, 18 September 1862. FCBL. (MHS).

20. Ibid.

21. Letter, Arabella Wharton Griffith Barlow to Maria Lydig Daly, 2 October 1862. Charles P. Daly Papers. Manuscripts and Archives Division. The New York Public Library. Astor, Lenox and Tilden Foundations.

22. Ibid.

23. Allan Nevins and Milton Halsey Thomas, eds., *The Diary of George Templeton Strong. Vol. III. The Civil War, 1860–65.* (New York: The Macmillan Company, 1952), 261.

24. Letter, FCB to APB, 8 March 1863. FCBL. (MHS).

25. Letter, Arabella Barlow to Maria Lydig Daly. 2 October 1862.

26. Isaac Plumb Memoir, United States Army Military Historical Institute, Carlisle Barracks, Pennsylvania.

27. Ibid.

28. Maria Lydig Daly, *Diary of a Union Lady,* ed. Harold Earl Hammond (New York: Funk & Wagnalls, 1962), 190.

29. Ibid.

30. Ibid., 228

31. Letter, FCB to APB, 24 April 1863. FCBL. (MHS).

32. A. C. Hamlin quoted. New York Monuments Commission. *In Memoriam. Francis Channing Barlow, 1834–1891,* (Albany, NY: J. B. Lyon Co., 1923), 88.

33. Letter, James Wood to Augustus Hamlin, 3 June 1891. Augustus C. Hamlin Collection, Houghton Library, Harvard University. MS Am 1084. Wood's problems with Barlow may have been personal. In his letter of 24 April 1863 Barlow records his satisfaction with three out of his four regimental commanders. "Col. Wood," he wrote," is disposed to be a little touchy and I shall have to take him down I fear." Letter, FCB to APB, 24 April 1863. FCBL. (MHS).

34. Letter, FCB to APB, 24 April 1863.

35. Edes, Edward Louis. Letter, 10 May 1863. Edward Louis Edes Letters. (MHS).

36. *O.R.*, 1, 25,1,183.

37. Letter, FCB to APB and brothers, 8 May 1863. FCBL. (MHS).

38. Fuller, for example, wrote " . . . a full blooded German organization was not, in this country, in those days, on a par with 'Yankee' troops." 42.

39. Ibid.

40. Letter, FCB to Robert Treat Paine, 12 August 1863. FCBL. (MHS).

41. Letter FCB to Gov. Horatio Seymour, 27 May 1863. New York State Adjutant General's Office. Register of Letters Received, 1862–66. New York State Archives.

42. Ibid.

43. Ibid.

44. Letter, FCB to APB, 2 June 1863. FCBL. (MHS).

45. Letter, FCB to APB, 29 May 1863. FCBL. (MHS).

46. He also referred to them as "miserable beasts." Letter, FCB to Charles Henry Dalton, 2 June 1863 in "The Charles Henry Dalton Papers," *Proceedings of the Massachusetts Historical Society, October 1922–June 1923* (Boston: Massachusetts Historical Society, 1923), 453.

47. Letter, FCB to APB, 26 June 1863. FCBL. (MHS).

48. Letter, FCB to Charles Henry Dalton, 2 June 1863, "Dalton Papers," 454.

49. Letter, FCB to APB, 2 June 1863. FCBL. (MHS).

50. Ibid.

51. Fuller, 89.

52. Russell Duncan ed. *Blue-Eyed Child of Fortune. The Civil War Letters of Robert Gould Shaw*. (Athens, GA: University of Georgia Press, 1992), 309.

53. Letter, FCB to APB, 24 April 1863. FCBL. (MHS)

54. Thomas Buell, *The Warrior Generals. Combat Leadership in the Civil War* (New York: Crown Publishers, Inc., 1997), 207

55. Cited in Buell, 208.

56. Duncan, *Blue-Eyed Child of Fortune,* 354.

57. Ibid., 355. Charles Russell Lowell (1835–1864) whose family was also part of the Transcendentalist-abolitionist circle in Boston was a close friend of Barlow and the Shaws. He married Shaw's sister, Josephine (known as "Effie"), creating a posthumous relationship with Barlow when Frank married Josephine's sister, Ellen in 1867. The Barlows thought so highly of Lowell that they named their second son after him.

58. Ibid., 382.

59. Letter, FCB to APB, 2 June 1863, 26 June 1863. FCBL. (MHS).

60. Letter, FCB to APB, 2 June 1863. FCBL. (MHS).

61. Letter, FCB to RB, 26 June 1863. FCBL. (MHS).

62. Ibid.

63. Letter, FCB to APB, 4 July 1863. FCBL. (MHS).

64. Woodworth, 244–54.

65. Letter, FCB to APB, 26 June 1863. FCBL. (MHS).

66. Larry Tagg, *The Generals of Gettysburg. The Leaders of America's Greatest Battle*. Website. "Civil War General of the Day." www.roadkill.com/~roser/tagg/generals/genral28.html

67. Karl Schurz, "Report on the Battle of Gettysburg." 20 August 1863. *OR,* 1, 27, 1, 728.

68. Letter, FCB to APB, 7 July 1863. FCBL. (MHS).

69. Adelbert Ames, "Report on Battle of Gettysburg," 28 July 1863. *OR* 1, 27, 1, 712.

70. Richard S. Ewell, "Report on Battle of Gettysburg," _____, 1863, *OR,* 1, 27, I, 445.

71. Jubal Early, "Report on Battle of Gettysburg," Ibid. 469.

72. Letter, FCB to APB, 7 July 1863. FCBL. (MHS).

73. The Barlow-Gordon encounter is taken largely from the account found in *Campfire and Battlefield.* (New York: Bryan, Taylor & Co. 1894), 466–67.

74. Conklin, 17.

75. Letter, FCB to APB, 7 July 1863. FCBL. (MHS).

76. Ibid.

77. Conklin, 17.

78. Letter, FCB to APB, 7 July 1863. FCBL. (MHS).

79. Ibid.

80. Scrymser, 12.

81. Ibid.

82. Cited in Conklin, 17

83. Edward H. Abbott, "Francis Channing Barlow," *Harvard Graduates Magazine,* June 1896, 4.

84. A letter printed in the *Sanitary Commission Bulletin* describes her as ministering "most tenderly" to a dying soldier. Cited in Conklin, 18. For detailed descriptions of army hospitals at Gettysburg see Cornelia Hancock, *Letters of a Civil War Nurse* (Lincoln, NE: University of Nebraska Press, 1998), 7–13.

85. Letter, Daniel Butterfield to Maj. General Newton, *OR,* 1, 27, III, 573.

86. Letter, FCB to APB, 4 July 1863. FCBL. (MHS).

87. Letter, FCB to Moses Blake Williams, 5 August 1863. FCBL. (MHS).

88. Letter, FCB to Robert Treat Paine, 12 August 1863. FCBL. (MHS).

89. Harriett Beecher Stowe described Mrs. Hawthorne's action as "picket duty." Randall Stewart, *Nathaniel Hawthorne. A Biography* (New Haven, CT: Archon Books, 1970), 222.

90. Letter, Arabella Barlow to Maria Lydig Daly, 28 October 1863. Charles P. Daly Papers. Manuscripts and Archives Division. The New York Public Library. Astor, Lenox, and Tilden Foundations.

91. Letter, FCB to APB, 4 July 1863. FCBL. (MHS).

92. Letter, FCB to Moses Blake Williams, 5 August 1863. FCBL. (MHS).

93. Ibid.

94. Letter, FCB to Robert Treat Paine, 12 August 1863. FCBL. (MHS).

95. Hancock, Winfield Scott. Letter to FCB, 12 December 1863. FCBL. (MHS).

CHAPTER 5. FROM THE RAPIDAN TO THE SALIENT

1. United States Department of War, *OR,* 1, 33, 1, 427.

2. A detailed examination of Grant's grand strategy for 1864 can be found in Herman Hathaway and Archer Jones, *How the North Won. A Military History of the Civil War* (Urbana, IL: University of Illinois Press, 1983), chapter 16.

3. For an example of how divided command and Meade's sense of humiliation affected the performance of the army see *Not War But Murder. Cold Harbor, 1864* (New York: Alfred A. Knopf, 2000), 234–40.

4. Bruce Catton, A *Stillness at Appomattox,* (Garden City: Doubleday & Company, Inc., 1953), 26–28.

5. Gilbert D. Frederick, *The Story of a Regiment. Being A Record of the Military Services of the Fifty-Seventh New York State Volunteer Infantry in the*

War of the Rebellion (Chicago: The Fifty-Seventh Veteran Association, 1895), 217.

6. Ibid.

7. Samuel S. Parmalee, Letter, 9 June 1864. Samuel Spencer Parmalee and Uriah N. Parmalee Papers. Duke University.

8. Letter, FCB to Brig. Gen. Alexander Webb, 9 April 1864. Webb Papers. Manuscripts and Archives. Yale University Library.

9. Letter, FCB to Almira Penniman Barlow, 9 April 1864. FCBL. (MHS).

10. Catton, 31.

11. Letter, FCB to APB, 9 April 1864. FCBL. (MHS).

12. Letter FCB to E. L. Godkin, *New York Evening Post,* 9 August 1890, 7. In this letter, Barlow related that when he was carried off the field at Antietam he had "been amazed to see the number of stragglers who were amusing themselves at the rear of the troops who were fighting at the front." However, accounts at the time state he was unconscious when brought in from the fighting. Possibly he returned to some state of consiousness as he was borne to the hospital, and the picture of the large number of shirkers bore into his memory.

13. Ibid.

14. Ibid.

15. Ibid.

16. Letter, FCB to APB, 9 April 1864. FCBL. (MHS).

17. Ibid.

18. Dr. William W. Potter, *One Surgeon's Private War. Dr William W. Potter of the 57th New York.* (Buffalo, NY: 1888); reprint Shippensburg, PA: White Mane Publishing Co., 1996), 97.

19. Cornelia Hancock, *Letters of a Civil War Nurse. Cornelia Hancock, 1863–1865.* Lincoln: University of Nebraska Press, 1998), 79.

20. Ibid., 80.

21. Letter, FCB to Richard Barlow, 22 April 1864. FCBL. (MHS).

22. Letter, FCB to APB, 19 April 1864. FCBL. (MHS).

23. Letter, FCB to RB, 22 April 1864. FCBL. (MHS).

24. Francis A. Walker, *History of the Second Army Corps in the Army of the Potomac* (New York: Charles Scribner's Sons, 1887; reprint Gaithersburg, MD, Butternut Press, 1985), 426.

25. Ibid.

26. Glenn Tucker, *Hancock the Superb* (Indianapolis, IN: Bobbs-Merrill Co., Inc., 1960), 171.

27. Gordon C. Rhea, *The Battles of the Wilderness & Spotsylvania,* (Fredericksburg, VA.: Eastern National Park and Monument Association, 1995), 29.

28. Catton, 97.

29. Letter, Winfield Scott Hancock to FCB, 9 May 1864, 5:50 P. M. FCBL. (MHS).

30. Walker, 449–50.

31. Letter, WSH to FCB, 10 May 1864. FCBL. (MHS).

32. Walker, 451.

33. Ibid., 452.

34. Report, C. A. Dana 10 May 1864. *OR,* 1, 36, 1, 66.

35. Hancock, Report on the Battle of Spotsylvania, *OR,* I, 36, 1, 331–32.

36. On the other hand, General Henry Hunt reported that Birney and Barlow ordered some artillery to fire from such a distance that the shells actually fell into the more advanced Federal batteries. Journal of General Henry J.

Hunt, artillery commander of the Army of the Potomac, 1864, 14. Library of Congress.

37. St. Clair A. Mulholland, *The Story of the 116th Regiment Pennsylvania Volunteers in the War of the Rebellion,* (Philadelphia: F. McManus Jr. & Co., 1903; reprint, Fordham University Press, 1996), 201.

38. J. W. Muffly, *The Story of Our Regiment. A History of the 148th Pennsylvania Vols.* (Des Moines, Iowa: The Kenyon Printing and Manufacturing Company; reprint, Baltimore, MD: Butternut and Blue, 1994), 120.

39. Ibid., 120–21.

40. Ibid., 121

41. General Henry J. Hunt, artillery commander of the Army of the Potomac's artillery, clearly placed the responsibility for the cannon's loss on Barlow's orders. Journal of General Henry J. Hunt, 1864, 14. Library of Congress.

42. Gordon C. Rhea, *The Battle of Spotsylvania and the Road to Yellow Tavern* (Baton Rouge: Louisiana University Press, 1997), 137.

43. Noah Andre Trudeau, *Bloody Roads South. The Wilderness to Cold Harbor, May–June, 1864* (Boston: Little, Brown and Company, 1989), 157–62.

44. Cited in Catton, 116.

45. FCB, "The Capture of the Salient, May 12, 1864." *Papers of the Military Historical Society of Massachusetts,* 1879, 246.

46. Ibid. 247.

47. Ibid.

48. Ibid.

49. John D. Black, "Reminiscences of the Bloody Angle." in *Glimpses of the Nation's Struggle.* Fourth Series. Papers Read before the Military Order of the Minnesota Commandery of the Loyal Legion of the United States. 1892–97. (St Paul: H. L. Collins, 1898; reprint Broadfoot Publishing: Wilmington, NC, 1992), 423.

50. Ibid.

51. Ibid.

52. Hancock, *OR,* I, 36, 1, 335.

53. Ibid., 423–24.

54. Ibid.

55. Walker, 469.

56. Rhea, *Battle of Spotsylvania,* 224–25.

57. Clifford Dowdey, *Lee's Last Campaign* (Boston: Little, Brown and Co., 1960), 200–201.

58. Muffly, 856.

59. Ibid.

60. Black, 424.

61. Barlow, 250.

62. Black, 424.

63. II Corps Memorandum, *OR,* 1, 36, 1, 358. Erasmus C. Gilbreath, of the 20th Indiana in Birney's Division recollected that a cheer went up when a colonel of the 99th Pennsylvania in that division was fired upon by what he thought was the main Confederate line. Erasmus C. Gilbreath Memoir, Erasmus C. Gibreath Papers. S2954, Indiana State Library, Indianapolis, Indiana.

64. Ibid. 426.

65. Barlow, 250.

66. Tucker, 172.

67. Nelson Miles. Letter, 6 January 1879 in Barlow, "Capture of the Salient," 259.

68. John R. Brooke, "Report on the Assault at Spotsylvania," *OR,* I, 36, 358.

69. Barlow, 256.

70. Ibid.

71. Brooke, "Spotsylvania," 410.

72. Ibid.

73. Black, 428.

74. Ibid.

75. Ibid., 433.

76. Ibid., 430.

77. Ibid.

78. Ibid, 431.

79. Miles in Barlow, 262.

80. David M. Jordan, *Winfield Scott Hancock* (Bloomington and Indianapolis: Indiana University Press, 1988), 31.

81. Black, 427.

82. Ibid., 433.

83. "Report of the Army of the Potomac Medical Directors Office" 28 November 1864, *OR,* I, 36, 1, 214.

84. Barlow, 251.

85. Ibid.

86. Winfield Scott Hancock, "Report of Spotsylvania-Cold Harbor," Baltimore, 21 September 1865. In *OR,* I, 36, 1, 339.

87. *OR,* I, 36, 2, 710.

88. Cited in Thomas Buell, *The Warrior Generals. Combat Leadership in the Civil War* (New York: Crown Publishers, Inc., 1997), 329.

89. Cited in Gordon Rhea, *Wilderness & Spotsylvania.* Civil War Series, 51.

90. Cited in Buell, 329.

91. Ibid.

92. Ibid.

93. Ibid., 76.

94. *OR,* I, 36, 1, 361.

95. Letter, FCB to APB, 18 May 1864. FCBL. (MHS).

96. Jordan, 131.

97. *OR,* I, 36, 1, 137.

98. Ibid., 119–20.

99. Ibid. 40.

100. Ibid.

101. Stephen B. Oates, *A Woman of Valor. Clara Barton and the Civil War* (New York: The Free Press, 1994), 318.

102. Brockett & Vaughan, *Women's Work in the Civil War* (Boston: R. H. Curran), cited in E. F. Conklin, *Women at Gettysburg, 1863* (Gettysburg, PA: Thomas Publications, 1993), 17.

103. Ibid.

104. Letter, FCB to RB, 20 May 1864. FCBL. (MHS).

CHAPTER 6. THE COLD HARBOR AND ACROSS THE JAMES

1. FCB to Charles Henry Dalton, May 24 1864. "Charles Henry Dalton Papers" in *Proceedings of the Massachusetts Historical Society, October 1922–June 1923* (Boston: Massachusetts Historical Society, 1923), 483.

2. Theodore Lyman, *With Grant and Meade from the Wilderness to Appomattox.* (Boston: Massachusetts Historical Society, 1922; reprint, Lincoln, NB: Bison Books, University of Nebraska Press, 1994), 107.

3. A physical description of Barlow is found on an affidavit he submitted when applying for a passport, 7 November 1864. National Archives.

4. Cited in Edward H. Abbot, "Francis Channing Barlow." *Harvard Graduates Magazine,* June, 1896, 5.

5. Noah Andre Trudeau, *Bloody Roads South. The Wilderness to Cold Harbor, May-June, 1864* (Boston: Little, Brown and Co., 1986), 220–26.

6. Lyman, 99–100.

7. Clifford Dowdey, *Lee's Last Campaign* (Boston: Little, Brown & Co., 1960), 265–68.

8. Trudeau, 243.

9. Russell F. Weigley, *A Great Civil War. A Military and Political History, 1861–65* (Indianapolis & Bloomington: University of Indiana Press, 2000), 344–45.

10. Captain Robert S. Robertson, "From Spotsylvania Onward," in *War Papers Read Before the Indiana Commandery Military Order of the Loyal Legion of the United States.* (Indianapolis: the Commandery, 1898; reprint, Wilmington, NC: Broadfoot Publishing Co., 1992), 353.

11. Winfield Scott Hancock, Cold Harbor Report, United States Department of War. *OR,* I, 36, 1, 343.

12. Francis A. Walker, *History of the Second Army Corps in the Army of the Potomac* (New York: Charles Scribner's Sons, 1887, reprint Gaithersburg, MD: Butternut Press, 1985,) 503.

13. Francis Channing Barlow to George Gordon Meade, *OR,* I, 36, III, 436.

14. Robertson, 356.

15. Ibid.

16. Ibid.

17. Ibid. 357.

18. *OR,* I, 36, 154.

19. Walker, 504.

20. Ibid.

21. Letter, FCB to Charles Henry Dalton, 24 May 1864. "Dalton Papers," 483.

22. Ibid.

23. Ibid.

24. Lyman 139.

25. Walker, 506.

26. Cited in Ernest B. Ferguson, *Not War But Murder. Cold Harbor, 1864* (New York: Alfred A. Knopf, 2000), 127.

27. Ibid.

28. Ibid.

29. Gordon C. Rhea, "'Butcher' Grant and the Overland Campaign," *North & South,* Volume 4, Number 1, 53–54.

30. Figures are from Glenn Tucker, *Hancock the Superb* (Indianapolis: Bobbs-Merrill, 1960), 221.

31. Robert Keating. *Carnival of Blood. The Civil War Ordeal of the Seventh New York Heavy Artillery.* (Baltimore, MD: Butternut and Blue, 1989), 21.

32. J. W. Muffly, *The Story of Our Regiment. A History of the 148th Pennsylvania Vols.* (Des Moines, Iowa: The Kenyon Printing & Mfg. Co, 1902; reprint, Baltimore, MD: Butternut and Blue, 1994), 129.

33. FCB, June 3, 1864, 7:30PM. *O.R.,* I, 36,1,369.

34. McDougall, Colonel Clinton D. Note to Hancock, 3 June 1864. FCBL. (MHS).

35. Hancock, *OR,* I, 36, 344–45. Barlow, Ibid., 369.

36. Tucker, 226.

37. Ibid., 227.

38. McDougall, 3 June 1864.

39. FCB to Hancock, 3 June 1864. 12:00 P. M. *OR,* I, 36, III, 533. On the other hand Gordon C. Rhea faults Barlow for not ordering MacGougall to support Brooke's Brigade. Gordon C. Rhea "Cold Harbor, Anatomy of a Battle" *North & South* vol. 5, no. 2, 59. Possibly Barlow feared repeating the situation at Spotsylvania when masses of men fed into a restricted space created disorder and impeded success. He may also have had enough of ill-conceived frantic assaults and declined the needless sacrifice of more of his men.

40. *OR,* I, 36, 1, 366. Hancock, however, never ordered Birney to attack. See Rhea, "Cold Harbor," 59.

41. Cited in Tucker, 231–32.

42. FCB to Hancock, 12:00 P. M., 3 June 1864. *OR,* I, 36, III, 533.

43. Ferguson, 175.

44. Hancock to Humphreys, 12:45 P. M., 3 June 1864. *OR,* I, 36, III, 533.

45. Ibid.

46. Cited in Tucker, 138.

47. Ibid.

48. Walker, 522.

49. Rhea, "Cold Harbor," 61.

50. *OR,* I, 36,1, 169.

51. Ibid., 166.

52. Tucker, 231.

53. Cited in Ferguson, 178.

54. Ferguson, 3.

55. Walker, 517.

56. Keating, 153.

57. FCB to Lt. Col. Francis Walker, *OR,* I, 36, III, 647.

58. Cited in Thomas Buell, *The Warrior Generals. Combat Leadership in the Civil War* (New York: Crown Publishers, Inc., 1997), 329.

59. Ibid., 333.

60. Cornelia Hancock, *Letters of a Civil War Nurse* (Lincoln: University of Nebraska Press, 1998), 98–99.

61. Ibid. See also Dr. William W. Potter, *One Surgeon's Private War. Doctor William W. Potter of the 57th New York.* (Buffalo, NY: 1888; reprint, Shippensburg, PA: White Mane Publishing Co., 1996), 107.

62. Lyman, 158.

63. Ibid., 157–58.

64. Walker, 523.

65. Muffly, 134.

66. Thomas J. Howe, *The Petersburg Campaign. Wasted Valor. June 15–18, 1864.* (Lynchburg, VA: H. E. Howard, Inc., 1988), 29.

67. Ibid., 27–28.

68. Muffly.

69. Ibid.

70. Howe, 42.

71. Ibid., 46.

72. Gilbert D. Frederick, *The Story of a Regiment. Being a Record of the Military Service of the Fifty-Seventh New York State Volunteer Infantry in the War of the Rebellion.* (Chicago: The Fifty-Seventh Veterans Association, 1895), 245–46.

73. Keating, 185.

74. Frederick, 536.

75. Howe, 57

76. Captain James Fleming, *OR,* I, 40, 1, 334.

77. Howe, 57.

78. Ibid., 68.

79. Ibid., 77

80. Ibid.

81. Ibid., 94–97.

82. FCB to WSH, *OR,* I, 40, II, 123.

83. Howe, 103.

84. FCB to WSH, *OR,* I, 40, II, 123.

85. Howe, 103.

86. Ibid., 104.

87. Walker, 540.

88. Howe, 120.

89. Ibid., 121.

90. Walker, 541.

91. Ibid.

92. Bruce Catton, *A Stillness at Appomattox* (Garden City: Doubleday & Co., 1957), 191. Smith claimed his men were too exhausted and disorganized to make an attack, and that the rebels had been reinforced. He stated that he had asked Hancock earlier in the day to form the II Corps on his left and assault the Confederate right. The first II Corps divisions did not arrive until after 11:00 P. M. Smith thought it would have been "madness" to have attacked unknown positions in the dark. Smith contended that an attack early on the 16th would have carried the city. He agreed with Hancock's statement that Birney's and Gibbon's divisions had been placed at his disposal. William Farrar Smith, *From Chattanooga to Petersburg Under Generals Grant and Butler* (Boston: Houghton, Mifflin and Company, 1893), 93, 102, 108–11.

93. Catton, 198.

94. Catton, 198. See also Howe, 131.

Chapter 7. Stalemate

1. Letter, FCB to Almira Penniman Barlow, 19 June 1864. FCBL. (MHS).

2. Ibid.

3. United States, Department of War, *OR,* I, 40, 1, 314.

4. Ibid.

5. Ibid.

6. Ibid., 315.

7. Ibid.

8. Letter, FCB to WSH, *OR, I, 40; II, 437.*

9. Ibid., 439.

10. Ibid., Col C. B. Morgan to WSH, 27 June 1864, 440.

11. Ibid., 29 June 1864, 442

12. Ibid., FCB to WSH, 1 July 1864, 443.

13. WSH to FCB, 3 July 1864. Ibid., 443.

14. Ibid., 444.

15. Letter, FCB to WSH, 4 July 1864. Ibid., 444.

16. Lyman, 173.

17. *OR,* I, 40; II, 277.

18. Ibid., 325–26.

19. Ibid., 328.

20. *OR,* I, 40, II, 310.

21. Frederick, 254.

22. St. Clair A. Mulholland, *The Story of the 116th Pennsylvania Volunteers in the War of the Rebellion* (Philadelphia, PA: F. McManus Jr. & Co., 1903; reprint, Fordham University Press, 1996), 277.

23. Frederick, 255.

24. Ibid.

25. Ibid., 319.

26. Walker, 546.

27. Letter, J. B. Hallinbeck to Robert S. Robertson, 21 June 1864. William C. Sparks, Jr. Collection.

28. Ibid.

29. Ibid., 327.

30. Frederick, 255.

31. Ibid., 329.

32. Robert Keating, *Carnival of Blood. The Civil War Ordeal of the Seventh New York Heavy Artillery* (Baltimore, MD: Butternut and Blue, 1998), 215.

33. Hallinbeck.

34. Ibid.

35. Keating, 93.

36. Ruth L. Silliker, ed., The *Rebel Yell and the Yankee Hurrah: The Civil War Journal of a Maine Volunteer: Private John W. Haley, 17th Maine Regiment* (Camden, ME: Down East Books, 1985), 175.

37. Ibid.

38. Bruce Catton, *A Stillness at Appomattox* (New York: Doubleday & Company, 1953), 212.

39. Ibid.

40. Ibid.

41. Mulholland, 278.

42. Letter, FCB to APB, 23 June 1864. FCBL. (MHS).

43. Ibid.

44. Ibid.

45. *OR,* I, 40, 1, 307.

46. Letter, FCB to APB, 23 June 1864. FCBL. (MHS).

47. Ibid.

48. Letter, FCB to RB, 2 July 1864. FCBL. (MHS).

49. Ibid.

50. *Harper's Weekly,* 9 July 1864, 445.

51. Lyman, 179.

52. Letter, FCB to RB, 9 July 1864. FCBL. (MHS).

53. Lyman, 186.

54. Ibid., 188.

55. Don Richard Lauter, "Winslow Homer and Friends in Prince George's County, Virginia, June, 1864." Privately printed, 1999, 1–8.

56. Letter, FCB to APB, 15 July 1864. FCBL. (MHS).

57. Ibid.

58. Ibid.

59. Potter, 109.

60. Lauter, 3, 5–6.

61. Ibid., 5.

62. Don Richard Lauter, "Once Upon a Time in the East. Arabella Wharton Griffith Barlow" in *The Journal of Women's Civil War History, vol. I* ed. Eileen Conklin (Gettysburg, PA: Thomas Publications, 2001), 22.

63. Potter, 111.

64. Letter FCB to APB, 15 July 1869. FCBL. (MHS).

65. Cornelia Hancock, *Letters of A Civil War Nurse* (Lincoln: University of Nebraska Press, 1998), 103.

66. Letter, FCB to APB, 19 July 1864. FCBL. (MHS).

67. Frederick Phisterer (compiler), *New York in the War of the Rebellion, Vol.V* (Albany: D. B. Lyon Co., 1912), 4270. Barlow seemed concerned to have familiar faces on his staff at this time and offered such a position to Robert Gould Shaw who declined, deciding to stay with his regiment.

68. Letter, FCB to Gen. Seth Williams, 8 May 1863. By permission of the Houghton Library, Harvard University. BMS Am 1649 25 (31).

69. Letter, FCB to APB, 19 July 1864. FCBL. (MHS).

70. Letter, FCB to Robert Treat Paine, 12 August 1863. Barlow wrote his old classmate that letters sent to Richard at The Brooklyn Navy Yard would always reach him.

71. Letter, FCB to APB, 19 July 1864. FCBL (MHS).

72. Ibid.

73. Ibid.

74. Weigley, 428.

75. Bryce A. Suderow, "Glory Denied. The First Battle of Deep Bottom, July 27th–29th, 1864," *North & South,* vol. 3, no. 7, 21.

76. Walker, 562.

77. Mitchell, Second Corps Memoranda, *OR,* I, 40, 1, 322.

78. Keating, 233.

79. Hancock's Report on Deep Bottom, Ibid., 310.

80. Mitchell, Memoranda, Ibid., 322. Barlow, Ibid.

81. *OR,* I, 40, 1, 312.1. Letter, FCB to Richard Barlow. 2 July 1864. FCBL. (MHS).

Chapter 8. Collapse and Resurgence

1. Letter, FCB to Richard Barlow, 2 July 1864. FCBL. (MHS).

2. Letter, FCB to Almira Penniman Barlow, 15 July 1864. FCBL. (MHS).

3. James A. Pomfret cited in Robert Keating, *Carnival of Blood. The Civil War Ordeal of the Seventh New York Heavy Artillery.* (Baltimore: Butternut and Blue, 1998), 234.

4. Cited in Thomas Buell, *The Warrior Generals. Combat Leadership in the Civil War* (New York: Crown Publishers, Inc., 1997), 342.

5. Dr. William W. Potter, *One Surgeon's Private War. Dr. William W. Potter of*

the 57th New York (Buffalo, NY: 1888; reprint Shippensburg, PA: White Mane Publishing Company, 1996), 117.

6. George Templeton Strong, *The Diary of George Templeton Strong. Vol. III. The Civil War, 1860–65.* eds. Allan Nevins and Milton Halsey Thomas (New York: The Macmillan Company, 1952), 468.

7. Cited in E. F. Conklin, *Woman at Gettysburg, 1863* (Thomas Publications, 1993), 23.

8. Ibid., 23.

9. "The Death of Mrs. General Barlow." *Harper's Weekly,* Vol. 8 (13 August 1864), 398.

10. Francis A. Walker, *History of the Second Army Corps in the Army of the Potomac* (New York: Charles Scribner's Sons, 1887; reprint, Gaithersburg, MD. Butternut Press, 1985), 572–73.

11. Bryce A. Suderow, "Nothing But A Miracle Could Save Us. Second Battle of Deep Bottom Virginia, August 14–20, 1864," *North & South,* vol. 4, No. 2, 12–31.

12. Ibid., 15.

13. *OR,* I, 42, 1, 216.

14. St. Clair A. Mulholland, *A History of the 116th Pennsylvania Volunteers* (New York: F. McManus & Co 1904; reprint, Fordham University Press, 1994), 281. See also Cornelia Hancock, *Letters of a Civil War Nurse* (Lincoln: University of Nebraska Press, 1998), 135.

15. Suderow, 19.

16. Walker, 572.

17. Ibid., 573.

18. Suderow, 19.

19. Ibid.

20. FCB, Report on the Second Deep Bottom Operation, *OR,* I, 42,I, 248.

21. Suderow, 21.

22. Ibid.

23. FCB, Report on Second Deep Bottom Operation, *OR,* I, 42, I, 248.

24. Suderow, 21.

25. Ibid.

26. *OR,* I, 42, 1, 248.

27. Winfield Scott Hancock, Report on the Second Deep Bottom Operation, *OR,* I, 42, I, 221.

28. *OR,* I, 42, I, 116–17.

29. Ibid.

30. Ibid., 218.

31. Ibid.

32. *OR,* I, 42, II, 173. See also Cornelia Hancock, who described the day of the Deep Bottom attack as "that awful hot day, last Sunday," 136.

33. By confirming the stalemate at Petersburg-Richmond, Second Deep Bottom may have marked the lowest point in Lincoln's administration. With the inability of Grant to achieve measurable success and Sherman stalled before Atlanta, Lincoln wrote his famous blind memorandum, in which he stated that it seemed probable he would not be reelected. See Suderow, 31.

34. *OR,* I, 42, II, 267.

35. Ibid., I, 42, I, 248.

36. Ibid., I, 42, I, 116–17.

37. Ibid., 263.

38. Theodore Lyman, *With Grant and Meade from the Rapidan to Appomattox* (Boston: Massachusetts Historical Society, 1922; Reprint, Lincoln: Bison Books/University of Nebraska Press, 1994,), 131.

39. Maria Lydig Daly, *Diary of a Union Lady,* ed. Harold Earl Hammond (New York: Funk & Wagnalls, 1962), 190, 379.

40. Paul Jones, *The Irish Brigade* (Washington-New York: Robert B. Luce, Inc., 1969), 236.

41. D. P. Conyngham, T*he Irish Brigade and Its Campaigns.* Section on the 1864 Campaign by William O' Meagher. (William McSorsey & Co.: 1867; reprint Bronx, NY: Fordham University Press, 1994), 474.

42. Ibid.

43. Ibid.

44. Cited in Buell, 342. Probably feeling humiliated that he had to relinquish his field command without a wound, Barlow appended the surgeon's diagnosis to his letter to Hancock, to prove to his commander, and himself, that the move was absolutely necessary.

45. Cornelia Hancock, 136.

46. Walker, 578.

47. Mulholland, 291.

48. *OR,* I, 42, II, 430.

49. WSH to FCB, 10 September 1864. FCBL. (MHS).

50. Letter, Brooks, Phillips to FCB, 12 October 1864. Shaw Papers. (MHS).

51. Ibid., 31 November 1864.

52. Ibid.

53. Ibid.

54. Death Certificate, David Hatch Barlow, 1 November 1869. Public Records Office, Philadelphia, Pa.

55. Letter, Winfield Scott Hancock to FCB, 3 November 1864. FCBL. (MHS).

56. Ibid.

57. Hammond, 345.

58. Ibid.

59. *OR,* I, 46, III, 170.

60. *OR,* I, 46, III, 460.

61. Chris M. Calkins, *The Appomattox Campaign, March 29–April 9, 1865* (Conshohocken, PA: Combined Books, 1997), 99.

62. Ibid. 101.

63. FCB, Report on the Appomattox Campaign. *OR,* I, 46, I, 758–59.

64. *OR,* I, 46, I, 583.

65. *OR,* I, 46, III, 1058.

66. Letter, FCB to Charles Henry Dalton, 24 May 1865. "Charles Henry Dalton Papers" in *Proceedings of the Massachusetts Historical Society, October 1922–June 1923* (Boston: Massachusetts Historical Society, 1923), 494.

67. Ibid.

68. Ibid., 495

69. *OR,* I, 46, III, 1194.

70. Ibid., 855.

71. Ibid, 1229.

72. Ibid., 1234.

73. Ibid., 1300.

CHAPTER 9. PEACEFUL PURSUITS

1. Maria Lydig Daly, *Diary of a Union Lady,* ed. Harold Earl Hammond (New York: Funk & Wagnalls, 1962), 379.

2. Ibid.

3. Interestingly, the previous June, Barlow had declined an invitation from an old college professor to speak at a memorial service in Cambridge. While he said he would like to attend the ceremony "to look tenderly upon the 'gathering of women', listen to the music, share the enthusiasm and *feel* the tears which is not given to man to shed," he begged off citing a fear of public speaking. "Seriously—the thought of a *speech* is dreadful to me," he wrote. This was a strange admission from a trial lawyer and may have been related to the strain of war or a disinclination to attend the ceremony. In his letter, Barlow expressed the hope that when the time came that he "had something to say to world . . . the gift [of public speaking] will come." It may be that having made up his mind to enter politics, Barlow found the gift. Letter, FCB to Professor Francis James Child, 3 June 1865. By permission of the Houghton Library, Harvard University. MS Am 1487, 9.

4. See Letter, FCB to Hon. John Bigelow, 6 November 1876. Samuel J. Tilden Papers. Manuscripts and Archives Division. The New York Public Library. Astor, Lenox and Tilden Foundations, quoted on page 209.

5. *Harper's Weekly,* 11 November 1865, 706.

6. Ibid.

7. Robert Shaw Barlow, obit. *New York Times,* 4 September 1943.

8. Edward H. Abbott, "Francis Channing Barlow," *Harvard Graduates Magazine,* June 1896, 13.

9. *New York Times,* 4 June 1869, 8.

10. Ibid., 4 July 1869, 5.

11. Ibid.

12. By way of illustration, to finance Lincoln's 1864 re-election cabinet members were asked to contribute $500, and workers at the New York City Custom House were assessed three percent of their yearly pay. Russell F. Weigley, *A Great Civil War. A Military and Political History, 1861–65,* (Bloomington: University of Indiana Press, 2000), 380.

13. "Francis Channing Barlow," *Dictionary of American Biography* (New York: Scribners and Sons, 1943), II, 609.

14. Ibid.

15. Letter, G. W. Curtis to FCB, 26 September 1869. Personal Miscellaneous File, Shaw Family Papers. Manuscripts and Archives Division. The New York Public Library. Astor, Lenox and Tilden Foundations. New York Public Library.

16. Francis Channing Barlow, obit., *New York Times,* 12 January 1896, 17.

17. New York State Monuments Commission. *In Memorium. Francis Channing Barlow, 1834–1896.* (Albany: J. B. Lyon Co., 1923), 133. See also letter from G. W. Curtis, 26 September 1869, which mentions Barlow's concerns in this matter.

18. David M. Ellis, James A. Frost, Harold A. Syrett, Harry J. Carman, *A History of New York State* (Ithaca: Cornell University Press, 1967), 357.

19. Letter, Robert A. Shaw, May 1943. D.R. Lauter Collection.

20. Ibid.

21. Ellis et al., 356.

22. Gen. Francis C. Barlow, *Facts for Mr. David Dudley Field.* (Albany, NY: Weed, Parson & Co., Printers, 1871), 8.

23. Ibid., 33.

24. Ibid., 33–34.

25. Ibid., 68.

26. Ibid., 70. Barlow left no stone unturned in his attempt to obtain evidence against Field. He even attempted to get his hands on a letter which Field had sent to the *North American Review* commenting on the American judiciary which Barlow thought might reveal damaging information about Field's relationship with Barnard. Letter, FCB to Charles E. Norton, 15 May 1871. By permission of the Houghton Library, Harvard University. BMS Am 1088.

27. Allen Johnson and Dumas Malone eds., *Dictionary of American Biography* (New York: Charles Scribner's Sons, 1959), 396.

28. New York State Monuments Commission, *In Memoriam. Francis Channing Barlow,* 133.

29. Letter, FCB to Samuel J. Tilden, 13 April 1872. Samuel J. Tilden Papers. Manuscripts and Archives Division. New York Public Library. Astor, Lenox and Tilden Foundations.

30. Tilden used his role in the overthrow of the Ring to come within an ace of the presidency. He was, however, only emboldened to attack Tweed openly after the Ring had been thrown on the defensive and was on the verge of cracking. See Alexander B. Callow, Jr,. *The Tweed Ring* (New York: Oxford University Press, 1966), 254.

31. *New York Times,* 23 August 1872, 1.

32. Ibid., 6 November 1871, 4.

33. Fisk himself was shot to death by his ex-mistress's suitor on 6 January 1872.

34. *New York Tribune,* 30 January 1872, 4.

35. Ibid., 4 February 1872, 10.

36. New York State Attorney General's Office, Letter Books (B0609), 1872–73. Letter FCB to Daniel Sickles, 2 January 1872. New York State Archives.

37. Ibid.

38. John Steele Gordon, *The Scarlet Woman of Wall Street* (New York: Weidenfield & Nicolson, 1988) 348–56.

39. *New York Times,* 15 May 1872, 8.

40. Ibid.

41. Reprinted in *New York Times,* 15 October 1872, 1.

42. Ibid., 4.

43. Ibid., 19 March 1873, 5.

44. Ibid.

45. While Tammany Hall fell into temporary disarray only Tweed and James H. Ingersoll ever spent any time in jail. Callow, 298.

46. *New York Times,* 16 August 1872.

47. Ibid.

48. Ibid.

49. Matthew P. Breen, *Thirty Years of New York Politics* (New York: privately printed, 1899), 424.

50. "Samuel J. Tilden" in Dumas Malone, ed., *Dictionary of American Biography* (New York: Scribner's, 1943), 540.

51. *Harper's Weekly,* 13 November 1875, 932.

52. Memorandum of cases under investigation by the New York State At-

torney General, Francis Channing Barlow, 31 December 1873. Fairchild Papers, Box 1, #63 New York Historical Society. 39–41.

53. Ibid.

54. *New York Times,* 20 August 1873, 4.

55. Ibid., 29 August 1873, 4

56. Ibid., 16 September 1873, 4.

57. Letter, FCB to James Russell Lowell, 20 May 1876. By permission of the Houghton Library, Harvard University. BMS Am, 765. In his letter, written before the Republican Convention met in 1876, Barlow asked Lowell to speak at a meeting of the Republican Reform Club. He thought Lowell would prove a major draw and explained that "We want to give a strong notice to the politicians at [the Convention] that there is a powerful body of Republicans here who will not tolerate a machine nomination."

58. *Harper's Weekly,* 11 October 1873, 890.

59. Ibid.

60. *New York Herald,* 25 September 1873, 4. Stillman got the nomination, but lost to Democrat Charles S. Fairchild in the general election.

61. Louis W. Koenig, "The Election That Got Away," *American Heritage,* October 1960, 6.

62. Ibid., 100.

63. Ibid.

64. Lloyd Robinson, *The Stolen Election. Hayes Vs. Tilden* (Garden City, NY: Doubleday and Co., Inc., 1968), 143.

65. Letter, FCB to Hon. John Bigelow, 6 November 1876. Samuel J. Tilden Papers. Manuscripts and Archives Division. New York Public Library. Astor, Lenox and Tilden Foundations.

66. A. M. Gibson. *A Political Crime. The History of the Great Fraud* (New York: William S. Gottsbereger publishers, 1885; reprint, Freeport, NY: Books for Libraries, 1969), 92.

67. Ibid.

68. Ibid., 93.

69. Ibid., 85.

70. House Committee on Alleged Electoral Frauds (Potter Committee), *Investigation of Alleged Electoral Frauds in the Late Presidential Election,* 43d Cong., 3d sess., Report no. 140, March 3, 1879, 18.

71. Ibid.

72. Gibson, 101. Noyes took over the presentation of the Republican case. In their Minority Report which was filed at the end of the hearings, the Republicans claimed Barlow was replaced "when [Republican] governor Stearns and his friends became dissatisfied with General Barlow." The Republicans did not give any reasons why the Governor and his "friends" became unhappy with Barlow's performance though their concerns are readily apparent. See Potter Committee, *Investigation of Alleged Electoral Frauds,* 83.

73. Gibson, 97.

74. Ibid. Cowgill, in the estimation of the *New York Herald,* was "the doubtful man of the [returning] board. No man in America ever held such power as now rests between the fingers of the gray-headed, gray-eyed, and gray-clad man who seems rather enjoying the consequence that is put on him." *New York Herald,* 4 December 1876. 4.

75. *New York Times,* 15 December 1876, 6.

76. Ibid.

77. Letter, FCB 15 December 1876 printed in the *New York Herald,* 18 December 1876. 4.

78. Ibid.

79. Ibid.

80. *New York Herald,* 19 December 1876, 5.

81. Gibson, 33.

82. Koenig, 100. Gibson, 105–13, gives a more detailed run down on the positions and favors given to those who helped secure Florida for Hayes. Needless to say, Barlow was not among the recipients. On the other hand, Frank P. Vazzano ("The Louisiana Question Resurrected: The Potter Commission and the Election of 1876," *Louisiana History,* vol. XVI, no. 1, Winter 1975, 49) believes that Hayes was unsure of what had happened in the contested southern states. If so, it seems to have been a case of not wanting to know.

83. Ibid., 104.

84. For a succinct explanation of the genesis of the Potter Commission see Vazzano, "The Louisiana Question Resurrected." Despite the charges, countercharges, reviewing of evidence and rehashing of arguments, the Potter Commission changed nothing. On 14 June 1878, a resolution passed the House which denied Congress the power to reverse the decision of the Electoral Commission which had given Hayes the presidency. Vazanno, 50.

85. *Harper's Weekly,* 15 March 1879, 202.

86. *New York Times,* 20 February 1879, 4.

87. Ibid.

88. Ibid., 22 February 1879, 2.

89. Ibid.

90. Ibid.

91. Ibid.

92. Ibid.

93. Ibid.

94. Ibid.

95. Ibid.

96. Ibid., 4.

97. Ibid.

98. Ibid.

99. Ibid., 24 February 1879,1.

100. Ibid.

101. *Harper's* chided the Republicans for making "a great mistake in not renominating General Barlow" in 1873, (11 October 1873, 890), and in their 13 March, 1875 issue charged that the Republicans, under the "malign influence" of corrupt interests and hacks "dropped his name from the ticket, and elbowed him out of its inner counsels," 13 October 1875, 932. *Harper's* was also sympathetic to Barlow's position in the Florida recount, 7 January 1877, 2.

102. *Harper's Weekly,* 15 May 1879, 202.

103. Ibid.

104. Abbott, 15.

105. Letter, FCB to Charles S. Fairchild, 30 June 1888. Fairchild Papers, Box 3, #125 New York Historical Society.

106. *Harper's Weekly,* 22 November 1884, 729. Ironically, Barlow's old law partner, George Bliss, sat with the Republican team. Democrat Grover Cleveland won the election.

107. *New York Times,* 4 January 1877, 6.

108. Ibid.

109. Ibid.

110. Ibid.

111. Ibid.

112. Ibid.

113. Ibid.

114. *New York Times,* 29 June 1877, Fairchild Papers, Box 1, #234, 4.

115. Letter, FCB to Charles S. Fairchild, 25 June 1877. NYHS.

116. Callow, 295.

117. Ibid., 296.

118. Ibid. 295.

119. Letter, FCB to Charles S. Fairchild, 5 March 1886. Fairchild Papers, Box 1, #152, NYHS.

120. Ibid.

121. Cited in *In Memoriam,* 133.

122. Ibid.

123. Ibid., 134.

124. Letter, FCB to Charles S. Fairchild, 30 June 1888. Fairchild Papers, Box 3, #125, NYHS.

125. Letter, FCB to Samuel J. Tilden, 7 January 1886. Samuel J. Tilden Papers. Manuscripts and Archives Division. New York Public Library. Astor, Lenox and Tilden Foundations.

126. Ibid.

127. Ibid.

128. Ibid.

129. Ibid.

130. Letter, Samuel J. Tilden to FCB, 26 January 1886. Samuel J. Tilden Papers. Manuscripts and Archives Division. New York Public Library. Astor, Lenox and Tilden Foundations.

131. Dumas Malone, ed., *Dictionary of American Biography,* XII, (New York: Scribner's and Son, 1943), 617.

132. Quoted in Natalie Spassky, *American Paintings in the Metropolitan Museum of Art.* vol II (New York: The Metropolitan Museum of Art,), 438.

133. A detailed account of the national and intra-GAR debate over the pensions is found in Stuart McConnell, *Glorious Contentment. The Grand Army of the Republic, 1865–1900* (Chapel Hill:University of North Carolina Press,1992) 149–62.

134. Letter, FCB to E. L. Godkin, 9 August 1890, *New York Evening Post,* 7.

135. Ibid.

136. Ibid.

137. Ibid.

138. Ibid.

139. Ibid.

140. Ibid.

141. Ibid.

142. Ibid.

143. Ibid.

144. Letter, Charles L. Barlow to Donald Pfanz, 21 March 1960. D. R. Lauter Collection.

145. Abbott, 10.

146. Ibid., 1.

147. James A. Scrymser, *Personal Reminiscences of James A. Scrymser. In Times of Peace and War* (New York: 1915), 13.

148. Ibid.

149. Ibid., 139–50. See chapter 9.

150. FCB, obit., *New York Herald,* 12 January 1896.

151. FCB, obit. *New York Times,* 12 January 1896.

152. Harriet Alma Cummings, compiler, *Burials and Inscriptions in the Walnut Street Cemetery of Brookline, Massachusetts* (Brookline, MA: Riverdale Press, 1920), 92–93. Almira died on 16 July 1868. Nothing is known of Edward and Richard after the Civil War.

CHAPTER 10. AFTERLIFE

1. This section is based on the *Boston Transcript* article as reprinted in the *Dublin* (Georgia) *Post,* 19 March 1879.

2. A variation of the story appears in James A. Scrymser's *In Times of Peace and War* (New York, 1915) 11–12. In Scrymser's account Early and Gordon rode by the fallen Barlow, and Gordon asked his commander whether they should do something for him. Early replied, "No he is too far gone," at which Barlow raised himself up and shaking his fist at Early said, "General Early I will live to lick you yet, damn you." Scrymser was not at Gettysburg, and his account does not explain how Barlow would have recognized Early. Nevertheless this version was repeated in Stegman's account in the 1923 New York State Monuments Commission book, *In Memoriam. Francis Channing Barlow.*

3. See William F. Hanna, "A Gettysburg Myth Exploded: The Barlow-Gordon Incident," *Civil War Times Illustrated,* 24,(May 1985),42–47,and John J.Pullen, "The Gordon Barlow Story, With Sequel," *Gettysburg Magazine,* 8 (January 1993), 5–8.

4. Letter, FCB to APB, 7 July 1863. FCBL. (MHS).

5. *New York Times,* 4 July 1888. 2.

6. Ibid.

7. Edward H. Abbott, "Francis Channing Barlow" in *Harvard Graduates Magazine* (June 1896), 135. Memorial Hall was subsequently renamed Annenberg Hall and currently serves as a freshman eating hall.

8. New York State Monuments Commission, *In Memoriam. Francis Channing Barlow* (Albany, NY: J. B. Lyon Company, Printers, 1923), 14.

9. Ibid.

10. Interestingly, in the most recent study of the opening day at Gettysburg, Harry W. Pfanz describes Barlow's stand on what was then "Blocher's Knoll" as a "blunder" that "ensured the defeat of the Corps." J. Matthew Gallman, review of *Gettysburg—The First Day,* by Harry W. Pfanz, *Civil War Book Review,* (Fall 2001): 10.

11. Ibid. 16–17.

12. Ibid

13. Scrymser, 139.

14. Ibid., 146.

15. *New York Times,* 6 December 1914, 6. Congress allocated $100,000, Mrs. Russell Sage, $150,000, the Rockefeller Foundation, $100,000 and Mrs. Edward

H. Harriman, $50,000. The building was designed in Beaux Arts style by Trowbridge and Livingston.

16. Ibid.

17. Scrymser, 150

18. Frederick Phisterer (complier), *New York in the War of the Rebellion, 1861–1865* (Albany: D. B. Lyon, 1912), III, 2274.

19. Frederick Gilbert, *The Story of a Regiment. Being a Record of the Military Services of the Fifty-Seventh New York State Volunteer Infantry in the War of the Rebellion.* (Chicago: The Fifty-Seventh Volunteer Association, 1895), 235.

20. Captain Robert S. Robertson, "From Spotsylvania Onward," *War Papers Read Before the Indiana Commandery of the Loyal Legion of the United States,* (Indianapolis: the Commandery, 1898), 344–58, reprint: Wilmington, NC: Broadfoot Publishing Co., 1992.

21. Robert Keating's recently published *Carnival of Blood* includes soldiers' comments sometimes critical of Barlow's leadership. Robert Keating, *Carnival of Blood. The Civil War Ordeal of the Seventh New York Heavy Artillery* (Baltimore, MD: Butternut & Blue, 1998).

22. Bruce Catton, *A Stillness at Appomattox,* (Garden City: Doubleday & Company, 1953), 199–120.

23. Stephen Sears, *Landscape Turned Red* (New York: Ticknor & Fields, 1983), 273–77.

24. Thomas Buell, *The Warrior Generals* (New York: Crown Publishers, Inc., 1997), xxxii.

Bibliography

Primary Materials

Manuscripts

DUKE UNIVERSITY, PERKINS LIBRARY

Letter, Samuel Spencer Parmalee 9 April, 1864. Samuel Spencer Parmalee and Uriah N. Parmalee Papers.

HARVARD UNIVERSITY, HOUGHTON LIBRARY

Data on the Barlow Family. Compiled by Louisa Barlow Jay.
Letter, Col. James Wood to Augustus Hamlin, 3 June 1891. Augustus C. Hamlin Collection.
Letter, David Hatch Barlow to James Russell Lowell, 30 December 1844.
Letters, Francis Channing Barlow, 1860–76.
Letters, Ralph Waldo Emerson, 1855–63.

INDIANA STATE LIBRARY

Erasmus C. Gilbreath Papers

MASSACHUSETTS HISTORICAL SOCIETY

Francis Channing Barlow Letters. Massachusetts Historical Society.
Edward Louis Edes Letters. Massachusetts Historical Society.

NEW YORK HISTORICAL SOCIETY

Charles S. Fairchild Papers.
War Letters, 1861–65.

NEW YORK PUBLIC LIBRARY

Charles Patrick Daly Papers.
Shaw Family Correspondence.
Samuel J. Tilden Papers.

NEW YORK STATE ARCHIVES

New York State Adjutant General's Office. Register of Letters Received, 1862–66.
New York State Attorney General's Office, Letter Books, 1872–73.

WILLIAM C. SPARKS COLLECTION

Letters, Lt. Robert Robertson, 16 April 1864–21 June 1864.

UNITED STATES ARMY MILITARY INSTITUTE,
CARLISLE BARRACKS, CARLISLE, PENNSYLVANIA

Diary, Lt. Isaac Plumb, 61st New York Infantry.

YALE UNIVERSITY LIBRARY

Webb Papers.
Bowles Papers.

Printed

Abbot, Edward H. "Francis Channing Barlow," in *Harvard Graduates Magazine.* June 1896.
Barlow, Francis. "The Capture of the Salient. May 12 1864." Papers of the Military Historical Society of Massachusetts. 1879.
_____. *Facts for Mr. David Dudley Field.* Albany, NY: Weed, Parsons & Co., 1871.
Breen, Matthew P., *Thirty Years of New York Politics.* New York: Breen, 1899.
Black, John. "Reminiscences of the Bloody Angle." In *Glimpses of the Nation's Struggle.* Fourth Series. Papers Read before the Military Order of the Minnesota Commandery of the Military Order of the Loyal Legion of the United States, 1892–1897. St. Paul, Minnesota: H. L. Collins, 1898; reprint: Wilmington, North Carolina: Broadfoot Publishing, 1992. 420–36.
Cooke, George Willis, ed. *Early Letters of George William Curtis to John S. Dwight. Brook Farm and Concord.* New York: Harper & Brothers Publishers, 1898.
Dalton, Charles Henry. "Charles Henry Dalton Papers." In *Proceedings of the Massachusetts Historical Society, October 1922–June 1923.* Boston: Massachusetts Historical Society, 1923.
Daly, Maria Lydig. *Diary of A Union Lady.* Edited by Harold Earl Hammond. New York: Funk & Wagnall's, 1962.
Duncan, Russell, ed. *Blue-Eyed Child of Fortune. The Civil War Letters of Robert Gould Shaw.* Athens, GA: University of Georgia Press, 1992.
Frederick, Gilbert D. *The Story of a Regiment. Being a Record of the Military Services of the Fifty-Seventh New York State Volunteer Infantry in the War of the Rebellion.* Chicago: The Fifty-Seventh Veterans Association, 1895.
Fuller, Charles A. *Personal Recollections of the War of 1861.* Sherburne, NY:

New Job Printing, 1906; reprint, Hamilton, NY: Edmonston Publishing, Inc., 1990.

Fuller, Margaret. *The Letters of Margaret Fuller.* Vol I: 1817–38. Edited by Robert N. Hudspeth. Ithaca, NY: Cornell University Press, 1983.

Hancock, Cornelia. *Letters of A Civil War Nurse.* Lincoln: University of Nebraska Press, 1998.

Lyman, Colonel Theodore. *With Grant and Meade from the Wilderness to Appomattox.* Boston: Massachusetts Historical Society, 1922; reprint, Lincoln, NB: University of Nebraska Press, 1994

Muffly, J. W. *The Story of Our Regiment. A History of the 148th Pennsylvania Vols.* Des Moines, IA: The Kenyon Printing & Mfg. Co., 1902; reprint Baltimore, MD.: Butternut and Blue, 1994.

Mulholland, St. Clair A. *The Story of the 116th Pennsylvania Volunteers in the War of the Rebellion.* 1903; reprint, New York: Fordham University Press, 1996.

Phisterer, Frederick, compiler. *New York in the War of the Rebellion.* 6 Volumes. Albany, NY: D. B. Lyon Co., State Printers, 1912.

Potter, Dr. William W. *One Surgeon's Private War. Doctor William Potter of the 57th New York.* Buffalo: 1888; reprint, Shippensburg, PA: White Mane Publications, 1996.

Robertson, Captain Robert S. "From Spotsylvania Onward." *War Papers Read Before the Indiana Commandery of the Loyal Legion of the United States.* Indianapolis, IN: Published by the Commandery, 1898; reprint, Wilmington, NC: Broadfoot Publishing Co., 1992.

Scrymser, James A. *Personal Reminiscences of James A. Scrymser. In Times of Peace and War.* New York: 1915.

Sears, John van der Zee. *My Friends at Brook Farm.* New York: Desmond Fitz-Gerald, Inc., 1912.

Sigman, Martin. The Diary of Martin Sigman, 64th New York Infantry. Cattaraugas County Museum, Little Falls, New York, n.d.

Silliker, Ruth L., ed. *The Rebel Yell and the Yankee Hurrah: The Civil War Journal of a Maine Volunteer: Private John W. Haley, 17th Maine Regiment.* Camden, ME: Down East Books, 1985.

Strong, George Templeton. *The Diary of George Templeton Strong.* III vols. Edited by Alan Nevins and Milton Halsey Thomas. New York: The Macmillan Company, 1952.

Thayer, James B. "Ezra Ripley." In *Harvard Memorial Biographies,* Vol. I, ed. Thomas Wentworth Higginson, 99–107. Cambridge, MA: Sever & Francis, 1867.

United States Congress. House Committee on the Alleged Electoral Frauds (Potter Committee). *Investigation of Alleged Electoral Frauds in the Late Presidential Election.* 43rd Cong., 3d Sess., Report no. 140. 3 March 1879.

United States War Department. *The War of the Rebellion. A Compilation of the Official Records of the Union and Confederate Armies.* 128 Volumes. Washington, DC: Government Printing Office, 1880–1901.

Newspapers and Periodicals

New York Herald.
New York Times.

Harper's Weekly.
New York Evening Post.

SECONDARY SOURCES

Books

BATTLE, REGIMENTAL, AND MILITARY STUDIES

Buell, Thomas. *The Warrior Generals. Combat Leadership in the Civil War.* New York: Crown Publishers, Inc., 1997.

Calkins, Chris M. *The Appomattox Campaign. March 29–April 29, 1865.* Conshocken, Pa: Combined Books, 1997.

Catton, Bruce. *A Stillness at Appomattox.* Garden City: Doubleday & Co., 1957.

Conklin, Eileen F. *Women at Gettysburg, 1863.* Gettysburg, PA: Thomas Publications, 1993.

Conyngham, D. P. *The Irish Brigade and Its Campaigns.* New York: McSorleye, 1867; reprint Fordham University Press, 1994.

Dowdey, Clifford. *Lee's Last Campaign.* Boston: Little, Brown & Co., 1960.

Duncan, Russell. *Where Death and Glory Meet. Colonel Robert Shaw and the 54th Massachusetts Infantry.* Athens, GA: University of Georgia Press, 1999.

Ferguson, Ernest B. *Not War But Murder. Cold Harbor 1864.* New York: Alfred A. Knopf, 2000.

Jones, Paul. *The Irish Brigade.* Washington and New York: Robert B. Luce, Inc., 1969.

Jordan, David M. *Winfield Scott Hancock.* Bloomington and Indianapolis: Indiana University Press, 1988.

Howe, Thomas J. *The Petersburg Campaign: Wasted Valor, June 15–18, 1864.* Lynchburg, Virginia: H. E. Howards, 1988.

Keating, Robert. *Carnival of Blood. The Civil War Ordeal of the Seventh New York Heavy Artillery.* Baltimore, MD: 1998.

Lauter, Don Richard. *Winslow Homer and Friends in Prince George County, Virginia, June, 1864.* Disputanta, VA: By the Author, 1999.

New York State Monuments Commission. *In Memoriam. Francis Channing Barlow. 1834–1896.* Albany, NY: J. B. Lyon Co., 1923.

Rhea, Gordon. *The Battle of Spotsylvania and the Road to Yellow Tavern.* Baton Rouge: Louisiana State University Press, 1997.

_____. *The Battles of the Wilderness & Spotsylvania.* Fredericksburg, VA: Eastern National Park and Monument Association, 1995.

Sears, Stephen W. *George B. McClellan. The Young Napoleon.* New York: Ticknor & Fields, 1988.

_____. *Landscape Turned Red.* New York: Ticknor & Fields, 1983.

Symonds, Craig L. *Joseph Johnston.* New York: W. W. Norton, 1992.

Thomas, Emory M. *Robert E. Lee. A Biography.* New York: W. W. Norton, 1995.

Trudeau, Noah Andre. *Bloody Roads South. The Wilderness to Cold Harbor, May–June, 1865.* Boston: Little, Brown & Co., 1989.

Tucker, Glenn. *Hancock the Superb.* Indianapolis, IN: Bobbs-Merrill, 1960.

Walker, Francis A. *History of the Second Army Corps in the Army of the Potomac.* New York: Charles Scribner's Sons, 1887.

Weigley, Russell F. *A Great Civil War. A Military and Political History, 1861–1865.* Indianapolis and Bloomington: Indiana University Press, 2000.

Woodworth, Steven E. *Davis & Lee At War.* Lawrence, KS: University of Kansas Press, 1995.

POLITICAL, CIVIL HISTORICAL, AND BIOGRAPHICAL STUDIES

Burton, Katherine. *Paradise Planters. The Story of Brook Farm.* New York and London: Longmans, Green & Co., 1939.

Callow, Alexander B., Jr. *The Tweed Ring.* New York: Oxford University Press, 1966.

Codman, John Thomas. *Brook Farm. Historical and Personal Memoirs.* Boston: Arena Publishing Co., 1897.

Ellis, David M., James A. Frost, Harold A. Syrett, and Harry J. Carman. *A History of New York State.* Ithaca: Cornell University Press, 1967.

Gibson, A. M. *A Political Crime. The History of the Great Fraud.* New York: William S. Gottsberger Publisher, 1885.

Gordon, John Steele. *The Scarlet Woman of Wall Street.* New York: Weichenfeld & Nicolson, 1988.

Holmes, Susan Barlow. *Barlow Clearinghouse.* Barlow Webpage. http://freepages.genealogy.rootsweb.com/~barlow

McConnell, Stuart. *Glorious Contentment. The Grand Army of the Republic, 1865–1900.* Chapel Hill: University of North Carolina Press, 1992.

Nielsen, Anna Barlow. "History of General Francis Channing Barlow's Family." Unpublished typescript, 1998.

Robinson, Lloyd. *The Stolen Election. Hayes Vs. Tilden.* Garden City: Doubleday & Co., 1968.

Spassky, Natalie. *American Painting in the Metropolitan Museum of Art.* vol. II. New York: The Metropolitan Museum of Art, 1985.

Stewart, Randall. *Nathaniel Hawthorne. A Biography.* New Haven, CT: Archon Books, 1970.

Swift, Lindsay. *Brook Farm and Its Members, Scholars and Visitors.* New York: Macmillan Co. 1900; reprint: New York: Corinth Books, 1961.

Articles

Andrus, Michael J. "The Battle of Beaver Dam Creek (Mechanicsville)." *Civil War* 51 (June 1995): 57–60.

Carmichael, Peter S. "The Battle of Savage's Station." *Civil War 51* (June 1995): 65–68.

Curtis, Edith P. Roelker. "A Season in Utopia." *American Heritage* (April 1959): 58–63, 98–100.

Hanna, William F. "A Gettysburg Myth Exploded: The Barlow-Gordon Incident." *Civil War Times Illustrated* 24, (May 1985): 42–47.

Hicks, Grenville. "A Conversation in Boston." *Sewanee Review,* vol. XXXIX, no. 2 (April–June 1921): 129–43.

Jamieson, Perry D. "Background to Bloodshed. The Tactics of the U.S.–Mexican War and the 1850s." *North & South* vol. 4, no. 6. (2001): 24–31.

Koenig, Louis W. "The Election That Got Away." *American Heritage* (October 1960): 4–7, 99–104.

Lauter, Don Richard. "Once Upon a Time in the East." In *The Journal of Woman's Civil War History.* Vol. I, ed. Eileen Conklin, 8–25. Gettysburg, PA: Thomas Publications, 2001.

Newton, Steven H. "The Battle of Seven Pines (Fair Oaks)." *Civil War* 51 (June 1995): 47–50.

Pullen, John J. "The Gordon-Barlow Story, With Sequel." *Gettysburg Magazine* 8 (January 1993): 5–7.

Quarstein, John V. "The Siege of Yorktown and the Engagements Along the Warwick River." *Civil War* 51 (June 1995): 29–34.

Rhea, Gordon. "'Butcher' Grant and the Overland Campaign." *North & South,* Vol. 4, No. 1 (2000): 44–55.

_____. "Cold Harbor. Anatomy of a Battle" *North & South,* Vol. 5, No. 2 (2002): 40–62.

Suderow, Bryce A. "Glory Denied. The First Battle of Deep Bottom," July 27–29, 1864." *North & South,* Vol.3, No.7 (2000): 17–32.

_____. "Nothing But A Miracle Could Save Us. The Second Battle of Deep Bottom Virginia, August 14–20, 1864." *North & South,* Vol. 4, No. 2 (2001): 12–32.

Vazzano, Frank P. "The Louisiana Question Resurrected. The Potter Commission and the Election of 1876." *Louisiana History,* Vol. XVL, No. 1 (Winter 1975), 39–57.

Welch, Richard F. "Boy General Francis Channing Barlow." *America's Civil War* (March 1998), 34–41, 69.

Index